Study Guide with Map Exercises

to accompany

American History: A Survey
Volume II

Twelfth Edition

Alan Brinkley
Columbia University

Prepared by

Michael V. Namorato
University of Mississippi

and

Charles Steven Palmer
University of Mississippi

Boston Burr Ridge, IL Dubuque, IA Madison, WI New York San Francisco St. Louis
Bangkok Bogotá Caracas Kuala Lumpur Lisbon London Madrid Mexico City
Milan Montreal New Delhi Santiago Seoul Singapore Sydney Taipei Toronto

The McGraw·Hill Companies

McGraw-Hill Higher Education

Study Guide with Map Exercises to accompany
American History: A Survey, Volume II
Alan Brinkley

Published by McGraw-Hill, an imprint of The McGraw-Hill Companies, Inc., 1221 Avenue of the Americas, New York, NY 10020. Copyright © 2007, 2003 by The McGraw-Hill Companies, Inc. All rights reserved. No part of this publication may be reproduced or distributed in any form or by any means, or stored in a database or retrieval system, without the prior written consent of The McGraw-Hill Companies, Inc., including, but not limited to, in any network or other electronic storage or transmission, or broadcast for distance learning.

4 5 6 7 8 9 0 QPD/QPD 0 9 8

ISBN-13: 978-0-07-312495-7
ISBN-10:   0-07-312495-8

www.mhhe.com

CONTENTS

INTRODUCTION iv

Chapter 15: Reconstruction and the New South 180

Chapter 16: The Conquest of the Far West 194

Chapter 17: Industrial Supremacy 205

Chapter 18: The Age of the City 216

Chapter 19: From Stalemate to Crisis 227

Chapter 20: The Imperial Republic 238

Chapter 21: The Rise of Progressivism 248

Chapter 22: The Battle for National Reform 259

Chapter 23: America and the Great War 270

Chapter 24: "The New Era" 283

Chapter 25: The Great Depression 293

Chapter 26: The New Deal 303

Chapter 27: The Global Crisis, 1921–1941 315

Chapter 28: America in a World at War 324

Chapter 29: The Cold War 335

Chapter 30: The Affluent Society 347

Chapter 31: The Ordeal of Liberalism 358

Chapter 32: The Crisis of Authority 371

Chapter 33: From "The Age of Limits" to the Age of Reagan 382

Chapter 34: The Age of Globalization 394

ANSWERS TO CHAPTER SELF TESTS 407

INTRODUCTION

Every history professor has heard hundreds of students complain that history is nothing but dry, irrelevant names and dates to be memorized quickly and just as quickly forgotten. To be sure, for students to have a good framework of historical understanding, they must have a basic knowledge of some important names and dates, but history is much more than that. It is society's memory, and society cannot function without history any more than an individual could function without his or her memory. The names represent real flesh-and-blood people, both famous and common, and the dates mark the time when those people lived and worked. This Study Guide will try to lead you toward the outcome of developing a historical perspective. You will be encouraged to go beyond the bare facts to think critically about the causes and consequences of historical decisions. Careful study of this guide in consultation with your instructor will help you use the text to its best advantage. With the guide, you can constantly test yourself to make sure that you have learned from what you have read.

Each chapter of the guide is composed of a number of parts: objectives, main themes, glossary, pertinent questions, identification, documents, map exercise, interpretive questions, summary, review questions, and chapter self test. Your instructor may assign specific items from the guide that best complement his or her approach to the course, or you may be expected to use the guide on your own. It will work well with either approach.

It is best to look over the appropriate chapter in the guide *before* you read your assignment so that you will be better attuned to what to look for as you read. The objectives and main themes that are listed at the beginning of each chapter of the Study Guide will give you a general idea of what the chapter is about. The object of your reading should be to see how the text develops these themes. The glossary contains historical terms used in the text but not fully defined therein. The identification items are names and terms covered in the text but not directly mentioned in the pertinent-questions section of the Study Guide. Of course, your instructor may add to and/or delete from these lists to meet the needs of the course.

The pertinent questions, review questions, and self tests are the heart of the Study Guide. The objective of these exercises is to provide you with a thoughtful method for self-assessment after you have read each chapter. Page numbers are provided for the pertinent questions so that you can check your answers and review if necessary. Some students will wish to write out their answers in full; some will jot down a few key ideas; and others will simply check themselves "in their heads." Experiment and use whichever method works best for you (assuming it is acceptable to your instructor.) The self test at the end of each chapter will help you check to be sure that you have learned the essential information being covered.

The document exercises in each chapter provide an opportunity for you to discover how important the analysis of documents can be to the historian's task. The questions on each document should be treated much like the pertinent questions. The map exercises let you see how geography can help you form historical perspective.

Used regularly with each chapter, this Study Guide will help you develop a system of study habits and analysis that will serve you well in this course and in many others as well.

STUDY GUIDE WITH MAP EXERCISES

Chapters 15–34

CHAPTER FIFTEEN
RECONSTRUCTION AND THE NEW SOUTH

Objectives

A thorough study of Chapter 15 should enable the student to understand

1. The conditions in the former Confederacy after Appomattox that would have made any attempt at genuine Reconstruction most difficult.

2. The differences between the Conservative and Radical views on the Reconstruction process and the reasons for the eventual Radical domination.

3. The functioning of the impeachment process in the case of President Andrew Johnson and the significance of his acquittal for the future of Reconstruction.

4. Radical Reconstruction in practice and southern (black and white) reaction to it.

5. The debate among historians concerning the nature of Reconstruction, its accomplishments, and its harmful effects on the South.

6. The national problems faced by President Ulysses S. Grant and the reasons for his lack of success as chief executive.

7. The diplomatic successes of the Johnson and Grant administrations and the role of the presidents in achieving them.

8. The greenback question and how it reflected postwar financial problems of the nation.

9. The alternatives that were available during the election of 1876 and the effects of the Compromise of 1877 on the South and on the nation.

10. The response of African Americans to conditions in the South following Reconstruction.

11. The reasons for the failure of the South to develop a strong industrial economy after Reconstruction.

12. The methods used in the South to regain control of its own affairs and the course of action it chose thereafter.

13. The ways in which southerners decided to handle the race question and the origin of the system identified with "Jim Crow."

14. The typical pattern of southern agriculture in the late nineteenth and early twentieth centuries and the impact this had on the region and its people.

15. The debate among historians over the origins of segregation after the Civil War.

Main Themes

1. That the defeat and devastation of the South presented the nation with severe social, economic, and political problems.

2. How Radical Reconstruction changed the South but fell short of the full transformation needed to secure equality for the freedman.

3. That white society and the federal government lacked the will to enforce effectively most of the constitutional and legal guarantees acquired by blacks during Reconstruction.

4. How the policies of the Grant administration moved beyond Reconstruction matters to foreshadow issues of the late nineteenth century.

5. How white leaders reestablished economic and political control of the South and sought to modernize the region through industrialization.

6. How the race question continued to dominate southern life.

Glossary

1. Whigs: A major political party between 1834 and the 1850s. The Whigs were unified by their opposition to Andrew Jackson and their support for federal policies to aid business. The party was strongest among the merchants and manufacturers of the Northeast, the wealthy planters of the South, and the farmers of the West most eager for internal improvements. Abraham Lincoln and many other Republicans had been Whigs before the issues of sectionalism destroyed the party.

2. veto/pocket veto: The president's refusal to sign a bill passed by Congress. He must send it back to Congress with his objections. Unless two-thirds of each house votes to override the president's action, the bill will not become law. A pocket veto occurs when Congress has adjourned and the president refuses to sign a bill within ten days. Because Congress is not in session, the president's action cannot be overridden. (See the Constitution, Article I, Section 7.)

3. spoils system: The political equivalent of the military axiom "To the victor belong the spoils." In the nineteenth century, the victorious political party in national, state, and local elections routinely dismissed most officeholders and replaced them with workers loyal to the incoming party. The "spoils" were the many patronage jobs available in the government. At the national level, this included thousands of post office and customs positions. Political organizations especially adept at manipulating spoils to remain in power were often called machines. Civil-service reformers demanded that nonpolicymaking jobs be filled on the basis of competitive examinations and that officeholders would continue in office as long as they performed satisfactorily.

4. Solid South: Refers to the fact that the South became overwhelmingly Democratic as a reaction to Republican actions during the Civil War and Reconstruction. Democratic domination of southern politics persisted for over a century despite occasional cracks, especially in presidential elections.

5. Unionists: Residents of the Confederate states who counseled against secession and who often remained loyal to the Union during the Civil War. Unionists were more common in upcountry regions of the South, where the slave-based plantation economy was less influential than in coastal areas of the South. Some Unionists left the South during the Civil War but many remained.

Pertinent Questions

THE PROBLEMS OF PEACEMAKING (402-406)

1. What effects did the Civil War have on the economy and social system of the South?

2. What special problems did the freedmen face immediately after the war? What efforts were made to help them?

3. What were the competing notions of freedom that existed in the post-war South?

4. What political implications did the readmission of the southern states pose for the Republicans?

5. What were the differences between the Conservative, Radical, and Moderate factions of the Republican Party during Reconstruction?

6. What were the objectives and provisions of Lincoln's plan for Reconstruction? How did the Radical Republicans respond to it?

7. Describe Andrew Johnson's approach to Reconstruction. How was it shaped by his political background and his personality?

RADICAL RECONSTRUCTION (406-409)

8. What did the southern state governments do during the "presidential Reconstruction" of 1865 and 1866?

9. How did Congress respond to the Black Codes and other southern state actions of 1865 and 1866?

10. What did the Congressional elections of 1866 reveal about the public attitude toward Reconstruction?

11. Explain the basic provisions of the Congressional plan of Reconstruction of 1867. On what principle was it based?

12. What measures did the Radical Republicans take to keep President Johnson and the Supreme Court from interfering with their plans?

13. Why did Radical Republicans want to impeach President Johnson and why did they fail?

THE SOUTH IN RECONSTRUCTION (409-414)

14. What three groups constituted the Republican Party in the South during Reconstruction?

15. What role did blacks play in southern political life during Reconstruction?

16. What was the balance between corruption and positive accomplishment by the Reconstruction-era state governments in the South?

17. What patterns of southern education began to emerge during Reconstruction?

18. What changes in land distribution occurred in the South after the Civil War? How were the hopes of blacks mostly dashed?

19. What economic advances did the freedmen make? How did the economic status of blacks compare with that of the average white southerner?

20. How did the crop-lien system overshadow the economic gains made by blacks and poor whites?

21. How did freedom affect black family life?

THE GRANT ADMINISTRATION (414-416)

22. How did Ulysses S. Grant's political accomplishments compare with his military ability?

23. What were the scandals that came to light during the Grant Administration? What role did Grant play in these?

24. People in what financial condition were most likely to favor expansion of the currency supply with greenbacks? What was done about the greenback issue?

25. What were the diplomatic accomplishments of the Grant administration?

THE ABANDONMENT OF RECONSTRUCTION (416-421)

26. What tactics did white southern Democrats use to restrict or control black suffrage?

27. Why did northern Republicans begin to take less interest in Reconstruction and the cause of the freedmen after about 1870?

28. Why was the presidential election of 1876 disputed? How was the controversy resolved by the "Compromise of 1877"?

29. What was President Rutherford B. Hayes's objective in the South? Did he succeed?

30. Compare white and black expectations for Reconstruction with the actual results.

THE NEW SOUTH (421-431)

31. What were the socioeconomic and political characteristics of the "Redeemers" (Bourbons)?

32. How did the policies of the "Redeemer" governments compare with those of the Reconstruction-era administrations?

33. In what particular products was industrialization in the South most advanced? What factors attracted industrial capital to the region after the war?

34. How did industrialization in the South compare with that in the North?

35. Describe the composition of the industrial workforce in the South. What problems did the workers face?

36. Describe the typical pattern of southern agriculture in the late nineteenth and early twentieth centuries. What problems confronted most farmers?

37. Describe the rise of the black middle class. How widespread were economic gains by southern blacks?

38. What was Booker T. Washington's prescription for black advancement?

39. How did the civil-rights cases of 1883 and *Plessy v. Ferguson* (1896) substantially negate the effect of the equal-protection clause of the Fourteenth Amendment?

40. What strategies and legal devices did the southern states use to evade the spirit of the Fifteenth Amendment?

41. Explain how southern whites used lynching to control the black population. How did some whites, both northern and southern, respond?

WHERE HISTORIANS DISAGREE (418-419)

42. How have historians differed over the nature of Reconstruction?

43. What part has the public played in this debate and why is the era so controversial?

44. How have historians attempted to explain the origins of segregation in America?

45. How have social and political development in the United States influenced the debate over the origins of segregation?

PATTERNS OF POPULAR CULTURE (422-423)

46. How was the minstrel show both a testament to the high awareness of race and the high level of racism in American society before the Civil War?

Identification

Identify each of the following and explain why it is important within the context of the chapter.

1. Thirteenth Amendment

2. O. O. Howard

3. Thaddeus Stevens

4. Charles Sumner

5. Wade-Davis Bill

6. John Wilkes Booth

7. Alexander H. Stephens

8. Joint Committee on Reconstruction

9. Fourteenth Amendment

10. Tenure of Office Act

11. Edwin M. Stanton

12. scalawag

13. carpetbagger

14. Blanche K. Bruce

15. Hiram R. Revels

16. sharecropping

17. crop lien system
18. Horatio Seymour
19. Hamilton Fish
20. "Grantism"
21. Liberal Republicans
22. Horace Greeley
23. Crédit Mobilier
24. "whiskey ring"
25. Panic of 1873
26. "Seward's Folly"
27. "redeemed"
28. Ku Klux Klan
29. Samuel J. Tilden
30. Readjuster
31. Henry W. Grady
32. the "Lost Cause"
33. Joel Chandler Harris
34. James B. Duke
35. standard-gauge
36. convict lease system
37. "fence laws"
38. The Atlanta Compromise
39. Jim Crow laws

Document 1

Read the portions of the chapter that discuss the Black Codes. Also read the section "Where Historians Disagree: Reconstruction." The following selection is taken from the writings of William A. Dunning. Consider the following questions: How does Dunning's account reveal his racist assumptions? How would accounts such as Dunning's lead white southerners in the twentieth century to conclude that they had been gravely wronged by Reconstruction? Which of the following positions is more convincing? Were the Black Codes a necessary and realistic response to the situation or were they a thinly disguised attempt to resubjugate the freedmen?

To a distrustful northern mind such legislation could very easily take the form of a systematic attempt to relegate the freedmen to a subjection only less complete than that from which the war had set them free. The radicals sounded a shrill note of alarm. "We tell the white men of Mississippi," said the *Chicago Tribune*, "that the men of the North will convert the state of Mississippi into a frog-pond before they will allow any such laws to disgrace one foot of soil over which the flag of freedom waves." In Congress, Wilson, Sumner, and other extremists took up the cry, and with superfluous ingenuity distorted the spirit and purpose of both the laws and the law-makers of the South. The "black codes" were represented to be the expression of a deliberate purpose by the Southerners to nullify the result of the war and reestablish slavery, and this impression gained wide prevalence in the North.

Yet, as a matter of fact, this legislation, far from embodying any spirit of defiance towards the North or any purpose to evade the conditions which the victors had imposed, was in the main a conscientious and straightforward attempt to bring some sort of order out of the social and economic chaos which a full acceptance of the results of war and emancipation involved. In its general principle it corresponded very closely to the actual facts of the situation. The freedmen were not, and in the nature of the case could not for generations be, on the same social, moral, and intellectual plane with the whites; and this fact was recognized by constituting them a separate class in the civil order. As in general principles, so in details, the legislation was faithful on the whole to the actual conditions with which it had to deal. The restrictions in respect to bearing arms, testifying in court, and keeping labor contracts were justified by well-established traits and habits of the negroes; and the vagrancy laws dealt with problems of destitution, idleness, and vice of which no one not in the midst of them could appreciate the appalling magnitude and complexity.

William A. Dunning, *Reconstruction: Political and Economic, 1865–1877* (1907; reprint, New York: Harper & Row [Harper Torchbooks], 1962), pp. 57–58.

Document 2

The crop lien system, initiated during Reconstruction, continued to be a major grievance of southern farmers well into the twentieth century. The following selection is taken from *The Ills of the South*, by Charles H. Otken, a Mississippi Baptist preacher and schoolteacher. Consider this document and the relevant parts of the text and answer the following questions: Why did the crop lien system arise? What were the consequences of the system on land ownership and crop selection? Could the system be fairly described as a "vicious circle"?

When all the cotton made during the year has been delivered and sold, and the farmer comes out in debt on the 31st of December, that farmer has taken the first step toward bankruptcy. If he is a small farmer, $25, $50, or $75 is a heavy burden to carry. Take these cases: Hezekiah Drawbridge owes $25 at the close of the year; his credit limit was $75. Stephen Goff owes $50; his credit limit ws $150. Buff Tafton owes $75; his credit limit was $250. The year during which these debts were made was fairly good, the purchases were moderate, there was no sickness in these families. The following year similar credit arrangements are made, and they purchase the full amount agreed upon between them and their merchants. From some unaccountable or accountable cause, the crop is a little worse, or the price of cotton is a little less. The winding up of the second year's farm operations finds Drawbridge, Goff, and Tafton with the following debts confronting them, respectively: $65, $115, $155. The outlook is blue for these farmers, and they feel blue. Thus, or nearly thus, this system operates in thousands of cases. Each year the plunge into debt is deeper; each year the burden is heavier. The struggle is woe-begone. Cares are many, smiles are few, and the comforts of life are scantier. This is the bitter fruit of a method of doing business which comes to the farmer in the guise of friendship, but rules him with despotic power. To a large class of men, the inscription printed in large, bold characters over the door of the credit system is: "The man who enters here leaves hope behind," and it tells a sad and sorrowful history. Anxious days, sleepless nights, deep wrinkles, gray hairs, wan faces, cheerless old age, and perhaps abject poverty make up, in part, the melancholy story.

Charles H. Otken, *The Ills of the South or Related Causes Hostile to the General Prosperity of the Southern People* (New York: Putnam, 1894).

Document 3

Read the section of the text concerning the case *Plessy v. Ferguson* which was decided by the Supreme Court in 1896. Included here are excerpts from the majority opinion and from Justice John Marshall Harlan's lone dissent. Consider the following questions: Which opinion is more convincing concerning the implication of the inferiority of blacks in the "separate but equal" doctrine? How does Harlan's dissent foreshadow the arguments of twentieth-century civil-rights crusaders? Is the United States Constitution today truly "color blind"?

The object of the [Fourteenth] amendment was undoubtedly to enforce the absolute equality of the two races before the law, but in the nature of things it could not have been intended to abolish distinctions based upon color, or to enforce social, as distinguished from political equality, or a co-mingling of the two races upon terms unsatisfactory to either. Laws permitting, and even requiring, their separation in places where they are liable to be brought into contact do not necessarily imply the inferiority of either race to the other, and have been generally, if not universally, recognized as within the competency of the state legislatures in the exercise of their police power. The most common instance of this is connected with the establishment of separate schools for white and colored children, which has been held to be a valid exercise of the legislative power even by courts of States where the political rights of the colored race have been longest and most earnestly enforced. . . .

Laws forbidding the intermarriage of the two races may be said in a technical sense to interfere with the freedom of contract, and yet have been universally recognized as within the police power of the State. . . .

So far, then, as a conflict with the Fourteenth Amendment is concerned, the case reduces itself to the question whether the statute of Louisiana is a reasonable regulation, and with respect to this there must necessarily be a large discretion on the part of the legislature. In determining the question of reasonableness it is at liberty to act with reference to the established usages, customs and traditions of the people, and with a view to the promotion of their comfort, and the preservation of the public peace and good order. . . .

We consider the underlying fallacy of the plaintiff's argument to consist in the assumption that the enforced separation of the two races stamps the colored race with a badge of inferiority. If this be so, it is not by reason of anything found in the act, but solely because the colored race chooses to put that construction upon it.

* * *

It was said in argument that the statute of Louisiana does not discriminate against either race, but prescribes a rule applicable alike to white and colored citizens. But this argument does not meet the difficulty. Everyone knows that the statute in question had its origins in the purpose, not so much to exclude white persons from railroad cars occupied by blacks, as to exclude colored people from coaches occupied by or assigned to white persons. . . . No one would be so wanting in candor as to assert the contrary. . . . In view of the Constitution, in the eye of the law, there is in this country no superior, dominant, ruling class of citizens. There is no caste here. Our Constitution is color-blind, and neither knows nor tolerates classes among citizens. . . . The destinies of the two races, in this country, are indissolubly linked together, and the interests of both require that the common government of all shall not permit the seeds of race hate to be planted under the sanction of law. . . . The arbitrary separation of citizens on the basis of race, while they are on a public highway, is a badge of servitude wholly inconsistent with the civil freedom and the equality before the law established by the Constitution.

Plessy v. Ferguson, 163 U.S. 537 (1896).

Map Exercise

Fill in or identify the following on the blank map provided. Use the map in the text as your source.

1. Former Confederate states.
2. First state to be readmitted, including the year.
3. Last three states to be readmitted, including the years. (Note that the other seven were readmitted in 1868.)
4. First three states to reestablish Conservative government, including the years.
5. States in which Conservative government was not reestablished until 1876.
6. The extent of the crop lien system in the South in 1880.

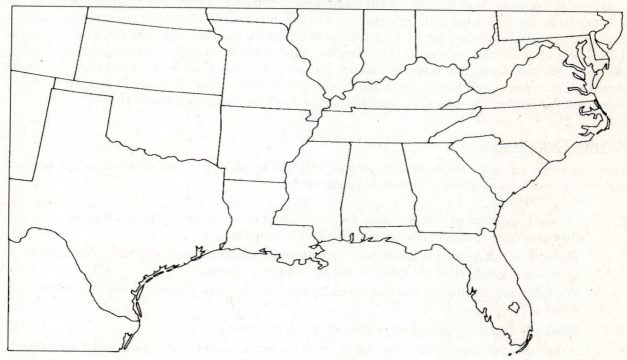

Interpretive Questions

Based on what you have filled in, answer the following. On some of the questions you will need to consult the narrative in your text for information or explanation.

1. Note the location of the first state to be readmitted by Congress and explain why it was restored to the Union so quickly.
2. What did the other ten states have to do to gain their readmissions in 1868–1870? What additional requirements did the last three face?
3. Note the first three states to experience the reestablishment of Conservative government and explain why the restoration of Democratic Party rule came so quickly there.
4. What forces delayed the reestablishment of Conservative government in the other states? What episode symbolically marks the end of the Reconstruction era?
5. Compare the crop lien system in 1880 to the location of cotton and slaves in 1860. What does this comparison tell you about the nature of postwar agriculture and labor in the New South?

Summary

The military aspect of the American Civil War lasted less than five years and ended in April 1865, but it would take another dozen years of Reconstruction to determine what the results of the war would be. The only questions clearly settled by the time of Appomattox were that the nation was indivisible and that slavery must end. The nation faced other issues with far-reaching implications. What would be the place of the freedmen in Southern society? How would the rebellious states be brought back into their "proper relationship" with the Union? The victorious North was in a position to dominate the South, but Northern politicians were not united in either resolve or purpose. For over two years after the fighting stopped, there was no coherent Reconstruction policy. Congress and the president struggled with each other, and various factions in Congress had differing views on politics, race, and union. Congress finally won control and dominated the Reconstruction process until Southern resistance and Northern ambivalence led to the end of Reconstruction in 1877. Whites who reasserted their economic and political control set out to industrialize the region but with little success. The South remained a troubled agricultural sector. No economic, political, or social issue in the South could escape the race question. The Jim Crow system of the southern establishment succeeded in evading the spirit of the Fourteenth and Fifteenth Amendments and many African Americans began to wonder just who won the Civil War. Meanwhile the South continued its colonial relationship with the North and southern plain folk, black and white, found themselves trapped by crop liens in circumstances some felt were almost as bad as slavery

Review Questions

These questions are to be answered with essays. This will allow you to explore relationships between individuals, events, and attitudes of the period under review.

1. Compare and contrast Lincoln's plan, the Wade-Davis Bill, Johnson's plan, and Radical Reconstruction. Consider provisions, motives, goals, and results.

2. Evaluate the successes and failures of Reconstruction. What decision could have been made to avoid the failures? What groundwork was laid for future changes?

3. What factors made the railroad the "central symbol of American progress" in the nineteenth century?

4. What was the ecological impact of the railroad on the American West?

5. Although many changes had occurred by 1900, the South remained an impoverished agricultural region, lagging well behind the rest of the nation. Describe the economic changes in the South and assess why they were not adequate to bring the old Confederacy into the national mainstream, as some of the region's spokespersons had hoped.

6. Explain the ways in which the southern white establishment was able to evade the spirit of the Fourteenth and Fifteenth Amendments to the Constitution.

Chapter Self Test

After you have read the chapter in the text and done the exercises in the Study Guide, take the following self test to see if you understand the material you have covered. Answers appear at the end of the Study Guide.

MULTIPLE-CHOICE QUESTIONS

Circle the letter of the response that best answers the question or completes the statement.

1. The Thirteenth Amendment to the U.S. Constitution:
   a. declared that the right to vote could not be denied on account of race.
   b. officially ended slavery.
   c. granted "citizenship" to the freedmen.
   d. provided that states could only count three-fifths (60%) of their black population when determining how many members they would be given in the U.S. House of Representatives.
   e. opened up the West to homesteading by African Americans.

2. The Fourteenth Amendment to the U.S. Constitution:
   a. declared that the right to vote could not be denied on account of race.
   b. officially ended slavery.
   c. granted "citizenship" to the freedmen.
   d. provided that states could only count three-fifths (60%) of their black population when determining how many members they could be given in the U.S. House of Representatives.
   e. opened up the West to homesteading by African Americans.

3. The Fifteenth Amendment to the U.S. Constitution:
   a. declared that the right to vote could not be denied on account of race.
   b. officially ended slavery.
   c. granted "citizenship" to the freedmen.
   d. provided that states could only count three-fifths (60%) of their black population when determining how many members they would be given in the U.S. House of Representatives.

4. Which faction of the Republican Party wanted Reconstruction to punish the former Confederacy, disenfranchise large numbers of southern whites, and confiscate the property of leading Confederates?
   a. Moderates.
   b. Conservatives.
   c. Redeemers.
   d. Scalybaggers.
   e. Radicals.

5. Which best describes Congressional reaction to the former Confederate states that had set up new governments under Andrew Johnson's "presidential Reconstruction"?
   a. They fully accepted all of the states except Georgia and South Carolina, which had elected no blacks to office.
   b. They conditionally accepted all of the states pending the results of local and state elections.
   c. They refused to seat the senators and representatives from the states and set up a committee to investigate and advise on Reconstruction.
   d. They fully accepted all of the states west of the Mississippi River, but required new constitutions in the others.

6. The "Black Codes" were a set of regulations established by:

   a. the Congress to protect the rights of the former slaves to own property and to find employment.

   b. the U.S. Supreme Court to enforce the provisions of the Thirteenth and Fourteenth Amendments to the U.S. Constitution.

   c. the northern states to prevent a massive influx of former slaves from entering their states and seeking homes and jobs.

   d. the southern states to promote white supremacy and to control the economic and social activities of the freedmen.

7. Which of the following, if any, was <u>not</u> a provision of the Congressional plan of Reconstruction enacted in early 1867?

   a. Dividing the South into military districts administered by military commanders.

   b. Requiring former Confederate states, as a condition of readmission to the Union, to ratify the Fourteenth Amendment to the U.S. Constitution.

   c. Mandating former Confederate states, as a condition of readmission to the Union, to hold a constitutional convention and prepare a constitution providing for black male suffrage.

   d. Declaring that each state must present a plan for distributing farm land to, or providing jobs for, the former slaves.

   e. <u>All</u> of the above were provisions of the Congressional plan of Reconstruction.

8. Critics of native southern whites who joined the Republican Party called them:

   a. carpetbaggers.

   b. whippersnappers.

   c. scalawags.

   d. white camellias.

   e. filibusterers.

9. Which best describes the extent of "Negro rule" in the southern states during Reconstruction?

   a. African Americans played a significant political role in several states but never elected a governor or controlled a state legislature.

   b. Some African Americans held local elective offices and a very few were elected to state legislatures but the numbers were politically inconsequential in every state.

   c. In the deep South, states where African Americans constituted a majority of the voters due to white disenfranchisement, blacks dominated both houses of the state legislatures and controlled state politics as long as federal troops remained in the South.

   d. African Americans did not actually hold many offices in any state, but they effectively dominated local offices in all but Tennessee and Arkansas through alliances with white Republicans.

10. What institution was the key point of contact in the agricultural credit system for most southern farmers, black and white, in the late nineteenth century?

    a. Small town banks owned by northerners.

    b. Large diversified planters.

    c. Finance companies in the larger cities such as Atlanta and Memphis.

    d. Local country-store merchants.

    e. Mail order mortgage companies operating out of New York.

11. In the late nineteenth century, the agricultural credit system in the South encouraged farmers to:
    a. rely heavily on cash crops—especially cotton.
    b. diversify away from cotton toward food grains and livestock.
    c. adopt the use of mechanization on increasingly larger farms.
    d. abandon farming and invest in capital-intensive manufacturing enterprises.

12. Ulysses S. Grant's election as president was largely a result of his being:
    a. governor of New York during the postwar economic boom.
    b. a triumphant commanding general of the Union army.
    c. the popular administrator of the Freedmen's Bureau.
    d. a flamboyant cavalry officer in the western Indian wars.

13. Which of the following, if any, was not associated with the "Compromise of 1877"?
    a. Removal of the last federal troops from the South.
    b. Increased federal aid for railroads and other internal improvements.
    c. Appointment of a southerner to the cabinet.
    d. Making Rutherford B. Hayes president.
    e. All of the above were associated with the "Compromise of 1877."

14. Which of the following, if any, is not cited by the text as a reason that Reconstruction failed to accomplish more to promote racial equality in the United States?
    a. Fear that harsh action might lead to resumed military action by the southern states, even though they had been defeated.
    b. Attachment to a states' rights view of the Constitution, even for the rebel states.
    c. Deep respect for private property rights, even for leading Confederates.
    d. Belief in black inferiority by many whites, even northern liberals.
    e. All of the above were cited as reasons that Reconstruction failed to accomplish more.

15. The "solid" South refers to the:
    a. work ethic values of southern whites.
    b. courage of Confederate soldiers during the war despite being outnumbered.
    c. steady returns that northern bankers could expect from investment in cotton.
    d. the fact that the Democratic Party could count on the votes of the southern states after Reconstruction.

16. In most states, the "Redeemers" or "Bourbons" were typically composed of:
    a. a newly emerging class of merchants, industrialists, railroad developers, and financiers.
    b. essentially the same old planter elite that had dominated antebellum politics.
    c. a coalition of poor, working-class whites and blacks.
    d. white farmers who owned small to medium farms.

17. Henry W. Grady was:
    a. the builder of the American Tobacco Company.
    b. an Atlanta editor who became a leading spokesman for the "New South" idea.
    c. the person principally responsible for Birmingham, Alabama, becoming an iron and steel production center.
    d. the governor of South Carolina who was most vociferous in advocating that blacks should migrate from the South to take industrial jobs in the North.

18. The "convict-lease" system was an arrangement whereby:

    a. southern states housed northern prisoners as a way to fund prisons without raising taxes.

    b. a white man convicted of a nonviolent crime could pay a poor person, usually black, to serve his time for him.

    c. the state rented cells to the convicts who then had to pay rent based on pittance wages paid in prison industry.

    d. private interests paid the state for the right to use groups of prisoners to work on railroad construction and other projects.

19. "Jim Crow" is a nickname for:

    a. white southerners who used violence or intimidation to restrict black activities.

    b. black people who curried favor with whites by acting excessively polite and deferential.

    c. the whole system of laws and customs that kept the races separate in schools, public buildings, housing, jobs, theaters, and the like.

    d. black people who pretended to be friendly toward whites but who secretly undermined white interests.

    e. the African-American culture of dance, music, food, and religion that grew up after slavery.

20. In *Plessy v. Ferguson* (1896) the U.S. Supreme Court established the general principle that:

    a. states could not prevent blacks from voting just because their grandparents had been slaves.

    b. states could require separate accommodations on trains, in schools, and the like, for blacks and whites as long as the accommodations were equal.

    c. Congress could take away a state's seats in the U.S. House of Representatives if the state refused to allow blacks to vote in Congressional elections.

    d. local governments could use zoning and building codes to enforce racial segregation by neighborhood.

21. Around the turn of the century, which of the following was most likely to attract northern white support?

    a. Increased enforcement of the Fifteenth Amendment.

    b. Statutes allowing whites and blacks to marry each other if they wished.

    c. A federal anti-lynching law.

    d. Congressional intervention to promote racial integration in southern public schools.

TRUE-FALSE QUESTIONS

Read each statement carefully. Mark true statements "T" and false statements "F."

1. As bad as the economic and physical situation was for southern blacks in the aftermath of the Civil War, conditions were even worse for the region's white population.

2. The Emancipation Proclamation ended slavery throughout the South in 1863.

3. Republicans were afraid that the quick return of the southern states to Congress would lead to more Democratic votes, thereby increasing the likelihood that Congress would establish protective tariffs and subsidize railroads.

4. President Lincoln believed that a lenient Reconstruction policy would encourage southern Unionists and other southern Whigs to become Republicans and build a stronger party in the South.

5. John Wilkes Booth acted completely on his own in plotting to murder President Lincoln.

6. Characteristics of Andrew Johnson's personality that hampered him as president were that he was too polite and deferential to assume any leadership initiative.

7. The Tenure of Office Act and the Command of the Army Act were passed by Congress to prevent southern states from sending former Confederates to Congress or from having them control the state militia companies.

8. Even though the House's impeachment charges were nominally based on specific "high crimes and misdemeanors," Andrew Johnson was actually convicted by the Senate and removed from the presidency for petty political reasons.

9. Despite the end of slavery, most black agricultural labor in the South in the late nineteenth century continued to emulate the gang-labor system in which slaves lived in concentrated quarters and worked in groups under the constant supervision of a white field boss suggestive of the prewar overseer.

10. During the period from just before the Civil War to just after Reconstruction, per capita income for African Americans rose significantly while per capita income for whites dropped.

11. In the 1870s, the expanded printing of greenback paper currency was advocated by those, especially debtors, who believed that inflation would help the economy.

12. In the context of Reconstruction, "redeemed" was used to refer to freedmen who had returned to their original slave plantations as workers after running away during or immediately following the war.

13. The Crédit Mobilier was a railroad construction company involved in scandal during the Grant administration.

14. Hamilton Fish was Grant's secretary of state whose action worsened relations between the United States and Great Britain.

15. Alaska was called "Seward's folly" or "icebox" because of Seward's abortive attempt to sell the territory to the Russian czar as a method of financing the cost of maintaining troops in the South during Reconstruction.

16. In the period from the end of Reconstruction into the twentieth century, the Democratic Party was the political party of the vast majority of southern whites.

17. In general, the "Redeemer"-"Bourbon" political regimes were inclined to raise taxes to expand services, especially public education.

18. By 1900 the portion of the nation's manufacturing output produced in the South was about three times what it had been on the eve of the Civil War.

19. The portion of southern farmers who were tenants, cash or sharecrop, increased markedly from Reconstruction to 1900.

20. In the period from Reconstruction to 1900, the crop lien system helped many southern back-country farmers in the piney woods and mountains move from cash-crop commercial farming into a ruggedly independent sort of subsistence farming.

21. By the late 1890s, a significantly smaller portion of southern blacks were allowed to vote than in the late 1860s.

CHAPTER SIXTEEN
THE CONQUEST OF THE FAR WEST

Objectives

A thorough study of Chapter 16 should enable the student to understand

1. The cultural characteristics of the varied populations of the West.
2. The pattern of settlement on the last American frontier and the significance of the frontier in American history.
3. The impact of the discovery of gold and silver in the West, both on the region and on the nation as a whole.
4. The development of the cattle industry in the American Southwest after 1860.
5. The methods used by the federal government to reduce the threat of the Plains Indians and the Indians' ultimate fate.
6. The reasons for the transition from subsistence farming to commercial farming and the effect of the change on the West.
7. The "Turner Thesis," its supporters, and its critics.

Main Themes

1. The varied and vibrant ethnic and racial cultures that characterized the American West and how Anglo-European whites enforced their dominant role by the latter part of the nineteenth century.
2. The transformation of the far West from a sparsely populated region of Indians and various early settlers of European and Asian background into a part of the nation's capitalistic economy.
3. The closing of the frontier as Indian resistance was eliminated, miners and cowboys spearheaded settlements, and railroads opened the area for intensive development.
4. The development of mining, ranching, and commercial farming as the three major industries of the West.
5. The problems faced by farmers as the agricultural sector entered a relative decline.

Glossary

1. territory: A geographical and governmental subdivision under the jurisdiction of the United States but not included within any state. Beginning with the Northwest Ordinance of 1787, the federal government divided the West into territories to facilitate control until the area was prepared for statehood. Territories were allowed some self-government by territorial legislatures, but the president appointed the territorial governor. Because of the peculiar circumstances surrounding their entry into the union, Texas and California never went through the territorial stage.

2. frontier: In the American sense, an unexplored, unsettled, or recently settled geographic region. The term also refers to any endeavor in which development possibilities seem unbounded—for instance, the urban frontier, frontiers of science. In the European sense, the frontier is the area near the border with another nation.

3. <u>placer mining</u>: The process of removing gold from the sand and gravel of stream beds. Gold, eroded from mountain lodes, washes into swift-flowing streams and is suspended in the water until the streams slow in certain places and the gold settles to the bottom. Placer mining is the easiest and cheapest method of gold mining because only a simple pan or wooden sluice box is required to separate the gold from the sand and gravel.

4. <u>quartz mining</u>: The process of removing gold or silver from lodes in ore-bearing rock and earth. It is an expensive process involving digging, blasting, crushing, and smelting.

5. <u>barrios</u>: Urban neighborhoods occupied, principally, by lower-class Mexican Americans. Spanish language dominates in the *barrio,* and businesses, churches, and other social institutions catering to Mexican Americans are concentrated in these neighborhoods. *Barrios* were often, but not always, located on the fringe of the city.

Pertinent Questions

THE SOCIETIES OF THE FAR WEST (434-442)

1. Describe the caste system that developed in the American Southwest under Spanish and Mexican rule. What role did the Pueblo Indians and other tribes play in this system?

2. Describe the culture of the Plains tribes, with particular emphasis on gender roles and the importance of the American bison (buffalo). What three tribes dominated the northern plains by the mid–nineteenth century?

3. Explain the advantages and disadvantages that the Plains Indians had in their conflicts with white settlers. Why did the whites eventually prevail?

4. How did Anglo-American dominance affect the nature of Hispanic culture in New Mexico from the 1840s to 1900?

5. What factors led to the decline of Mexican-American economic and social dominance in California and Texas? What was the socioeconomic status of most Mexican Americans by the end of the nineteenth century?

6. Up to 1869, in what two fields did the greatest number of Chinese immigrants work? How did employment tendencies, residence patterns, and social relationships change in the Chinese community later in the nineteenth century?

7. Why was Anglo-European hostility toward the Chinese so high in California? What actions resulted from this hostility? How did the Chinese Americans respond?

8. What factors led to the massive increase in Anglo-European settlement of the Far West after the Civil War?

9. Describe the vision of the Homestead Act and how it was flawed. What changes were made to try to remedy weaknesses in the act?

10. Describe the process of evolution from territory to state. What areas still lacked statehood by the turn of the century? Why?

THE CHANGING WESTERN ECONOMY (442-447)

11. What was the composition of the western labor force? How was it shaped by racial prejudice and gender imbalance?

12. Describe the typical pattern of development and decline in the western mining industry. What was life like for the men and women who lived and worked in the mining regions?

13. Describe the origins, purposes, and practices of the "long drive" and "open range" periods of the "cattle kingdom." What ended this colorful but brief boom?

14. Why did women tend to gain the right to vote in the western states and territories before they did in the East?

THE ROMANCE OF THE WEST (447-453)

15. To what two factors does the text attribute much of the romantic image of the Far West? Explain.

16. How accurate was Frederick Jackson Turner's thesis about the American frontier?

THE DISPERSAL OF THE TRIBES (453-457)

17. Describe the evolution of traditional national Indian policy up to the 1880s. What did the policies accomplish? How were the policies and their implementation flawed?

18. What happened to the great buffalo (bison) herds, and how did it affect Indian life?

19. Describe how the influx of white settlers into the West led to violence and warfare. What were the major encounters? Why did the whites ultimately prevail?

20. What was the basic objective of the Dawes Act, and how did it try to accomplish this goal?

THE RISE AND DECLINE OF THE WESTERN FARMER (457-461)

21. Describe the building of the transcontinental railroads and subsidiary lines. Why can it be said that the western railroads were essentially public projects, despite their private ownership?

22. How did the railroads stimulate settlement of the Great Plains?

23. What unfamiliar problems did farmers encounter on the Great Plains? What methods and devices helped solve these problems?

24. How were market forces changing the nature of American agriculture? What was the result?

25. What were the three main grievances of the late-nineteenth century farmer? To what extent did psychological factors compound these problems?

PATTERNS OF POPULAR CULTURE: THE WILD WEST SHOW (448-449)

26. What role did Buffalo Bill and the Wild West Show phenomenon play in shaping and preserving an image of the American West that is at odds with that presented by most modern historians?

WHERE HISTORIANS DISAGREE: THE "FRONTIER" AND THE WEST (450-451)

27. Why do the "new western historians" argue that Anglo-European Americans did not so much settle the West as conquer it? Is this a fair characterization of the course of events?

Identification

Identify each of the following, and explain why it is important within the context of the chapter.

1. Great American Desert

2. Indian Territory

3. "territorial rings"

4. *californios*

5. "coolies"

6. "tongs"

7. Washoe district/Comstock Lode

8. vigilantes

9. "range wars"

10. Albert Bierstadt

11. Mark Twain

12. Frederic Remington

13. Theodore Roosevelt

14. Bureau of Indian Affairs
15. Sand Creek massacre
16. Crazy Horse and Sitting Bull
17. George A. Custer
18. Battle of the Little Bighorn
19. Nez Percé
20. Geronimo
21. Wounded Knee
22. barbed wire
23. Annie Oakley

Document 1

At the Medicine Lodge Council of 1867 representatives of the Kiowa, Comanche, Cheyenne, Arapaho, and Plains Apache tribes met with a United States delegation including the Commissioner of Indian Affairs, a U.S. senator, and various generals and other officials. Over 7,000 Indians were gathered along Medicine Lodge Creek in southern Kansas just outside Indian Territory. Several chiefs spoke eloquently of their anguish at having to give up territory. The excerpt below comes from the statement of Kiowa Chief Satanta. Consider the following questions: Did all the land south of the Arkansas River really belong to the southern Plains tribes? Was there a realistic way for Satanta's vision to have been granted by federal policy?

> All the land south of the Arkansas [River] belongs to the Kiowas and Comanches, and I do not want to give away any of it. I love the land and the buffalo and I will not part with any. . . . I have heard that you intend to settle us on a reservation near the [Wichita] mountains [in southwestern Oklahoma]. I do not want to settle there. I love to roam over the wide prairie, and when I do it, I feel free and happy, but when we settle down we grow pale and die. . . . A long time ago this land belonged to our fathers, but when I go up to the river, I see a camp of soldiers, and they are cutting my wood down, or killing my buffalo. I do not like that, and when I see it, my heart feels like bursting with sorrow.

Document 2

The *Atlanta Constitution* was one of the leading Bourbon voices of the postwar South, especially during the editorship of Henry Grady (1879–1889). The following editorial, written before Grady's period, celebrates the completion of the first transcontinental railroad. Consider the following questions: How does the editorial reveal the psychological importance of the transcontinental railroad to the American sense of nationhood? How does it show that the railroad would lead to the end of the frontier? What does the writer reveal about southern jealousy of northern industrial accomplishment and southern resolve to advance economically (see Chapter Fifteen)?

> This mammoth enterprise is completed at last. It has no equal in modern history for magnitude, importance, and the energy of its execution. Bold in conception and stupendous in realization, it stands a monument among the monster achievements of the age. It links the oceans with its iron bond. It brings the continents into close social and commercial communion. It nullifies the area of immense distances and overleaps the impediments of boundless wilderness. It pierces savage realms with the probe of civilization. It hitches progress on to the barren dominion of the uncultured Indian. It connects the buffalo with the water-fall. With the speed of lightning it transmits the refinements of high polish and the improvements of progressive art and science broad-cast over a country that must have remained otherwise a free range of wild forest. It redeems from disuse millions of acres of virgin

land, and is the "opening up" [of] a stream of commerce and development that will beneficially inundate one of the magnificent portions of the world.

It is useless to dispute the wonderful spirit of energy and skill that has put this herculean enterprise through. The difficulties have been almost invincible, and the nerve to overcome them has been grand.

But this success has some grave drawbacks concerned with it. . . . It might have been built elsewhere with less money and served the purposes of its construction better. . . . The Southern Pacific route is destined to be the successful road between the two oceans. It is shorter than the one now built, runs through a milder climate, has less obstacles of mountain and river, and can be used all the year round. . . . We regard the Southern Pacific as one of the necessities of Southern effort. It will do more to build up our Southern States than any other one business movement. When we get to be the channel for the stupendous tide of commerce and trade that will surge over the land from the Pacific coast, we will spring into potent importance, and we will absorb and assimilate unreckonable wealth and population. Let us grasp for the huge prize. Let us no longer sit confessed sluggards in contrast with Northern energy. Let us not sit supinely and see our Northern neighbor pick fruits that belong to us legitimately.

Atlanta Constitution, 12 May 1869, p. 1.

Map Exercise

Fill in or identify the following on the blank map provided. Use the maps in the text and appendix as your source.

1. Indicate the area of the Great Plains by means of diagonal lines.
2. Draw lines indicating the general flow of the "long drives."
3. Indicate the Rocky Mountains and the Sierra Nevada-Cascade Range by drawing inverted *V*s along their positions.
4. Place boxes with dates to indicate the general areas of the gold and silver rushes of 1849, 1858 to 1859, and 1874. Tell what state each strike was in.
5. Draw a line along the approximate route of the first transcontinental railroad. Place a star at the point where the two lines joined.
6. Locate Denver and San Francisco.
7. Identify the following: Indian Territory (Oklahoma); the Dakotas; New Mexico; and California.

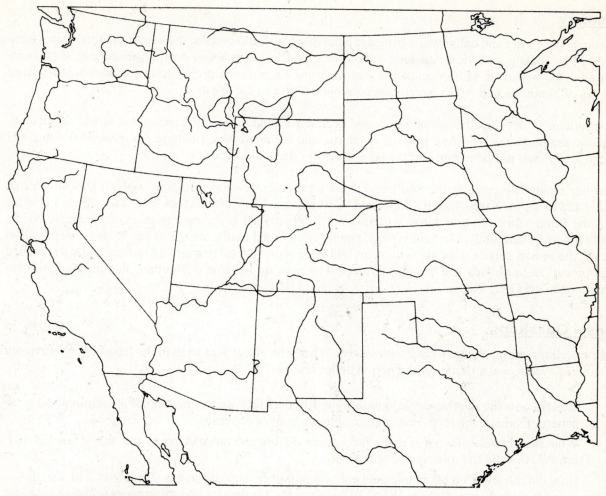

Interpretive Questions

Based on what you have filled in, answer the following. On some of the questions you will need to consult the narrative in your text for information or explanation.

1. How was the pre–Civil War settlement along the Pacific coast isolated from the rest of the nation?
2. Why did the post–Civil War gold and silver rushes involve considerable west-to-east as well as east-to-west migration?
3. What two major cities of the twentieth century obtained significant early boosts from the mining rushes?
4. What were the long-term results from the days of the long cattle drives?
5. Why were the Plains Indians so resentful of the reservations they were provided?
6. What areas of the nation were best served by the first transcontinental railroad? Why was the South resentful?
7. What special challenges did agriculture of the Great Plains present to farmers?

Summary

Far from being empty and unknown, significant parts of what would become the western United States were populated by Indians and Mexicans long before the post-Civil War boom in Anglo-European settlement. Even after the waves of white occupation and in face of significant prejudice from those whites, large numbers of Mexicans and Asian Americans continued to live in the West.

White settlement developed in initial boom and decline patterns in three industries that would do much to shape the region in the long run: mining, ranching, and commercial agriculture. Asians, Mexicans, and African Americans provided much of the labor force for these industries.

In the late nineteenth century, the South and West were underdeveloped regions with an almost colonial relationship to the industrial, heavily populated Northeast and Midwest. Except for a few pockets in the far West, the frontier line of agricultural settlement in 1860 stopped at the eastern edge of the Great Plains. Hostile Plains Indians and an unfamiliar environment combined to discourage advance. By the end of the century, the Indian barrier to white settlement had been removed, cattlemen and miners had spearheaded development, and railroads had brought farmers, who, despite nagging difficulties, had made significant adaptations to the Great Plains.

Review Questions

These questions are to be answered with essays. This will allow you to explore relationships between individuals, events, and attitudes of the period under review.

1. Explain how the mining, cattle, and farming frontiers followed something of a boom-and-bust pattern. Evaluate the long-term impact of these frontier activities.

2. What was the role of women in the far western mining and railroad towns and on the ranches and farms? How did the role change with time?

3. How did the white racial, ethnic, and cultural prejudice against Indians, Mexicans, and Asians shape the development of the West? What were the similarities and differences in the experiences of these three groups?

Chapter Self Test

After you have read the chapter in the text and done the exercises in the Study Guide, take the following self test to see if you understand the material you have covered. Answers appear at the end of the Study Guide.

MULTIPLE-CHOICE QUESTIONS

Circle the letter of the response that best answers the question or completes the statement.

1. Because the area was arid to semiarid and thought to be unfit for Anglo-European civilization, many nineteenth-century Americans called the Far West the:
   a. Trans Mississippi Wasteland.
   b. Intermountain Barrens.
   c. Prairie Wilderness.
   d. Great American Desert.

2.   Indian Territory, to which several eastern Indian tribes including the Cherokees and Creeks were removed, is now the state of:

    a. South Dakota.

    b. Kansas.

    c. Oklahoma.

    d. Wyoming.

3.   Which of the following best represents the "caste system" that prevailed in the American Southwest before the arrival of Anglo-European settlement? (highest status first)

    a. Pueblos, Spanish/Mexicans, Apaches/Navajos

    b. Apaches/Navajos, Pueblos, Spanish/Mexicans

    c. Spanish/Mexicans, Pueblos, Apaches/Navajos

    d. Spanish/Mexicans, Apaches/Navajos, Pueblos

4.   What northern Plains Indian nation was the strongest?

    a. Comanche

    b. Sioux

    c. Pawnee

    d. Blackfeet

5.   The groups of local businessmen and politicians who had Washington connections and who dominated the government of New Mexico and other territories were often called

    a. "range bosses."

    b. "territorial rings."

    c. "ranch kings."

    d. "capitol cowboys."

6.   What happened to the *californios* who dominated California prior to the gold rush of 1849?

    a. Most died due to epidemic diseases brought in by the miners.

    b. The ones who could speak English adapted well and continued to dominate real estate ownership.

    c. Most emigrated back to Mexico or Arizona.

    d. Many lost status and land and were excluded from the prosperity of the statehood period.

7.   Which of the following was *not* a reason for Anglo-American resentment of Chinese immigrants?

    a. They tended to congregate together and maintain Chinese culture.

    b. Some secret societies ("tongs") engaged in crime.

    c. Many of the early female Chinese immigrants had been sold into prostitution.

    d. The Chinese were perceived as lazy slackers who would not work hard.

8.   Which of the following was *not* a flaw in the Homestead Act?

    a. One hundred sixty acres was not enough land in the West.

    b. The law did not provide capital for machines and the like.

    c. The land was too costly for most settlers.

9. Which type of mining came first as new fields opened?
   a. placer (pan)
   b. quartz (lode)
   c. strip (open pit)
   d. hydraulic (water pressure)

10. Which of the following states/territories did *not* experience significant mining development from the 1850s to 1880s?
   a. Nevada
   b. Colorado
   c. Kansas
   d. South Dakota
   e. Montana

11. The "long drive" in the open-range cattle industry referred to the process of:
   a. rounding up the cattle from great distances all over the range for branding in the spring.
   b. moving the cattle south to Texas in the winter and north to Colorado, Wyoming, and Montana in the spring to take advantage of the best pasture.
   c. using cattle as oxen to pull covered wagons for settlers seeking homesteads in the West.
   d. herding cattle from the ranges in Texas and other remote areas to the nearest accessible railroad loading point so that the cattle could be shipped to slaughterhouses in the East.

12. What *two* groups constituted most of the cowboys in the open range era? (Mark *two* letters.)
   a. southern Whites
   b. Native Americans
   c. African Americans
   d. Hispanics
   e. Chinese

13. The historian who influenced many with his paper on "The Significance of the Frontier in American History" was:
   a. Oliver Wendell Holmes.
   b. C. W. McCune.
   c. Albert Bierstadt.
   d. Frederick Jackson Turner.
   e. Charles A. Beard.

14. The federal government agency vested with management of Indian relations and the reservations was the:
   a. Indian Lands Commission.
   b. Native American Administration.
   c. Office of Assimilation and Concentration.
   d. Bureau of Indian Affairs.

15. Who were the *two* principal Indian chiefs who led the forces that massed in the northern plains in 1875–1876 following the Black Hills gold rush? (Mark *two* letters.)

    a. Black Kettle

    b. Sitting Bull

    c. Crazy Horse

    d. Geronimo

    e. Red Eagle

16. The purpose of the Dawes Severalty Act of 1887 was to:

    a. weaken tribes, allot land to individual Indians, and promote assimilation.

    b. geographically disperse the reservations so it would be more difficult for Indian warrior forces to unite.

    c. increase tribal loyalty and reduce violence by allowing chiefs and tribal councils to act autonomously on the reservations.

    d. restore economic viability to the nomadic way of Plains Indian life by revitalizing the bison herds.

17. Construction of the early transcontinental railroad lines was financed mainly by:

    a. European investors excited about the developing American West.

    b. Wall Street investors with close ties to cattle and mining interests.

    c. small investors such as farmers and local merchants who wanted to attract rail lines to their communities.

    d. government subsidies in the form of favorable loans and land grants.

18. What fencing material revolutionized agriculture on the prairie and plains?

    a. split rails

    b. chain link

    c. pickets

    d. barbed wire

19. By the end of the century, agriculture on the Great Plains was increasingly:

    a. subsistence in nature.

    b. commercially oriented.

    c. truck farming.

    d. being displaced by industry.

20. Which of the following are listed in the text as farmers' three principle grievances? (Mark three letters.)

    a. High interest charges

    b. Persistent production shortfalls

    c. Inequitable freight rates

    d. Inadequate currency

    e. Poor-quality farm machinery produced by American factories

TRUE-FALSE QUESTIONS

Read each statement carefully. Mark true statements "T" and false statements "F."

1. As late as 1900, the Far West remained essentially outside America's capitalist economy.

2. Except in warfare, American Indian tribal culture made little distinction between the genders in family and work roles.

3. Although most historians have previously presented the buffalo (bison) as critical to Plains Indian culture prior to the 1880s, recent anthropological work has revealed that this is a myth and that the buffalo was actually relatively unimportant for these tribes.

4. Prior to the arrival of significant numbers of English-speaking settlers, an elite group of large landowning Hispanics dominated life in New Mexico.

5. A *barrio* was a Mexican American who cooperated with Anglo settlers and often supervised poor farm workers.

6. "Coolies" were Chinese indentured servants whose status was close to slavery.

7. In the late nineteenth century, most white Californians favored increased Chinese immigration because there was a labor shortage and the Chinese would work cheaply.

8. The Timber Culture Act, Desert Land Act, and Timber and Stone Act provided avenues for westerners to acquire larger tracts of land than were allowed under the Homestead Act.

9. By 1900 all of the present states except Alaska, Hawaii, and Utah had been admitted to the Union.

10. The working class in the American West was racially diversified and stratified.

11. Vigilantes were groups of citizens in mining towns organized to enforce justice in the absence of official legal authority.

12. Prostitution was common in the mining "boom towns."

13. When the "long-drive" era began, there was an excess of cattle in Texas, so cowboys drove huge herds to rail centers in Louisiana, especially New Orleans, for shipment to the East.

14. Since the majority of western cowboys were veterans of the Confederate army, African Americans were seldom allowed to work on ranches or the long drives.

15. The so-called "Range Wars" were fought between the big railroad companies and their workers over harsh working conditions and low wages.

16. The text regards Frederick Jackson Turner's thesis of the West as an empty, uncivilized frontier awaiting settlement and which was essentially settled by 1890, as the best explanation for the region's transformation.

17. Although the Bureau of Indian Affairs was chronically under funded and understaffed, the reform-minded whites who ran it established a solid reputation for honesty, efficiency, and sincere concern for the well-being of the Native Americans they served.

18. On the West Coast, in California in particular, whites sometimes hunted down Indians and killed them without provocation.

19. Although small, the Nez Percé tribe was composed of particularly effective warriors who engaged in raids throughout the southern plains until Chief Joseph was finally captured in 1877.

20. The first transcontinental railroad was completed shortly before the beginning of the Civil War, but due to the war the railroad didn't carry much traffic until the end of the 1860s.

CHAPTER SEVENTEEN
INDUSTRIAL SUPREMACY

Objectives

A thorough study of Chapter 17 should enable the student to understand:

1. The reasons for the rapid industrial development of the United States in the late nineteenth century.
2. The specific impact of technological innovations in promoting industrial expansion.
3. The role of the individual entrepreneur in the development of particular industries.
4. The changes that were taking place in the organization and management of American business.
5. The ways in which classical economics and certain ideas of Darwin were used to justify and defend the new industrial capitalism.
6. The critics of the new industrial capitalism and the solutions they proposed.
7. The conditions of immigrants, women, and children in the work force.
8. The several efforts of organized labor to form national associations.
9. The reasons that organized labor generally failed in its efforts to achieve its objectives.

Main Themes

1. How various factors (raw materials, labor supply, technology, business organization, growing markets, and friendly governments) combined to thrust the United States into worldwide industrial leadership.
2. How this explosion of industrial capitalism was both extolled for its accomplishments and attacked for its excesses.
3. How American workers, who on the average benefited, reacted to the physical and psychological realities of the new economic order.

Glossary

1. monopoly: A business situation in which one company controls virtually the entire market for a particular good or service. The monopoly may be regional or national. (When a few businesses control the market, it is called an *oligopoly*.)
2. patent: An official government grant, given as an incentive for technological advancement, which entitles an inventor to exclusive right to the proceeds of his or her work for a limited number of years. (See U.S. Constitution, Article I, Section 8.)
3. capitalism: A national economic and business system in which the great majority of the basic means of production and distribution of goods are privately owned and managed for profit.
4. law of supply and demand: An economic axiom that asserts that when the demand for goods and services exceeds the supply, prices will rise, and when supply surpasses demand, prices will fall.
5. socialism: An economic theory that emphasizes the importance of class and argues that the interests of workers and capitalists are inherently antagonistic. Socialists believe that a more equitable distribution of the economic benefits of society will result if the people as a whole, through their government, own and manage the basic means of production and distribution.

6. <u>Marxism/communism</u>: A variety of extreme socialism, based on the writings of Karl Marx, that assumes that the inherent conflict between labor and capital will inevitably lead to socialist revolution, the collapse of capitalism, and the emergence of a classless society.

7. <u>collective bargaining</u>: A system in which a labor union negotiates with management to set the wages and working conditions of all members of the union. This is in contrast to the traditional system in which each worker dealt individually with management.

8. <u>Adam Smith</u>: Scottish philosopher and economist who advocated laissez faire. Scottish-born Smith was the author of the extremely influential book *The Wealth of Nations* (1776) which argues that the "invisible hand" of competition will best produce wealth and that governments should not interfere with business.

9. <u>craft and industrial unionism</u>: Craft unions are organized according to a worker's skill—for example, plumbing. Industrial unions are organized according to the industry in which a worker toils, regardless of his or her particular responsibility—for example, coal mining.

Pertinent Questions

SOURCES OF INDUSTRIAL GROWTH (464-472)

1. What technological innovations of the late nineteenth century transformed communications and business operations?

2. What new methods were developed for the large-scale production of durable steel? Where were the principal American centers of steel production and ore extraction?

3. What was the relationship between the steel industry and the railroads?

4. How did the railroad impact the United States? Specifically, in what areas especially did railroad growth change the status quo?

5. Describe the early oil industry in the United States, indicating what the main uses of petroleum were at first. What technological development profoundly changed the oil industry?

6. Although the age of the automobile would not fully arrive until the 1920s, what developments of the 1890s and early 1900s laid the basis for the later boom?

7. Although the Wright Brothers developed the first practical airplane in the U.S., what nation led in early development? What led to further development in America?

8. Describe the emergence of organized corporate research and its impact on American economic development. What role did universities play in this process?

9. Explain the concepts of "scientific management" and "mass production." Who were the leading pioneers of these new approaches to industry?

10. How did the railroad transform American economically and ecologically? Were the changes that the railroad caused ecologically beneficial or not? Explain.

11. What was the main legal principle that made buying stock in the modern corporation attractive to investors?

12. Explain the new approach to management and business organization that accompanied the rise of large corporations. What industries led in these developments?

13. Compare and contrast the vertical and horizontal integration strategies of business combination. Which approaches did Andrew Carnegie and John D. Rockefeller use initially? How did they evolve toward using both strategies?

14. Explain how financiers and industrialists used pools, trusts, and holding companies to expand their control. What was the result of this trend toward corporate combination?

CAPITALISM AND ITS CRITICS (472-477)

15. How did popular culture keep alive the "rags-to-riches" and "self-made man" hopes of the American masses? How realistic were such dreams?

16. Explain how the theories of Social Darwinism and classical economics complemented each other. Who formulated these theories? How did the great industrialists embody such concepts?

17. Describe the "alternative visions" to the business-dominated view of society. How influential were such radical voices?

18. What were the visible symptoms that many Americans blamed on the trend toward "monopoly?" How did monopoly threaten the individual and men in particular?

INDUSTRIAL WORKERS IN THE NEW ECONOMY (477-487)

19. What were the two sources of the massive migration into the industrial cities of the late nineteenth and early twentieth centuries?

20. Contrast the earlier immigrants to the United States with those who dominated after the 1880s. What attracted these migrants? What tensions ensued?

21. What happened to the standard of living of the average worker in the late nineteenth century? What physical hardships and psychological adjustments did many workers face?

22. Why did industry increasingly employ women and children? How were they treated? What attitudes toward working women were exhibited by many adult male workers and their unions?

23. Why did Americans consider it inappropriate for women to work in industry? Who saw children working in industry as a problem?

24. What was the significance of the railroad strike of 1877?

25. Compare and contrast the organization, leadership, membership (especially the role of women) and programs of the Knights of Labor and the American Federation of Labor. Why did the AFL succeed, while the Knights disappeared?

26. Compare and contrast the Haymarket affair, Homestead Strike, and Pullman Strike. On balance, what was their effect on the organized labor movement?

27. What several factors combined to help explain why organized labor remained relatively weak before World War I?

PATTERNS OF POPULAR CULTURE (474-475)

28. What parts of Horatio Alger's message often got lost in the public's mind at the time he wrote and later? Why?

29. What is the significance of *Little Women*? How did it affect America in its time?

Identification

Identify each of the following and explain why it is important within the context of the chapter.

1. Alexander Graham Bell

2. Thomas A. Edison

3. Bessemer Process

4. Charles and Frank Duryea

5. Henry Ford

6. Wilbur and Orville Wright

7. Frederick Winslow Taylor

8. Cornelius Vanderbilt

9.   I. M. Singer

10.   J. P. Morgan

11.   Chicago Union Stockyard

12.   standard time

13.   Herbert Spencer

14.   "invisible hand"

15.   *The Gospel of Wealth*

16.   Henry Georgia

17.   Socialist Labor Party/American Socialist Party

18.   Ellis Island

19.   padrones

20.   National Labor Union

21.   Molly Maguires

22.   Samuel Gompers

23.   "anarchism"

24.   Eugene V. Debs

25.   Women's Trade Union League

Document 1

Refer back to the section of the chapter under the heading "Capitalism and its Critics." The great industrialist Andrew Carnegie built his fortune on steel, but he also built a lasting reputation as a philanthropist because he spent millions of dollars on the establishment of libraries. Carnegie's *Gospel of Wealth* was a call for other rich people to share their wealth with the worthy poor. Consider the following questions: How does Carnegie's view exemplify Social Darwinism? What is the essence of Carnegie's argument against socialism? On what social values and assumptions about human nature was the gospel of wealth based?

> The price which society pays for the law of competition, like the price it pays for cheap comforts and luxuries, is also great; but the advantages of this law are also greater still, for it is to this law that we owe our wonderful material development, which brings improved conditions in its train. But, whether the law be benign or not, we must say of it, as we say of the change in the conditions of men to which we have referred: It is here; we cannot evade it; no substitutes for it have been found; and while the law may be sometimes hard for the individual, it is best for the race, because it insures the survival of the fittest in every department. We accept and welcome, therefore, as conditions to which we must accommodate ourselves, great inequality of environment, the concentration of business, industrial and commercial, in the hands of a few, and the law of competition between these, as being not only beneficial, but essential for the future progress of the race. . . .

> Objections to the foundations upon which society is based are not in order, because the condition of the race is better with these than it has been with any others which have been tried. Of the effect of any new substitutes proposed we cannot be sure. The Socialist or Anarchist who seeks to overturn present conditions is to be regarded as attacking the foundation upon which civilization itself rests, for civilization took its start from the day that the capable, industrious workman said to his incompetent and lazy fellow, "If dost not sow, thou shalt not reap," and thus ended primitive Communism by separating the drones from the bees. One who studies this subject will soon be brought face to face with the conclusion that upon the sacredness of property civilization itself depends—the right of the laborer to his hundred dollars in the savings bank, and equally the legal right of the millionaire to his millions. . . .

This, then, is held to be the duty of the man of Wealth: First, to set an example of modest, unostentatious living, shunning display or extravagance; to provide moderately for the legitimate wants of those dependent upon him; and after doing so to consider all surplus revenues which come to him simply as trust funds, which he is called upon to administer, and strictly bound as a matter of duty to administer in the manner which, in his judgment, is best calculated to produce the most beneficial results for the community—the man of wealth thus becoming the mere agent and trustee for his poorer brethren, bringing to their service his superior wisdom, experience, and ability to administer, doing for them better than they would or could do for themselves.

Andrew Carnegie, *The Gospel of Wealth* (1889).

Document 2

In 1883, the United States Senate Committee on Education and Labor conducted hearings on labor-management relations. The committee took testimony from labor leaders, factory owners, and other observers. The following selection excerpts the testimony of Dr. Timothy D. Stow, a physician in Fall River, Massachusetts, an important textile-mill center since before the Civil War. In 1890, almost half the population of Fall River was foreign-born. Read this document and refer to the section in the text called "Wages and Working Conditions," and consider the following questions: Was the Fall River experience typical of industrial centers? How does Dr. Stow recognize the psychological as well as the physical problems of the Fall River workers? Would Fall River have been a fertile field for labor-union organizers?

The Chairman: We want to find out how the working people of Fall River are living and doing. You can tell us that in the way in which one gentleman would talk to another, the one understanding the subject and the other not understanding it. Just tell us the condition of the operatives there, in your own way, bearing in mind that we would rather have it without premeditation than as a prepared statement.

The Witness: I have been in Fall River about eleven years, though I have been one year absent during that time. As a physician and surgeon, of course, I have been brought into contact with all classes of people there, particularly the laboring classes, the operatives of the city.

With regard to the effect of the present industrial system upon their physical and moral welfare, I should say it was of such a character as to need mending, to say the least. It needs some radical remedy. Our laboring population is made up very largely of foreigners, men, women, and children, who have either voluntarily come to Fall River or who have been induced to come there by the manufacturers.

As a class they are dwarfed physically. Of course there are exceptions to that; some notable ones. On looking over their condition and weighing it as carefully as I have been able to, I have come to the conclusion that the character and quality of the labor which they have been doing in times past, and most of them from childhood up, has been and is such as to bring this condition upon them slowly and steadily.

They are dwarfed, in my estimation, sir, as the majority of men and women who are brought up in factories must be dwarfed under the present industrial system; because by their long hours of indoor labor and their hard work they are cut off from the benefit of breathing fresh air and from the sights that surround a workman outside a mill. Being shut up all day long in the noise and in the high temperature of these mills they become physically weak.

Then, most of them are obliged to live from hand to mouth, or, at least, they do not have sufficient food to nourish them as they need to be nourished. Those things, together with the fact that they have to limit their clothing supply—this constant strain upon the operative—all tend to make him, on the one hand, uneasy and restless, or, on the other hand, to produce discouragement and recklessness. They make him careless in regard to his own condition. All those things combined tend to produce what we have in Fall River.

Now, first, as to the moral condition of the operatives of Fall River. I think so far as crime is concerned we have quite as little crime there as in any city of its size. We have a population rising on 50,000. There is a disposition at times, and under certain pressure, for some operatives to violate the law, to pilfer, or something of that kind, and I think it grows out of not what is called "pure cussedness" but a desire to relieve some physical want. For instance, a man wants a coat and has not the means of earning it, and he is out of employment, and being pinched with the cold, and with no prospect of getting employment, or of getting a coat by honest means, he steals one. Or perhaps he steals food on the same principle.

But so far as crime is concerned, we have comparatively little. But what I do say, and what has been on my mind ever since I came to Fall River, with reference to operatives there, is the peculiar impress they seem to bear, a sort of dejected, tired, worn-out, discouraged appearance, growing out of the bad influences of long hours of labor, the close confinement of the mills, the din of the machinery, [and] their exclusion from social intercourse, except at night.

U.S. Congress, Senate Committee on Education and Labor, *Report of the Committee of the Senate Upon the Relations Between Labor and Capital* (Washington, D.C., 1885).

Map Exercise

Fill in or identify the following on the blank map provided.

1. Area of the country best served by railroads as of 1870.
2. Area of the country that experienced the most significant railroad development from 1870 to 1890.
3. Main area of the early iron and steel industry.

Summary

Although some economists place the industrial "take-off" of America in the years before the Civil War, it was in the three decades following that great conflict that the United States became the world's leading industrial power. A fortunate combination of sufficient raw materials, adequate labor, enviable technological accomplishments, effective business and entrepreneurial leadership, nationwide markets, and supportive state and national governments boosted America past its international rivals. The industrial transformation had a profound impact on the lives of the millions of workers who made the production revolution possible. Some who were distrustful of industrial power turned toward socialism; others tried to organize workers into powerful unions. But in these early years of industrial conflict, the forces of business usually triumphed.

Review Questions

These questions are to be answered with essays. This will allow you to explore relationships between individuals, events, and attitudes of the period under review.

1.   What were the several main factors that combined to produce America's impressive rise to industrial supremacy?

2.   Both the success-oriented novels of Horatio Alger and the utopian works of Edward Bellamy were best sellers in late-nineteenth-century America. What might explain this paradox of Americans' wanting to read about both how great their country was and how greatly it needed to improve?

3.   The great industrialists and financiers praised unfettered free enterprise while at the same time they tried to eliminate competition through corporate consolidation. How can these apparently conflicting positions be reconciled?

Chapter Self Test

After you have read the chapter in the text and done the exercises in the Study Guide, take the following self test to see if you understand the material you have covered. Answers appear at the end of the Study Guide.

MULTIPLE-CHOICE QUESTIONS

Circle the letter of the response that best answers the question or completes the statement.

1.   Three of the following are advantages that the United States enjoyed in its rise to industrial supremacy in the late nineteenth century. Which is the *exception?*

   a.   favorable government policies

   b.   an abundance of basic raw materials

   c.   a growing labor supply and expanding market

   d.   a high level of basic research in pure science

2.   Both the Bessemer-Kelly process and the open-hearth process are methods of:

   a.   mining coal.

   b.   producing steel.

   c.   pasteurizing milk.

   d.   refining petroleum.

3. The internal combustion engine was invented

    a. in the late 19th century

    b. 1901-1910

    c. 1911-1920

    d. in the 1920s

4. Charles and Frank Duryea were pioneers in what industry?

    a. railroads

    b. petroleum

    c. aircraft

    d. automobile

5. The term "Taylorism" refers to:

    a. scientific management in industry.

    b. a revival of pride in craftsmanship.

    c. a movement to organize unskilled labor.

    d. a movement away from mass-produced clothing.

6. Henry Ford's main contribution to American industrialism was his:

    a. invention of the internal combustion engine.

    b. introduction of structured management organization.

    c. investment in research and development.

    d. use of the moving assembly line to achieve mass production.

7. Andrew Carnegie made his principal fortune in the field of:

    a. steel.

    b. banking.

    c. shipping.

    d. petroleum.

8. The legal principle that made investment in corporations attractive and made the growth of huge corporations possible was:

    a. *caveat emptor.*

    b. accelerated depreciation.

    c. limited liability.

    d. exemption allowances.

9. A "vertically integrated" system of production is one in which:

    a. all the employees belong to one big union organized by industry rather than by craft.

    b. management and labor share equally in the profits through an elaborate sharing arrangement.

    c. employees of different ethnic origins work together on the assembly line.

    d. a single company controls the entire industrial process from source of raw materials to the final market.

10. John D. Rockefeller made his principal fortune in the field of:

    a. steel.

    b. banking.

    c. shipping.

    d. petroleum.

11. What new type of business organization permitted a small group of capitalists to control the stock of a large number of individual corporations without actually becoming one company? The term later came to refer generally to any huge economic concentration.

    a. trust

    b. monopoly

    c. holding company

    d. joint-stock company

12. "Social Darwinism" was based on what aspect of Charles Darwin's theory of biological evolution?

    a. social gospel

    b. intelligent creation

    c. biblical inerrancy

    d. survival of the fittest

13. Both Social Darwinism and classical economics agree that:

    a. humans are descended from lower animals.

    b. free competition promotes human progress.

    c. the government should ease the lot of the poor.

    d. government ownership of the majority of the means of production is desirable.

14. Which of the following emphasizes most strongly the duty of the rich to do good works for the public?

    a. socialism

    b. social Darwinism

    c. classical economics

    d. gospel of wealth

15. The theme of virtually all of Horatio Alger's novels was:

    a. the rich get richer; the poor get poorer.

    b. poor boy makes good by hard work, perseverance, and luck.

    c. average guy gets wealthy through cunning, guile, and questionable business practices.

    d. rich man has conversion and realizes that philanthropy and government regulation are the only ways to promote an equitable society.

16. In the late nineteenth century, the American working classes suffered from three of the following conditions. Which is the *exception?*

    a. Little or no worker's compensation for injury.

    b. No government health and safety regulations.

    c. Declining standard of living, in both absolute and relative terms.

    d. No job security; layoffs due to seasonal, cyclical, or technological factors.

17. The significance of the railroad strikes of 1877 was that:

a. the workers won union recognition on most lines.

b. anarchists rose to domination of the railroad unions.

c. it was the first strike to be so national in scope.

d. the federal government for the first time served as neutral mediator.

18. A major feature of the program of the American Federation of Labor was its emphasis on:

a. encouraging females to join the industrial workforce.

b. reforming and altering the capitalist system so that workers would own part of the corporations they worked for.

c. immediate gains for its members, such as higher wages, shorter hours, and better working conditions.

d. mass organization of all laborers—skilled, unskilled, and agricultural.

19. The significance of the Haymarket Square incident in 1886 was that:

a. unions won their demand for an eight-hour day.

b. the American socialist movement received a great boost.

c. the use of Pinkerton guards as strikebreakers was outlawed.

d. it stimulated a hysterical wave of fear of anarchism and its alleged connection with unionism.

20. The Homestead strike of 1892 and the Pullman strike of 1894 were similar in that:

a. both involved the American Railway Union.

b. federal troops were used to restore order in both.

c. both started when management ordered pay cuts for some workers.

d. strikers fought Pinkerton guards in violent pitched battles at both locations.

TRUE-FALSE QUESTIONS

Read each statement carefully. Mark true statements "T" and false statements "F."

1. The principal use of petroleum up to the 1890s was as oil for lubrication of machines rather than for fuel.

2. The early steel industry concentrated in western Pennsylvania and eastern Ohio because iron ore and coal deposits were abundant in that area.

3. J. P. Morgan is credited with inventing the most efficient technology for mass production of steel.

4. Many Americans were reluctant to invest in corporations in the late nineteenth century because if the corporation went bankrupt the creditors of the corporation had a legal claim to all the personal assets of the investor.

5. John D. Rockefeller began building Standard Oil by concentrating on the refining stage of the petroleum industry.

6. Although the term "trust" technically referred to a specific form of business organization, the term came to be generally applied to any great economic combination.

7. In the developing economy of the late nineteenth century, the majority of the business tycoons accurately personified the "rags-to-riches" rise to wealth and power.

8. The theory of Social Darwinism argued that great concentrations of wealth in the late nineteenth century violated the principles of evolution and that a great economic collapse was inevitable.

9. The "Gospel of Wealth" referred to the idea that the rich had a responsibility to use their money to promote social well-being.

10. The Knights of Labor favored a broad program of social reform including a cooperative system whereby workers would control much of the economy.

11. Although there were significant problems facing workers and there were many areas of poverty, the average standard of living for the American worker increased during the late nineteenth century.

12. Most European immigrants who came to the eastern United States up to the 1880s arrived from northern Europe and the British Isles, but by 1900 southern and eastern Europeans dominated.

13. In general, railroads, mining companies, and industrial employers tried to discourage the immigration of workers from Europe.

14. Because most industrial work required mechanical skills and body strength, few women and children were employed in factories in late-nineteenth-century America.

15. The American Federation of Labor stressed the idea of "one big union" for all workers, while the Knights of Labor was basically a coalition of individual craft unions.

16. Molly Maguire was the principal founder of the Women's Trade Union League.

17. Samuel Gompers was the leader of the American Federation of Labor.

18. The Haymarket affair increased fears of "anarchism" among middle-class Americans.

19. Although unions lost most strikes in the 1890s, the labor victory in the Pullman strike led to a rapid increase in union membership.

20. The steady influx of new immigrants from Europe was a source of stability and strength for the labor-union movement.

CHAPTER EIGHTEEN
THE AGE OF THE CITY

Objectives

A thorough study of Chapter 18 should enable the student to understand:

1. The patterns and processes of urbanization in late-nineteenth-century America.
2. The changes in the pattern of immigration in the late nineteenth century.
3. The new economic and social problems created by urbanization.
4. The relationships of both urbanization and immigration to the rise of boss rule.
5. The early rise of mass consumption and its impact on American life, especially for women.
6. The changes in leisure and entertainment and the growth of mass-culture opportunities including organized sports, vaudeville, movies, and other activities.
7. The main trends in literature and art during the late nineteenth and early twentieth centuries.
8. The impact of the Darwinian theory of evolution on the intellectual life of America.
9. The profound new developments in American educational opportunities.

Main Themes

1. How the social and economic lure of the city attracted foreign and domestic migrants, and how these newcomers adjusted to urban life.
2. How rapid urban growth forced adaptations to severe problems of government mismanagement, poverty, crime, inadequate housing, and precarious health and safety conditions.
3. How the urban environment served as the locus for new philosophical ideas, expanded leisure opportunities, fresh approaches to education, rapid expansion in journalism, and a new consumerism.
4. How the new order of "high" urban culture inspired both serious writers and artists to render realistic portrayals of the seamy side of city life, while many middle- and upper-class Americans were engaging in expanded forms of leisure and entertainment.

Glossary

1. suburb: A residential area adjacent to, and dependent on, a city. In some cases, suburbs are absorbed (annexed) into the city as it grows; in other instances, suburbs form their own municipal governments or draw services from county governments.
2. urban: Unless otherwise specified, a Census Bureau term referring to any city or town with a population exceeding 2,500. The term must be used with care because this definition includes many places normally thought of as small towns. The "urban" developments described in this chapter occur mostly in big cities with populations exceeding 100,000.

Pertinent Questions

THE URBANIZATION OF AMERICA (490-497)

1. What were the attractions of the city that led to population expansion? What were the main sources of urban growth?

2. What were the factors that inspired the exodus of southern African Americans into cities, especially northern cities, that began in the late nineteenth century?

3. How did the foreign immigrants of the 1890s and later differ from most of the earlier immigrants? What attracted them to the United States? (See Chapter Seventeen also.)

4. What social institutions and community actions helped facilitate immigrant adjustment to urban life in America? What were the barriers? Which groups seemed to adapt better than most others?

5. Describe the desire for assimilation and the strains it often caused. In general, how did native-born Americans regard assimilation?

6. What efforts were made to restrict immigration in the late nineteenth century? What ethnic groups and other types of immigrants were specifically restricted?

THE URBAN LANDSCAPE (497-501)

7. What inspired the move toward the creation of expanded public spaces and public buildings in large American cities? What were the lasting legacies of this impulse?

8. What led to the development of residential suburbs around big cities?

9. Contrast the residential pattern of the working class and the poor with that of the wealthy and moderately well-to-do. What was big city life like for the poor?

10. How did urban mass transit technology evolve from the Civil War era to the turn of the century?

11. What technological innovations made the development of the skyscraper possible and desirable?

STRAINS OF URBAN LIFE (501-504)

12. How did big cities cope with the urban hazards of fire, disease, and sanitation? What were the environmental implications of dense urban development?

13. What was the typical middle-class attitude toward the problem of widespread urban poverty?

14. How prevalent was violent crime in turn-of-the-century America? How did cities respond?

15. Explain the factors that contributed to the rise of political machines and their bosses, and describe the typical operation of a political machine. What were the positive as well as the negative aspects of boss rule in large cities?

THE RISE OF MASS CONSUMPTION (504-506)

16. Describe the changes in income and purchasing power of the urban middle and working classes. Who made the greater gains?

17. How did the emergence of mass-market products along with chair stores, mail-order outlets, and large department stores impact the lives of American families, especially women?

LEISURE IN THE CONSUMER SOCIETY (506-513)

18. How did Americans begin to change their attitudes toward leisure and consumption? What factors contributed to this new view? How did the approaches to leisure vary by class?

19. Compare and contrast the rise of baseball with that of football. What other spectator sports became popular as Americans came to enjoy more leisure time?

20. What changes were beginning to emerge in women's sports?

21. What were the main sorts of popular entertainment activities available to urban dwellers of the late nineteenth and early twentieth centuries? How did class considerations shape the types of activities enjoyed?

22. Why was the Fourth of July such an important holiday? How was it different in the South?

23. What important changes occurred in journalism and publishing in the decades after the Civil War?

HIGH CULTURE IN THE AGE OF THE CITY (513-519)

24. What issues did the realist novelists explore, and how did they approach them?

25. By the early 1900s what movements in American visual art were becoming evident? How did these movements reflect the contrast between the genteel and modern approaches?

26. How did Darwinism challenge traditional American faith and contribute to the growing schism between cosmopolitan, mostly urban, and traditional, mainly rural, values? (See also Chapter Seventeen on Social Darwinism.)

27. How did the new social science disciplines of economics, sociology, and anthropology impact the intellectual view of contemporary and historic America?

28. Describe the evolution of free public schooling in the United States. What parts of the nation lagged in education?

29. What government and private actions combined to lead to the establishment or significant expansion of universities and colleges after the Civil War?

30. What opportunities for higher education were available to women in this era? What were the distinctive characteristics of the women's colleges?

AMERICA IN THE WORLD: GLOBAL MIGRATIONS (493)

31. What is meant by "push" and "pull" factors in population migrations?

32. How did 19th and early 20th century immigration to the United States fit in the context of worldwide, especially European, migration?

PATTERNS OF POPULAR CULTURE: CONEY ISLAND (508-509)

33. What impulses among urban Americans explain the attraction that Coney Island had to so many people? What classes were most attracted to its charms? Why did its relative popularity begin to wane after World War I?

Identification

Identify each of the following, and explain why it is important within the context of the chapter.

1. immigrant ghettoes
2. Reform Judaism
3. American Protective Association/Immigration Restriction League
4. Frederick Law Olmstead
5. Columbian Exposition
6. "streetcar suburbs"
7. tenement
8. Jacob Riis
9. Brooklyn Bridge
10. Louis Sullivan
11. Public Health Service

12. Salvation Army

13. William M. Tweed

14. Sears Roebuck

15. National Consumers League

16. World Series

17. National College Athletic Association (NCAA)

18. James A. Naismith

19. George M. Cohan

20. Irving Berlin

21. vaudeville

22. D. W. Griffith

23. Scott Joplin

24. William Randolph Hearst

25. "yellow journalism"

26. Theodore Dreiser

27. "pragmatism"

28. Carlisle School

29. "land-grant" college

Document 1

Read the section of the text under the heading "The Urban Landscape," and then read the excerpt below, taken from *How the Other Half Lives* (1890), the famous book by Jacob Riis. Consider the following questions: How does Riis's account compare with the "melting pot" thesis? What ethnic/racial group that would later occupy the slums of northern cities is absent from this mixed crowd? What comparisons could be made between the poor neighborhoods of the late nineteenth century and those of today?

When once I asked the agent of a notorious Fourth Ward alley how many people might be living in it I was told: one hundred and forty families, one hundred Irish, thirty-eight Italian, and two that spoke the German tongue. Barring the agent herself, there was not a native-born individual in the court. The answer was characteristic of the cosmopolitan character of lower New York, very nearly so for the whole of it, wherever it runs to alleys and courts. One may find for the asking an Italian, a German, a French, African, Spanish, Bohemian, Russian, Scandinavian, Jewish, and Chinese colony. Even the Arab, who peddles "holy earth" from the Battery as a direct importation from Jerusalem, has his exclusive preserves at the lower end of Washington Street. The one thing you shall vainly ask for in the chief city of America is a distinctively American community. There is none; certainly not among the tenements. . . .

The once unwelcome Irishman has been followed in his turn by the Italian, the Russian Jew, and the Chinaman, and has himself taken a hand of opposition, quite as bitter and quite as ineffectual, against these later hordes. Wherever these have gone they have crowded him out, possessing the block, the street, the ward with their denser swarms. . . .

A map of the city, colored to designate nationalities, would show more stripes than the skin of a zebra, and more colors than any rainbow.

Jacob Riis, *How the Other Half Lives* (New York: Charles Scribner's Sons, 1890). Reprint, "The Mixed Crowd," in F. Cordasco, ed., *Jacob Riis Revisited* (Garden City, NY: Anchor Books, Doubleday & Co., 1968). pp. 18–19.

Document 2

Read the section of the text describing the rise of mass-circulation magazines, and then read the following editorial, which is from one of the first issues of the *Ladies' Home Journal*. Consider the following questions: Why was the low price of the magazine so important? (A yearly subscription was fifty cents, and single copies cost a nickel.) In the age of realism, why did the publishers believe that the readers wanted "a pure and high-toned family paper?" How did popular magazines such as the *Ladies' Home Journal* differ from established literary journals?

We want 50,000 subscribers on our books by February 1st, 1884, and we ask as a favor that you will help us get them. Will you not show this copy to your friends and neighbors and ask them to subscribe?

The price is very low, and they can afford it, no matter how many other papers they may take. We aim to publish a pure and high-toned family paper, and think we deserve your support. We have no lottery scheme on hand, no one cent chromos, no prizes or premiums of any kind except to club-raisers. We have no frauds to distribute, no lies to tell. Then how are we to marshal that army of recruits, fifty thousand strong, from Maine and Oregon, from Minnesota and Florida, from the hills of Pennsylvania and the prairies of Illinois?

First, The Ladies Home Journal shall be made without a peer. We propose to make it a household necessity—so good, so pure, so true, so brave, so full, so complete, that a young couple will no more think of going to housekeeping without it than without a cook-stove. The best pens that money can put in motion shall fill its editorial pages and various departments with many facts in few words.

Such a paper will take. The people will want it, children will cry for it; and we shall get the 50,000 subscribers.

Ladies' Home Journal and Practical Housekeeper, January 1884, p. 4.

Map Exercise

Fill in or identify the following on the blank map provided. Use the map in the text as your source.

1. Urban population centers of over a half-million (500,000) in 1900.
2. Smaller but important regional cities: Buffalo; Cleveland; Detroit; Washington, D.C.; Atlanta; New Orleans; Memphis; Minneapolis; Cincinnati; Louisville; Kansas City; Dallas; Houston; Denver; Seattle; San Francisco; and Los Angeles.
3. The area of heaviest industrial concentration.

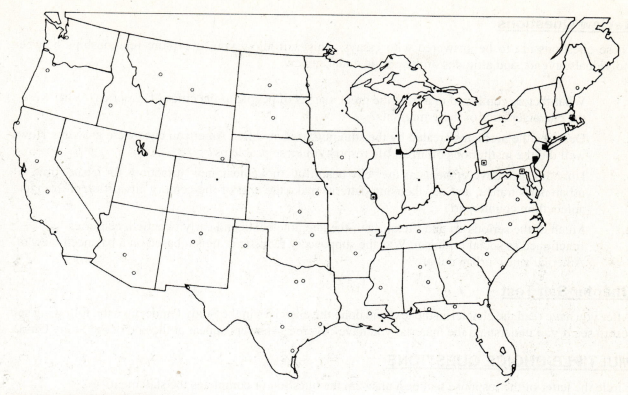

Interpretive Questions

Based on what you have filled in, answer the following. On some of the questions you will need to consult the narrative in your text for information or explanation.

1. Using this map and the railroad map in Chapter Seventeen, explain the relationship between railroads, industry, and large cities.
2. In what part of the nation, and specifically in what large cities, did the bulk of the post-1880 foreign immigrants settle?
3. Within the area indicated by the map as settled, which well-populated region of the country was most lacking in large cities of 100,000 or more? Why?
4. Note that all of the major urban areas of the late twentieth century were already established by 1900. What does this indicate about the maturity of the national economic and transportation system by the turn of the century?

Summary

In the years after the Civil War, America's cities boomed as people left the rural areas of Europe and the United States to seek jobs and other attractions offered by American cities. The rapid growth of cities caused many problems in housing, transportation, and health. Technological attacks on these problems barely kept pace, and city governments often resorted to boss rule to cope. The booming cities were places of intellectual ferment and cultural change. Urban dwellers found many ways to enjoy increased leisure time. Many Americans wanted to prove to skeptical Europeans that the nation had cultural as well as economic accomplishments to admire. American culture became more uniform through free public education, mass-market journalism, and standardized sports. Higher education, especially new state universities, reached out to a wider market. More and more women attended college in coeducational and single-sex institutions.

Review Questions

These questions are to be answered with essays. This will allow you to explore relationships between individuals, events, and attitudes of the period under review.

1. What factors combined to attract the great masses of people to the cities of America? What were the characteristics of these migrants?

2. Describe the problems created by the stunning pace at which American cites were growing. How well did the institutions of urban life respond to these problems?

3. How did such developments as the "city beautiful" movement, new attractions for leisure time, urban mass transit, and new housing patterns make the turn-of-the-century city different from its antebellum counterpart?

4. Much of the serious art and literature of the late nineteenth and early twentieth centuries functioned as social criticism. Was the supposedly realistic criticism based on a balanced view of America's new urban culture?

Chapter Self Test

After you have read the chapter in the text and done the exercises in the Study Guide, take the following self test to see if you understand the material you have covered. Answers appear at the end of the Study Guide.

MULTIPLE-CHOICE QUESTIONS

Circle the letter of the response that best answers the question or completes the statement.

1. Which of the following population trends occurred in the United States from 1860 to 1910?
   a. Gradual decline of the rural population in absolute numbers.
   b. Shift of the majority of the urban population from central city to suburbs.
   c. Significant shift of the population from the North to the South.
   d. Faster rate of growth for the cites than for the general population.

2. Because of rapid growth in the latter nineteenth century, American cities:
   a. protected traditional social and cultural values.
   b. provided services and facilities inadequate to demands.
   c. witnessed the flight of factories and corporate offices to newer, less crowded locations.
   d. supported efficient and honest governments.

3. American urban population growth from 1860 to 1910 resulted mainly from a(n):
   a. low rate of infant mortality.
   b. increasing fertility rate.
   c. low death rate from disease.
   d. large influx of new residents.

4. The large-scale movement of African Americans from the rural South to industrial cities began during the latter nineteenth century mainly because of the:

   a. poverty and oppression of the South.

   b. prospective professional opportunities in the cities.

   c. abundance of factory jobs there for African Americans.

   d. absence of racial discrimination in the North.

5. The new immigrants of the latter nineteenth century settled primarily in eastern industrial cities because they:

   a. lacked the capital to buy land and begin farming in the West.

   b. found immediate employment as unskilled factory workers.

   c. found refuge and camaraderie among fellow nationals there.

   d. did all of the above.

6. The formation of ethnic neighborhoods by immigrants in American cities:

   a. tended to reinforce the cultural values of their previous societies.

   b. resulted primarily from discriminatory zoning restrictions.

   c. prevented their identification with, and advancement in, American society.

   d. intensified a sense of not belonging to a coherent community.

7. Nativist reaction against European immigrants of the latter nineteenth century resulted from all of the following factors *except* the:

   a. arrival of such vast numbers of immigrants.

   b. refusal of most immigrants and their children to attempt to assimilate themselves into American culture.

   c. generalized fears of, and prejudices against, foreigners.

   d. economic concern that immigrant workers would threaten the wages and positions of American workers.

8. The Immigration Restriction League:

   a. blamed foreigners for all the disorder and corruption of the urban world.

   b. advocated the screening of immigrants through literacy tests.

   c. adopted crude theories of conspiracy and a stance of rabid xenophobia.

   d. enlisted the support of President Grover Cleveland for their proposals.

9. Which of the following groups were excluded or severely restricted from immigration to the United States by laws passed in the 1880s and 1890s? (Mark one or more letters.)

   a. Chinese

   b. convicts, paupers, and mental incompetents

   c. illiterates

   d. Irish

10. The majority of big-city residents in latter-nineteenth-century America:
   a. could afford their own houses, thanks to the availability of cheap labor and low building costs.
   b. took advantage of less expensive lands on the edges of the city and settled in suburbs.
   c. stayed in the city centers and rented living space.
   d. exacted high standards from urban landlords.

11. By the 1890s, a million New Yorkers lived in tenements, which were:
   a. slum dwellings with inadequate light, plumbing, and heat.
   b. helping relieve and disperse population growth.
   c. rental buildings designed for single-family residences.
   d. transformed by state laws into model housing units for the poor.

12. What late-nineteenth-century technological developments made "skyscrapers" practical? (Mark two letters.)
   a. electric elevators
   b. air conditioning
   c. concrete
   d. steel girder construction

13. The most famous and notorious city "boss" of the late nineteenth century was:
   a. Louis Sullivan.
   b. Theodore Dreiser.
   c. John A. Roebling.
   d. William M. Tweed.

14. The political machines of the bosses were able to retain power for all of the following reasons *except:*
   a. immigrant voters were more concerned with receiving services than with middle-class standards of political morality.
   b. some wealthy and influential citizens profited from dealings with the bosses.
   c. city government structure often had structural weaknesses that kept it from meeting citizen needs.
   d. the absence of reform groups to mobilize public outrage against boss rule.

15. Which of the following was *not* a trend contributing to the rise of mass consumption in the latter nineteenth century?
   a. The emergence of ready-made clothing as a basis of the American wardrobe.
   b. The breakup of marketing monopolies held by national chain stores.
   c. The development of canned food and refrigerated railroad cars.
   d. The emergence of large department stores and mail-order houses.

16. Vaudeville shows were composed of:

   a. traveling dramatists who performed Shakespeare and other classic plays in small towns and cites.

   b. a variety of acts including musicians, singers, comedians, magicians, jugglers, dancers, and the like.

   c. a mixture of primitive motion pictures with music by a small live orchestra.

   d. gypsies and other unsavory characters who used the shows to attract crowds to sell patent medicines and other fraudulent products.

17. The emergence of national press services in the latter nineteenth century contributed most significantly to:

   a. increased salaries for reporters.

   b. standardization of the news.

   c. separation of news from opinions.

   d. a professional identity for American journalists.

18. In the late-nineteenth and early-twentieth century:

   a. writers such as Stephen Crane tended to ignore the new urban reality.

   b. many women formed new book clubs dedicated to the discussion of literature.

   c. artists returned to the "genteel tradition" of painting.

   d. novels such as *The Jungle* and *The Awakening* praised American society.

19. The theory of evolution:

   a. supported traditional American beliefs about the nature of man and history.

   b. met uniform resistance from middle-class Protestant religious leaders.

   c. gained greater acceptance in rural areas than in urban areas.

   d. influenced new ways of thinking in the social sciences.

20. According to the philosophy of pragmatism, modern society, for guidance, should primarily rely on:

   a. inherited ideals.

   b. scientific inquiry.

   c. moral principles.

   d. religious beliefs.

21. Which of the following trends in American education did *not* take place in the latter nineteenth century?

   a. The spread of universal free public education.

   b. Passage by states of compulsory attendance laws.

   c. Rapid proliferation of colleges across the nation.

   d. Increased emphasis on the classical curriculum at the university level.

TRUE-FALSE QUESTIONS

Read each statement carefully. Mark true statements "T" and false statements "F."

1. The 1920 census was the first one in which a majority of the American population lived in "urban" areas of 2,500 or more residents.

2. Cities offered people privacy and social space that were unavailable in small towns.

3. Most of the European immigrants who came to American cities from 1860 to 1910 came from rural backgrounds.

4. Urban African Americans males in the late nineteenth century usually held skilled industrial jobs.

5. The "streetcar suburbs" of Boston and other northeastern cities mainly provided cheap housing for low-paid factory workers and domestics.

6. Jacob Riis was a newspaper reporter and photographer who exposed the wretched conditions in the slums of New York.

7. In the late nineteenth and early twentieth centuries, large-scale popular baseball was professionalized, whereas big-time football remained a college and university activity.

8. The political bosses and the machines they operated were usually popular with the people in the poor and working-class neighborhoods of the large cities.

9. Realist novelists tended to explore and write about the seamy side of urban life.

10. "Yellow journalism" referred to breezy magazines that printed family-oriented fare and avoided reminding their readers of poverty, scandal, or political controversy.

11. The "Armory Show" was a major exposition of the development of the nation's modern scientific technology.

12. Darwin's theories were opposed by all organized Christian religious groups.

13. Because of the lack of private schools available, the South led the nation in the establishment of tax-supported public schools for all children.

14. By granting large amounts of land to state governments, the federal government encouraged states to establish universities and colleges that would emphasize practical learning, especially in agriculture and mechanics.

15. The neighborhood saloon was most popular in middle class areas since the men had more time to frequent such establishments.

16. Minstrel shows were local classical groups that laid the groundwork for the emergence of serious symphony orchestras in the early twentieth century.

17. D. W. Griffith was a pioneer in the production of motion pictures.

18. William Randolph Hearst was the founder of the "reform" movement within Judaism.

19. John Dewey stressed reforming education to place less emphasis on rote learning of traditional knowledge and more on a flexible approach that would prepare students to be effective citizens who could deal with the realities of society.

20. The Carlisle School was one of the first post-secondary institutions to admit African Americans.

21. The rise of "coeducation" in public colleges and universities in the late nineteenth century led to a marked decline in the number and influence of women's colleges in the period.

CHAPTER NINETEEN
FROM STALEMATE TO CRISIS

Objectives

A thorough study of Chapter 19 should enable the student to understand:

1. The nature of American party politics in the last third of the nineteenth century.

2. The problems of political patronage in the administrations of Rutherford B. Hayes, James A. Garfield, and Chester A. Arthur that led to the passage of the Pendleton Act.

3. The circumstances that permitted the Democrats to gain control of the presidency in the elections of 1884 and 1892.

4. The origins, purposes, and effectiveness of the Interstate Commerce Act and the Sherman Antitrust Act.

5. The positions of the two major parties on the tariff question and the actual trend of tariff legislation in the 1880s and 1890s.

6. The rise of agrarian discontent as manifested in the Granger movement, the Farmers' Alliances, and the Populist movement.

7. The rise of the silver question from the "Crime of '73" through the Gold Standard Act of 1900.

8. The significance of the presidential campaign and election of 1896.

9. The reasons for the decline of agrarian discontent after 1898.

Main Themes

1. How evenly balanced the Democratic and Republican parties were during the late nineteenth century and how this balance flowed from differing regional and sociocultural bases.

2. The inability of the political system and a limited national government to respond effectively to the nation's rapid social and economic changes.

3. How the troubled agrarian sector mounted a powerful but unsuccessful challenge to the new directions of American industrial capitalism and how this confrontation came to a head during the crisis of the 1890s.

Glossary

1. dark horse: A political candidate who is not considered a front runner and whose victory would be surprising to most observers.

2. cooperatives: Business enterprises owned by members of an organization and operated for members' benefit and profit. Farmers hoped to avoid reliance on businessmen by forming their own cooperatives, but most of these enterprises failed.

3. laissez faire: The theory that the economy functions best when it is free from governmental interference. In a strict laissez-faire system, the government neither helps nor hinders business, but many American businessmen who professed laissez-faire doctrines were happy to accept government aid in the form of protective tariffs and railroad subsidies.

Pertinent Questions

THE POLITICS OF EQUILIBRIUM (522-527)

1. How well balanced were the two major political parties between the Civil War and the turn of the century—especially from the mid-1870s to the early 1890s?

2. What role did politics play for the typical eligible voter of the late nineteenth century? How does that compare with the importance of politics in the life of the present-day voter?

3. What regional, religious, and ethnic factors distinguished the two major parties? Despite basic issue agreement, what culturally related issues tended to divide the parties?

4. Aside from its providing Civil War pensions and the postal service, how significant was the role of the national government in the late nineteenth century?

5. How did the patronage system lead to dominance of national politics by local and state political organizations and factions in the national parties? What was the impact on the presidency of Rutherford B. Hayes?

6. In what way was President James Garfield a martyr to civil service? How did Chester A. Arthur react?

7. How did the presidential election of 1888 differ from the typical fare of that period? What was the key issue, how did it become so, and what was the result?

8. What led to passage of the Sherman Antitrust Act? Why did it have so little impact?

9. What caused the significant Republican reverses in the 1890 and 1892 elections? What was the result of Cleveland's effort to lower tariffs after his reelection?

10. How was the demise of the Granger Laws related to the passage of the Interstate Commerce Act? Why was the Interstate Commerce Commission so ineffective?

THE AGRARIAN REVOLT (527-533)

11. Explain how the emphasis of the Grange gradually shifted. Why did the organization eventually fade in importance?

12. What was the vision of the Farmers' Alliance? What role did women play? What was their position on women's suffrage?

13. How did the Farmers' Alliance transform into the People's Party?

14. What kind of person was most attracted to Populism? What were the leaders like?

15. What were the basic elements of Populist ideology and how were they reflected in the party's platform? Why did the movement fail to obtain significant labor support?

THE CRISIS OF THE 1890S (533-537)

16. What were the immediate and long-range causes of the Panic of 1893? How serious was the depression that followed?

17. What developments after 1873 led to the coalition of farmers and miners on behalf of silver coinage? Why did "free silver" seem to be the answer?

A CROSS OF GOLD (537-541)

18. Why did the gold-standard issue divide the Democratic Party?

19. How did William Jennings Bryan win the Democratic presidential nomination in 1896 and how did his candidacy put the Populists in a dilemma?

20. Describe the passions of the 1896 campaign. Where did Bryan do well? Why did he lose?

21. How did President William McKinley handle the bimetallism question? What happened during his administration to help resolve the issue?

PATTERNS OF POPULAR CULTURE: THE CHAUTAUQUAS (530-531)

22. Why was the Chautauqua movement so popular at the turn of the century? What societal changes led to the movement's demise?

WHERE HISTORIANS DISAGREE: POPULISM (534-535)

23. To what extent have historians' own views about capitalism, democracy, and popular movements shaped their views about Populism? Also, what are the most recent interpretations saying about Populism and the modern regulatory state?

Identification

Identify each of the following and explain why it is important within the context of the chapter.

1. Civil War pensions
2. James G. Blaine
3. Pendleton Act
4. Benjamin Harrison
5. McKinley Tariff
6. Montgomery Ward & Co.
7. Mary Lease
8. Tom Watson
9. James B. Weaver
10. "Colored Alliances"
11. "Bourbons"
12. Coxey's Army
13. specie
14. "Crime of 1873"
15. Currency/Gold Standard Act of 1900

Document 1

The tariff issue came to the forefront in the election of 1888, with Grover Cleveland favoring lower rates. Read the following excerpt from President Cleveland's State of the Union message in December 1887. Also read the short excerpt from the Minority Report of the House Ways and Means Committee in which the Republicans expressed their opposition to the Mills bills, which embodied many of Cleveland's tariff revision suggestions. Consider the following questions: How does the first part of the address reveal Cleveland's political philosophy? Is Cleveland's characterization of the protective tariff as a tax on consumers an accurate one? Although in another part of the speech Cleveland disclaims any support for completely "free trade," would that be the logical culmination of his ideas? The Republican Minority Report implies that American prosperity flowed from the protective tariff. Was this a valid claim?

You are confronted at the threshold of your legislative duties with a condition of the national finances which imperatively demand immediate careful consideration.

The amount of money annually exacted, through the operation of present laws, from the industries and necessities of the people largely exceeds the sum necessary to meet the expenses of the Government.

When we consider that the theory of our institutions guarantees to every citizen the full enjoyment of all the fruits of his industry and enterprise, with only such deduction as may be his share toward the careful and economical maintenance of the Government which protects him, it is plain that the exaction of more than this is indefensible extortion and a culpable betrayal of American fairness and justice. This wrong inflicted upon those who bear the burden of national taxation, like other wrongs, multiplies a brood of evil consequences. The public Treasury, which should only exist as a conduit conveying the people's tribute to its legitimate objects of expenditure, becomes a hoarding place of money needlessly withdrawn from trade and the people's use, thus crippling our national energies, suspending our country's development, preventing investment in productive enterprise, threatening financial disturbance, and inviting schemes of public plunder. . . .

But our present tariff laws, the vicious, inequitable, and illogical source of unnecessary taxation, ought to be at once revised and amended. These laws as their primary and plain effect, raise the price to consumers of all articles imported and subject to duty by precisely the sum paid for such duties. Thus the amount of the duty measures the tax paid by those who purchase for use these imported articles. Many of these things, however, are raised or manufactured in our own country, and the duties now levied upon foreign goods and products are called protection to these home manufacturers, because they render it possible for those of our people who are manufacturers to make these taxed articles and sell them for a price equal to that demanded for the imported goods that have paid customs duty. So it happens that while comparatively few use the imported articles, millions of our people, who never used and never saw any of the foreign products, purchase and use things of the same kind made in this country, and pay therefore nearly or quite the same enhanced price which the duty adds to the imported articles. Those who buy imports pay the duty charged thereon into the public Treasury, but the great majority of our citizens, who buy domestic articles of the same class, pay a sum at least approximately equal to this duty to the home manufacturer. This reference to the operation of our tariff laws is not made by way of instruction, but in order that we may be constantly reminded of the manner in which they impose a burden upon those who consume domestic products as well as those who consume imported articles, and thus create a tax upon all our people.

* * *

The bill is a radical reversal of the tariff policy of the country, which for the most part has prevailed since the foundation of the Government, and under which we have made industrial and agricultural progress without a parallel in the world's history. If enacted into law it will disturb every branch of business, retard manufacturing and agricultural prosperity, and seriously impair our industrial independence.

William O. Stoddard, *Grover Cleveland* (New York: Stokes, 1888), pp. 248–250, 252–253.

Document 2

From the Farmer's Declaration of Independence of 1873 through the Ocala Demands of 1890 to the Populist Party's Omaha platform of 1892, the farmers of the South and West expressed their frustration with an increasingly industrial corporate society that they felt was leaving them behind. Read the selection below which is taken from the Omaha platform and consider the following questions: Were the Populist demands reasonable and rational responses to the problems facing the Populist constituency? What elements of socialism can be found in the Populist program? How was the platform designed as an attempt to broaden the appeal of Populism beyond farmers?

We declare, therefore—

First.—That the union of the labor forces of the United States this day consummated shall be permanent and perpetual; may its spirit enter into all hearts for the salvation of the Republic and the uplifting of mankind.

Second.—Wealth belongs to him who creates it, and every dollar taken from industry without an equivalent is robbery. "If any will not work, neither shall he eat." The interests of rural and civil labor are the same; their enemies are identical.

Third.—We believe that the time has come when the railroad corporations will either own the people or the people must own the railroads; and should the government enter upon the work of owning and managing all railroads, we should favor an amendment to the constitution by which all persons engaged in the government service shall be placed under a civil-service regulation of the most rigid character, so as to prevent the increase of the power of the national administration by the use of such additional government employes [sic].

FINANCE.—We demand a national currency, safe, sound, and flexible, issued by the general government only, a full legal tender for all debts, public and private, and that without the use of banking corporations; a just, equitable, and efficient means of distribution direct to the people, at a tax not to exceed 2 per cent, per annum, to be provided as set forth in the sub-treasury plan of the Farmers' Alliance, or a better system; also by payments in discharge of its obligations for public improvements.

1. We demand free and unlimited coinage of silver and gold at the present legal ratio of 16 to 1.

2. We demand that the amount of circulating medium be speedily increased to not less than $50 per capita.

3. We demand a graduated income tax.

4. We believe that the money of the country should be kept as much as possible in the hands of the people, and hence we demand that all State and national revenues shall be limited to the necessary expenses of the government, economically and honestly administered.

5. We demand that postal savings banks be established by the government for the safe deposit of the earnings of the people and to facilitate exchange.

TRANSPORTATION.—Transportation being a means of exchange and a public necessity, the government should own and operate the railroads in the interest of the people. The telegraph and telephone, like the post-office system, being a necessity for the transportation of news, should be owned and operated by the government in the interest of the people.

LAND.—The land, including all the natural sources of wealth, is the heritage of the people, and should not be monopolized for speculative purposes, and alien ownership of land should be prohibited. All land now held by railroads and other corporations in excess of their actual needs, and all lands now owned by aliens, should be reclaimed by the government and held for actual settlers only.

Omaha Platform of the Populist Party, 1892.

Map Exercise

Fill in or identify the following on the blank map provided. Use the map in the text as your source.

1. Using the maps in previous chapters, identify the Great Plains, the silver-mining regions, and the cotton-tobacco belt.
2. Fill in territories not yet states as of 1896.
3. Identify states carried by Bryan.

Interpretive Questions

Based on what you have filled in, answer the following. On some of the questions you will need to consult the narrative in your text for information or explanation.

1. Where was the Grange strongest? In what parts of the country did the Populist movement have the most impact? Why?
2. Why were the states carried by Bryan mainly those of the Great Plains, the silver-mining regions, and the cotton-tobacco belt? Why did he fail to make inroads in the Midwest and the Northeast?

Summary

Close elections and shifting control of the White House and Congress characterized the politics of the period from 1876 to 1900. Regional, ethno-cultural, and economic factors helped determine party affiliation and elections often turned on consideration of personality. But there were real issues too. Tariff, currency, and civil-service questions arose in almost every election. Discontented farmers in the People's party briefly challenged the Republicans and Democrats, but the two-party system remained intact. The election of 1896, the great battle between the gold standard and the silver standard, firmly established the Republican party as the majority party in the United States. Agrarian and mining interests were unable to convince voters that currency inflation through the free coinage of silver would lead the nation out of the depression of the 1890s. By fusing with the Democrats, the Populists ended any chance they might have had to become a major force in American politics. By the end of the nineteenth century, business forces had triumphed. They had secured a gold-based currency and a rigorously protective tariff. Efforts to regulate railroads and trusts were half-hearted to begin with and were weakened even further by court decisions.

Review Questions

These questions are to be answered with essays. This will allow you to explore relationships between individuals, events, and attitudes of the period under review.

1. What were the differences between the Republicans and the Democrats? To what extent did regional and ethnic differences translate into serious differences on the issues?

2. Compare and contrast the three major farm groups: the Grange, the Farmers' Alliances, and the Populists. Do you agree with the recent historians who believe that Populism was a reasonable and realistic response to agrarian grievances?

3. In a series of cases, including the *Wabash* case and *United States v. E. C. Knight Co.,* the United States Supreme Court severely restricted efforts to regulate business. What logic did the Court use in these and similar cases and what effect did the decisions have on business?

Chapter Self Test

After you have read the chapter in the text and done the exercises in the Study Guide, take the following self test to see if you understand the material you have covered. Answers appear at the end of the Study Guide.

MULTIPLE-CHOICE QUESTIONS

Circle the letter of the response that best answers the question or completes the statement.

1. A significant characteristic of American politics at the national level during the late nineteenth century was the:
   a. development of a true multiparty system.
   b. dominance of the Republican Party in popular support.
   c. dominance of the Democratic Party in popular support.
   d. nearly equal division of popular support for the Democratic and Republican parties.

2. In the late nineteenth century, which of the following groups would *least likely* vote Democratic?
   a. Roman Catholics of immigrant origin
   b. Protestant farmers of the South
   c. unskilled wage earners
   d. northern blacks

3. Before the passage of civil service-reform legislation, there were about 100,000 civilian federal government jobs to be filled by presidential appointment. Of these, the greatest percentage were in the:

   a. post office.
   b. Department of the Army.
   c. attorney general's office.
   d. Department of the Treasury.

4. Which of the following acts was passed to a considerable extent as a result of the assassination of Garfield?

   a. the Mills Tariff Act
   b. the Pendleton Civil Service Act
   c. the Sherman Antitrust Act
   d. the Dependent Pension Act

5. Which president served two nonconsecutive terms in office?

   a. Rutherford B. Hayes
   b. Benjamin Harrison
   c. Grover Cleveland
   d. William McKinley

6. The most significant issue in the presidential election of 1888 was:

   a. civil service reform.
   b. the Mulligan letters.
   c. free silver.
   d. the tariff.

7. Congress justified its passage of the Sherman Antitrust Act on the basis of its constitutional power to:

   a. levy taxes.
   b. promote the general welfare.
   c. regulate interstate commerce.
   d. forbid any business practice that impaired free competition or threatened the capitalist system.

8. What was the result of the 1892 national elections?

   a. the House and Senate were controlled by different parties for the first time since the Civil War.
   b. for the first time since the end of 1878 the Democratic Party controlled both houses of Congress and the presidency.
   c. the Populists carried enough Congressional seats to prevent either party from having a majority.
   d. the Supreme Court intervened to resolve an electoral vote dispute and awarded the presidency to Grover Cleveland.

9. The so-called Granger Laws were designed to regulate:
   a. child labor.
   b. the export of farm crops.
   c. railroad and warehouse rates.
   d. minimum wages and maximum hours.

10. The Chautauqua movement represented the:
   a. aspirations of the urban poor to seek better environment.
   b. thirst of many Americans for entertainment, education, and enlightenment.
   c. coalition of bankers and industrial leaders to resist populist reforms.
   d. emerging interest in using governmental action to end racial discrimination.

11. The company that emerged in the 1870s to provide goods to farmers via mail order was:
   a. R. H. Macy Company.
   b. Bloomingdales, Inc.
   c. F. W. Woolworth Ltd.
   d. Montgomery Ward and Company.

12. During the 1860s and 1870s, the Grangers carried out three of the following activities. Which is the *exception?*
   a. They established cooperatives.
   b. They forged a political coalition with organized labor.
   c. They supported political candidates sympathetic to the farmers' needs.
   d. They disseminated information about new scientific agricultural techniques.

13. One of the most important leaders of the Southern Farmers Alliance and People's Party was:
   a. Roscoe Conkling.
   b. Marcus Hanna.
   c. Tom Watson.
   d. James G. Blaine.

14. The Populists in 1892 favored three of the following. Which is the *exception?*
   a. The direct election of senators.
   b. The abolition of the graduated income tax.
   c. Government ownership of railroads, telephones, and telegraphs.
   d. The establishment of "subtreasuries" that would advance loans against stored crops.

15. Three of the following were contributory causes of the Panic of 1893. Which is the *exception?*
   a. The tax policies of the federal government on big business.
   b. Excessive capital investments, especially by railroads.
   c. The loss of American markets abroad due to depressed conditions in Europe.
   d. Weakened purchasing power of farmers due to depressed prices in agriculture.

16. In order to alleviate unemployment produced by the Panic of 1893, Jacob S. Coxey proposed:
    a. a new dependent pensions bill.
    b. drafting the unemployed into the Army.
    c. creating jobs by means of government public works programs.
    d. a welfare program of unemployment compensation.

17. The expression "Crime of '73" refers to the:
    a. discontinuance of silver coinage.
    b. adoption of a bimetallic standard.
    c. inflation produced by the unlimited coinage of silver.
    d. fixing of the ratio between silver and gold at 16 to 1.

18. The most important issue in the 1896 presidential campaign was:
    a. the tariff.
    b. foreign policy.
    c. the civil service.
    d. the money question.

19. The significance of the "cross of gold" speech was that:
    a. it ended the "battle of the standards."
    b. it inspired the Populists to oppose free silver.
    c. it led to William Jennings Bryan's Democratic presidential nomination.
    d. it helped persuade Congress to adopt the Gold Standard Act of 1900.

20. The issue of free coinage of silver rapidly declined in importance among farmers after 1896 partly because:
    a. farm prices began to rise.
    b. farmers lost interest in politics.
    c. tariff rates declined and imports increased.
    d. voters became more knowledgeable about economic issues.

TRUE-FALSE QUESTIONS

Read each statement carefully. Mark true statements "T" and false statements "F."

1. Compared to today, a much higher percentage of eligible voters went to the polls in the late nineteenth century.

2. In the late nineteenth century, the Republican Party was more likely than the Democratic to favor the restriction of immigration.

3. Although most congressmen apparently expected the Sherman Antitrust Act to be mainly symbolic, the Supreme Court interpreted it very strictly and the Justice Department used it vigorously to prosecute monopolies.

4. The Republican-sponsored high protective tariff of 1890 was popular with the voters and led to Republican control of both houses of Congress for the first time since the Civil War.

5. The Interstate Commerce Act of 1887 was haphazardly enforced and narrowly interpreted by the courts so that it had little or no practical effect.

6. The Grange was strongest in the Midwestern states.

7. The assassination of William McKinley by an office seeker provided impetus to the passage of the Pendleton Civil Service Act.

8. The Sherman Antitrust Act applied initially only to railroads.

9. The Farmers' Alliance organizations provided the foundation from which the Populist Party emerged.

10. Reflecting conservative rural values, the Farmers Alliance movement allowed no role for women and African Americans.

11. Many aged Civil War veterans of the Union army lived in severe poverty because of the lack of a widespread pension program.

12. Some southern white Populists sought to build political connections with black farmers, but the efforts did not prove lasting.

13. The Populists tried to build political connections with industrial workers but were generally unsuccessful in doing so.

14. Most industrialized nations of the world recognized *both* gold and silver as backing for their monetary systems.

15. In the 1896 election, William Jennings Bryan carried most of his votes from the farming areas of the Midwest and mid-Atlantic states.

16. The Chautauqua movement provided many reformers with a platform to spread their ideas to a wide audience.

17. James B. Weaver was the leader of the Stalwart faction of the Republican party.

18. Several influential Populist orators were women.

19. Increased gold production from new discoveries and improved techniques helped improve the U.S. economy around the turn of the century.

20. The Farmers' Alliance promoted the idea of having farmers form marketing cooperatives to eliminate the middleman.

CHAPTER TWENTY
THE IMPERIAL REPUBLIC

Objectives

A thorough study of Chapter 20 should enable the student to understand:

1. The new Manifest Destiny and how it differed from the old Manifest Destiny.
2. The objectives of American foreign policy at the turn of the century with respect to Europe, Latin America, and Asia.
3. The variety of factors that motivated the United States to become imperialistic and how the American variety of imperialism followed that of other nations.
4. The relationship between American economic interests, especially tariff policy, and developments in Hawaii and Cuba.
5. The causes of the Spanish-American War.
6. The military problems encountered in fighting the Spanish and, subsequently, the Filipinos.
7. The problems involved in developing a colonial administration for America's new empire.
8. The motives behind the Open Door notes and the Boxer intervention.
9. The nature of the military reforms carried out following the Spanish-American War.

Main Themes

1. Why Americans turned from the old continental concept of Manifest Destiny to a new worldwide expansionism.
2. How the Spanish-American War served as the catalyst to transform imperialist stirrings into a full-fledged empire.
3. How the nation had to make attitudinal, political, and military adjustments to its new role as a major world power.

Glossary

1. Monroe Doctrine: President James Monroe's declaration in 1823 that the Western Hemisphere was off limits to further European colonization and that the United States would consider any effort by the European powers "to extend their system to any portion of this hemisphere as dangerous to our peace and safety." This policy of opposing outside interference in Western Hemisphere affairs has been the enduring cornerstone of United States policy toward Latin America.
2. filibustering: The launching of invasions or attacks by private individuals organized as a military force. Anti-Spanish Cubans used the United States as a base for filibustering expeditions against the Spanish government of Cuba.

Pertinent Questions

STIRRINGS OF IMPERIALISM (544-549)

1. What intellectual, economic, philosophical, and racial factors helped create a new national mood more receptive to overseas expansionism?

2. Describe Alfred Thayer Mahan's thesis of national power. To what extent did the United States implement his ideas?

3. What were James G. Blaine's objectives in promoting a Pan-American cooperation? How successful were his efforts?

4. How did Hawaii gradually get drawn into America's economic and political sphere? What was the impact on the indigenous Hawaiian people?

5. How did the Venezuelan and Samoan incidents demonstrate that imperialism necessarily involved America in diplomatic maneuvers with European powers?

WAR WITH SPAIN (549-558)

6. What were the causes of American involvement in Cuban affairs? Could the United States have achieved its objectives by means short of war?

7. What two incidents combined to finally pull the United States into war with Spain? What were the broader motives that led the United States into the war?

8. Describe the American plans and preparations for the Spanish-American War. How effective was the effort?

9. Explain the importance of the action by the navy's Asiatic fleet. How did such action change the character of the war?

10. Explain how ground and sea forces combined for quick victory in Cuba. How intense was the Spanish resistance?

11. What role did African-American troops play in the United States' war effort? What social conflicts arose?

12. Describe the relationship between Puerto Rico and the United States. What tensions emerged?

13. What arguments were raised for and against imperialism in general and annexation of the Philippines in particular? Why did annexation prevail?

THE REPUBLIC AS EMPIRE (558-563)

14. What forms of government did the United States establish for its newly obtained possessions other than Cuba? What particular challenges and conflicts did governing Cuba pose?

15. Were early American actions in the Philippines a repudiation of the ideals that had led the United States to help Cuba secure its independence? What happened in the longer run?

16. How was the Open Door policy calculated to provide maximum commercial and diplomatic advantage at minimum cost? What did the costs turn out to be?

17. Summarize the major military reforms instituted between 1900 and 1903. What were the problems that these changes were designed to solve?

AMERICA IN THE WORLD: IMPERIALISM (546-547)

18. How did the new imperialism of the Nineteenth Century differ from the older style empires?

19. What were the justifications for imperialism put forth by its most ardent advocates?

20. Briefly describe the British Empire. How did it influence American thinking?

PATTERNS OF POPULAR CULTURE: YELLOW JOURNALISM (550-551)

21.   What is meant by "yellow journalism?" How was it spurred by the Spanish-American War? What was its legacy?

Identification

Identify each of the following, and explain why it is important within the context of the chapter.

1.   Henry Cabot Lodge
2.   Pan-American Union
3.   Pearl Harbor
4.   Queen Liliuokalani
5.   "Butcher Weyler"
6.   Joseph Pulitzer and William Randolph Hearst
7.   George Dewey
8.   Rough Riders
9.   Treaty of Paris
10.   Election of 1900
11.   Emilio Aguinaldo
12.   Arthur MacArthur
13.   William Howard Taft
14.   John Hay
15.   Boxer Rebellion
16.   Elihu Root

Document 1

Read the section of the text under the heading "Stirrings of Imperialism." The selection below is taken from an article by Senator Henry Cabot Lodge (R-Mass.) in the March 1895 issue of *Forum* magazine. Then in the second of his more than thirty years in the Senate, Lodge criticized President Cleveland for his failure to annex Hawaii and stated his general position on American expansionism. Consider the following questions: What motives for imperialism are reflected in Lodge's article? How would Lodge's argument fit with that of Josiah Strong and the Social Darwinists? How much of Lodge's dream became reality during his long service in the Senate?

In the interests of our commerce and of our fullest development, we should build the Nicaragua Canal, and for the protection of that canal and for the sake of our commercial supremacy in the Pacific we should control the Hawaiian Islands and maintain our influence in Samoa. England has studded the West Indies with strong places which are a standing menace to our Atlantic seaboard. We should have among those islands at least one strong naval station, and when the Nicaragua Canal is built, the island of Cuba, still sparsely settled and of almost unbounded fertility, will become to us a necessity. Commerce follows the flag, and we should build up a navy strong enough to give protection to Americans in every quarter of the globe and sufficiently powerful to put our coasts beyond the possibility of successful attack.

The tendency of modern times is toward consolidation. It is apparent in capital and labor alike, and it is also true of nations. Small states are of the past and have no future. The modern movement is all toward the concentration of people and territory into great nations and large dominions. The great nations are rapidly absorbing for their future expansion and their present defense all the waste places of the earth. It is a movement which makes for civilization and the advancement of the race. As one of the great nations of the world, the United States must not fall out of the line of march.

For more than thirty years we have been so much absorbed with grave domestic questions that we have lost sight of these vast interests which lie just outside our borders. They ought to be neglected no longer. They are not only of material importance but they are matters which concern our greatness as a nation and our future as a great example. They appeal to our national honor and dignity and to the pride of country and of race.

Henry Cabot Lodge, *Forum*, March 1895.

Document 2

Read the passages of the text and the Patterns of Popular Culture section that discuss the "yellow press" of Joseph Pulitzer and William Randolph Hearst. Not all major newspapers engaged in such journalistic tactics. One of the nation's most conservative papers was the *New York Herald Tribune*. Although the *Herald Tribune* supported the Spanish-American War when it finally came, it constantly editorialized for peace. Staunchly Republican, the *Herald Tribune* supported McKinley's every move. After the de Lôme letter, the paper counseled caution. Following the explosion of the *Maine,* the paper downplayed calls for war. The following editorials were written about two weeks before McKinley's war message. The *Herald Tribune* once again called for peace and then launched a bitingly satirical attack on its "yellow" competitors, the *New York World* and *New York Journal.* After reading the editorials, consider the following questions: Were the probabilities on the side of peace in early April 1898? Did the report on the sinking of the *Maine* satisfy the people? Does it appear that the *Herald Tribune* was jealous of the circulation gains made by its competition? Were the excesses of the "yellow press" as extreme as the second editorial indicates?

The balance of probabilities is still on the side of peace. That is to be said with confidence, despite the alarmist rumors and truculent menaces so generally extant. Delay is making for peace by giving reason time to conquer passion. Men do not keep at white heat permanently. They either cool off or are consumed. A dozen times since the Cuban war began there has been a fierce clamor for intervention. Those who were loudest then see now that such action would have been a deplorable mistake. When Antonio Maceo was killed, men demanded war. But peace was kept, and with it the credit and honor of this Nation. When the *Maine* was destroyed indignation rose to fever pitch. But seven weeks have passed, and the peace is still unbroken. Again, the report on the *Maine* was to be the signal for hostilities. But it was not. It was a report that satisfied the American people. So did the Message [from President McKinley] that accompanied it. And they are now a week old and there is no war. The chances are that, thus kept off week after week, the dreaded catastrophe will be altogether averted. . . . The honor and welfare of the Nation are safe in William McKinley's hands. It will be well to leave them there.

Not least of all, the outlook is still peaceful, and we trust increasingly so, because peace—so long as justice is supreme—is right, and war—unless justice and honor are at stake—is wrong.

* * *

It is to be feared that the exceedingly able and energetic manner in which the newspapers intrusted with the National honor have conducted the war up to the present time may lead to overconfidence on the part of the seventy million American citizens who catch the newspapers on the fly as they come from the press and read them while they are hot. . . . If it isn't war that we have been enjoying at the comparatively low price of twenty-four pages for a cent then nothing is war; all the verities have vanished; truth crushed to earth under job type six inches deep cannot rise again. An Error clad in the most gorgeous garb of the spacewriter's opulent vocabulary, instead of writhing and dying, just stalks abroad with several bands in front of a procession of her worshippers.

War: Of course it's war. If it isn't war then the newspapers which have consented in the most self-sacrificing way to become the custodians of the National honor have been emitting lies at the rate of about a million a minute, and that is simply inconceivable. That is to say, it was inconceivable before the possibility of issuing and selling for cash a million newspapers a minute had been demonstrated by the actual affidavits of well-known votaries [devoted adherents] of the truth. . . . So as soon as the issue can be made plain to the American people, and the fact is established beyond a doubt that President McKinley has violated the unwritten law of the Republic which makes it obligatory upon him to declare war whenever any newspaper with a circulation of a million a minute demands it, this war will be concluded with the impeachment of McKinley and the general uprising of the outraged sentiment of the American people under Joseph Bailey of Texas against the Republican party.

New York Herald Tribune, 5 April 1898.

Map Exercise

Fill in or identify the following on the blank map provided. Use the map in the text as your source.

1. Cuba, Puerto Rico, Hawaii, Samoa, Midway, Guam, the Philippines, and Alaska.
2. The area of the Venezuelan border dispute.
3. The area of the Chinese coast that was divided into European spheres of influence.

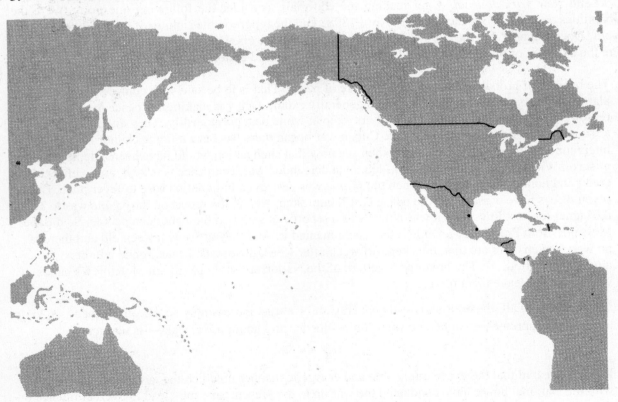

Summary

Turning its interest from the continental United States to the world at large, America in the years after the Civil War fought a war with Spain and acquired a far-flung empire. By 1900, American possessions included Alaska, Hawaii, the Philippines, Puerto Rico, and a string of Pacific islands. In addition, Cuba was essentially an American protectorate. The nation was suddenly a world power with worldwide responsibilities and burdens. The empire had been acquired for economic and philosophical reasons. Expansionism could provide an outlet for a perceived glut of American goods and an arena in which to demonstrate the supposed superiority of Western civilization. To accommodate its new role, the nation had to devise ways to improve its military establishment and govern its overseas territories.

Review Questions

These questions are to be answered with essays. This will allow you to explore relationships between individuals, events, and attitudes of the period under review.

1. Compare and contrast the old and new concepts of the Manifest Destiny. Look especially at the economic, philosophical, cultural, and racial motives for overseas expansion. Were these factors at work in the older continental expansionism?

2. What hesitations and doubts about imperialism did Americans evince between 1865 and 1898? How did the Spanish-American War change all this?

3. Was the Spanish-American conflict indeed a "splendid little war?" What was splendid about it? What was sordid, racist, seamy, or ill-conceived?

4. What parallels can be drawn between America's imperial aspirations and actions and the way white Americans dealt with the American Indian?

Chapter Self Test

After you have read the chapter in the text and done the exercises in the Study Guide, take the following self test to see if you understand the material you have covered. Answers appear at the end of the Study Guide.

MULTIPLE-CHOICE QUESTIONS

Circle the letter of the response that best answers the question or completes the statement.

1. The new Manifest Destiny of the 1890s differed from traditional American expansionism in that the territories acquired in the 1890s were:
   a. not likely to become states.
   b. not contiguous with existing states or territories.
   c. not considered suitable for massive American settlement.
   d. all of the above.

2. The text lists three factors that contributed directly or indirectly to the development of the new Manifest Destiny at the turn of the century. Which of the following is *not* one of the three?
   a. The depression of 1893.
   b. The concept of the closing of the frontier.
   c. The declining volume of American foreign trade.
   d. The Populist movement and other class protests.

3. Alfred Thayer Mahan was significant to the development of American imperialism through his writings on:
   a. sea power.
   b. Social Darwinism.
   c. Christian Missions.
   d. dialectical materialism.

4. As a result of the naval building program begun in the 1870s, by 1900 the U.S. Navy was:
   a. the most powerful in the world.
   b. the third most powerful in the world.
   c. the tenth most powerful in the world.
   d. actually weaker than in 1880 because of corruption in spending naval appropriations.

5. Which of the following was *not* a result of increasing American influence in the Hawaiian Islands beginning in the 1830s?
   a. The native population declined significantly due to disease.
   b. Native religion was undermined by Christian missionaries.
   c. Asian immigrants were prevented from residing in Hawaii.
   d. American sugar plantations dominated the economy.

6. In 1893, a revolution in Hawaii overthrew the government of Queen Liliuokalani. This revolution was instigated mainly by:
   a. Spanish imperialists.
   b. native inhabitants of Hawaii.
   c. Asian immigrants to Hawaii.
   d. American plantation interests.

7. The provisional government following the revolution in Hawaii that overthrew Queen Liliuokalani:
   a. was dominated by Hawaiians despite American economic superiority.
   b. enacted trade barriers with the United States.
   c. rapidly collapsed when American troops withdrew.
   d. sought annexation to the United States.

8. Three of the following were competitors for control of the Samoan Islands in the 1880s and 1890s. Which is the *exception?*
   a. Germany
   b. Great Britain
   c. Japan
   d. United States

9. The Wilson-Gorman tariff of 1894 had disastrous effects on the economy of Cuba because of its very high duties on:
   a. rum.
   b. cotton.
   c. tobacco.
   d. sugar.

10. The expression "yellow journalism" refers to the newspapers that emphasized:

    a. unwavering loyalty to the Democratic Party in the South.

    b. pacifism in foreign affairs.

    c. lurid and sensational news.

    d. the dangers of Oriental immigration.

11. Which of the following newspaper publishers were accused of using "yellow journalism" in their coverage of the trouble in Cuba in the 1890s? (Mark *two* letters.)

    a. William Randolph Hearst.

    b. Josiah Strong.

    c. Valeriano Weyler.

    d. Joseph Pulitzer.

12. The de Lôme letter had the effect of:

    a. discrediting the McKinley administration in U.S. eyes.

    b. worsening United States-Spanish relations.

    c. exposing United States imperialistic ambitions.

    d. temporarily improving United States-Spanish relations.

13. Commodore George Dewey was noteworthy to the Spanish-American War for:

    a. capturing Puerto Rico.

    b. sinking the Spanish fleet in Manila Bay.

    c. sinking the Spanish fleet in Santiago harbor.

    d. preventing Spanish reinforcements from reaching Cuba.

14. American preparation and mobilization for the military operations against Cuba in 1898 may most accurately be described or characterized as:

    a. remarkably inefficient and incompetent.

    b. adequate, but lacking in popular enthusiasm and support.

    c. remarkably quick and efficient in spite of poor planning and leadership.

    d. highly professional, well-organized, and efficient in both planning and execution.

15. The use of African-American troops in the United States Army during the Spanish-American War had the effect of:

    a. leading to the complete desegregation of the United States military.

    b. promoting a significant, if temporary, wave of racial unity throughout the nation.

    c. arousing racial tensions among troops and with communities around posts, especially in several southern states.

    d. none of the above, for there were no African American troops in the United States military at this time.

16. In addition to waging military expeditions against the Spanish in Cuba and the Philippines, the United States invaded:

    a. Morocco.

    b. Barcelona.

    c. Puerto Rico.

    d. El Salvador.

17. The Treaty of Paris of 1898, which ended the Spanish-American War, provided for Spain to transfer to the United States three of the following. Which is the *exception?*

    a. Guam.

    b. Virgin Islands.

    c. Philippines.

    d. Puerto Rico.

18. The most serious issue in the debate over ratification of the Treaty of Paris of 1898 was:

    a. the status of the Philippines.

    b. political rights of Puerto Rican natives.

    c. American commercial rights in Cuba.

    d. the sum of money to be paid by Spain to the United States.

19. The motive of the United States in contributing troops to the rescue of the besieged diplomats during the Boxer Rebellion was to:

    a. punish China.

    b. demonstrate American power to the Europeans.

    c. gain a foothold in China for an American sphere of influence.

    d. have a voice in the final settlement and prevent the dismemberment of China.

20. The reforms of Elihu Root in the period between 1900 and 1903 were significant in:

    a. improving the federal bureaucracy.

    b. modernizing the United States Army.

    c. curbing monopolistic business practices.

    d. cleaning up corruption in the Navy Department.

TRUE-FALSE QUESTIONS

Read each statement carefully. Mark true statements "T" and false statements "F."

1. Some influential writers supported American imperialism on the grounds that white Anglo-Saxon and Teutonic peoples were destined to dominate portions of the world occupied mainly by the darker-skinned races.

2. The United States helped organize the Pan-American Union.

3. In the 1895 dispute between Great Britain and Venezuela, the United States' position was favorable to Great Britain.

4. In the 1890s Senator Henry Cabot Lodge led the isolationist faction of Congress that argued that the United States should not have any significant interests beyond the nation's existing borders.

5. The American attack on the Spanish fleet at Manila resulted in the most difficult and bloodiest engagement of the Spanish-American War.

6. The United States fought a brief naval war with Great Britain over access to trade in Jamaica and the Bahamas.

7. By 1895 almost all the population of Hawaii's main islands was of European ancestry.

8. The main commodity of trade between the United States and Cuba was cotton.

9. The Spanish-American War was called the "splendid little war" because military plans and arrangements went smoothly and efficiently even though there was diplomatic controversy.

10. The largest ground-forces encounter of the Spanish-American War actually took place in the Dominican Republic.

11. Emilio Aguinaldo was the principal leader of the Cuban nationalists until he died in a Spanish detention camp prior to American intervention.

12. A provision was incorporated into Cuba's constitution that gave the United States the right to intervene in Cuba to preserve independence, life, and property.

13. Whereas the Spanish-American War lasted only about three and a half months, the American effort to suppress the subsequent Filipino insurrection lasted more than three years.

14. Because of the publicity that had accompanied Spanish atrocities in Cuba, the U.S. Army carefully avoided harsh tactics in the Philippine War.

15. William Howard Taft acquired his initial national reputation as the commander of the "Rough Rider" regiment.

16. The victory of William McKinley over William Jennings Bryan in the 1900 presidential election can be interpreted as a national endorsement of America's imperialism.

17. U.S. troops intervened in Cuba and occupied key parts of the island on occasion between 1900 and World War I.

18. The U.S. governors of the Philippine colony gave the Filipinos broad local autonomy and oversaw significant development of roads, schools, and the like.

19. As secretary of state, John Hay encouraged western nations and Japan to respect each others' spheres of influence in China and to allow all nations equal access to trade in their spheres.

20. The so-called Open Door policy was designed to protect American interests in Panama, in particular, and Central America, in general.

247

CHAPTER TWENTY-ONE
THE RISE OF PROGRESSIVISM

Objectives

A thorough study of Chapter 21 should enable the student to understand:

1. The social justice reforms of the period and the role of the church in carrying out the Social Gospel.
2. The origins of the progressive impulse.
3. The progressive emphasis on scientific expertise, organizational reform, and professionalism.
4. The role of women's groups in promoting reform.
5. The significance of the women's suffrage movement.
6. The desire of the progressives to limit the role of political party organizations and the measures they advocated to accomplish this goal.
7. The temperance movement and its relationship to other progressive reforms.
8. The origins of the NAACP and the importance of W.E.B. DuBois.
9. The movement to restrict immigration, and how allowing fewer immigrants was regarded as a reform.
10. The alternate approaches to the problems of the trusts: socialism, regulation, and trust busting.

Main Themes

1. How progressivism was a reaction to the rapid industrialization and urbanization of the United States in the late nineteenth century.
2. That all progressives shared an optimistic vision that an active government could solve problems and create an efficient, ordered society.
3. That progressives wanted to reduce the influence of party machines on politics.
4. How temperance, immigration restriction, and women's suffrage movements took on crusade-like aspects.

Glossary

1. at-large election: An election in which each candidate for a city council (or other representative body) is voted on by all the voters within a city (or other jurisdiction) rather than by only the residents of a specific ward (or district).
2. encyclical: A letter on a current issue of church concern circulated to Roman Catholic clergy by the pope. Encyclicals, such as *Rerum Novarum,* are considered to constitute official church policy.

Pertinent Questions

THE PROGRESSIVE IMPULSE (566-572)

1. What were the key reform "impulses" that characterized progressivism?
2. What did the muckrakers do to help prepare the way for progressivism?

3. What contribution did the Social Gospel movement make to progressivism?

4. Contrast the Social Darwinist view of society with the progressive vision. How did the settlement house movement and the social work profession illustrate the difference?

5. What were the characteristics of the so-called new middle class and the new professionalism? What kinds of organizations were formed? Who was usually excluded?

6. In what professions did women dominate? What were the hallmarks of those professions?

WOMEN AND REFORM (572-577)

7. What was meant by the "new woman"? What professions did women enter? Why?

8. What were the accomplishments of the women's club movement? How did the clubs reflect both the influence of women and the restrictions upon them?

9. What were the principal arguments used for and against women's suffrage?

10. Explain how the debate over the "sphere" of women shaped the suffrage movement. Which position was probably the most influential in finally obtaining the vote for women? Why was the West different?

11. What happened to the women's movement after suffrage was accomplished in 1920? Explain the significance of the 19th amendment.

THE ASSAULT ON THE PARTIES (577-581)

12. Compare and contrast the proponents and opponents of municipal government reform.

13. How were reform measures such as the commission plan, the city-manager plan, nonpartisanship, and at-large elections designed to destroy the power of the urban party bosses?

14. What was the basic purpose of the initiative, referendum, direct primary, and recall?

15. How did key progressive governors demonstrate that effective leadership was the key to successful reform? Who was the most celebrated of this group?

16. What was the relationship between the weakening of political parties and the rise of interest groups? Specifically identify progressive demands for workers.

SOURCES OF PROGRESSIVE REFORM (581-584)

17. What role did organized labor play in progressive reform efforts?

18. By what means did some urban political machines, such as Tammany Hall, manage to survive the progressive era? What was the impact of the Triangle Fire on reform?

19. Why was progressivism especially strong in the western states?

20. How did the race relations views of Booker T. Washington contrast with those of W. E. B. DuBois?

21. How did the NAACP get started? What were its early victories?

CRUSADE FOR SOCIAL ORDER AND REFORM (584-587)

22. Explain the importance of lynching in the early 20th century and explain the position of the NAACP and southern women in particular on this issue.

23. Today, antiliquor laws are often thought of as conservative. Why was prohibition regarded as a progressive issue? What forces usually opposed prohibition?

24. Most progressives abhorred the urban disorder resulting from the influx of immigrants, but they differed about the appropriate response to the problem. Which one dominated? Why?

CHALLENGING THE CAPITALIST ORDER (587-590)

25. Both progressives and socialists believed that the enormous industrial combinations were at the core of many of the nation's problems, but they certainly did not agree on the appropriate solutions. How did the socialist agenda differ from the typical progressive program? On what issues did the socialists disagree among themselves?

26. Describe the two different progressive approaches to the perceived problem of economic consolidation and centralization. What solutions did advocates of each approach favor?

WHERE HISTORIANS DISAGREE: PROGRESSIVE REFORM (568-569)

27. What have the different emphases of historians revealed about the diversity of motives and interests reflected in progressivism? Also, focusing on the most recent studies (1993 on), what are these scholars saying about progressivism?

AMERICA IN THE WORLD: SOCIAL DEMOCRACY (578)

28. Compare and contrast progressivism in America with social democracy in Europe.

<u>Identification</u>

Identify each of the following and explain why it is important within the context of the chapter.

1. Ida Tarbell

2. Lincoln Steffens

3. Salvation Army

4. Walter Rauschenbusch

5. *Rerum Novarum*

6. Jacob Riis

7. Hull House/Jane Addams

8. Thorstein Veblen

9. Taylorism

10. American Medical Association

11. "Boston Marriage"

12. Women's Trade Union League

13. Anna Howard Shaw

14. Carrie Chapman Catt

15. Nineteenth Amendment

16. Equal Rights Amendment

17. secret ballot

18. Robert M. La Follette

19. Triangle Shirtwaist fire

20. Niagara Movement

21. grandfather clause

22. "talented tenth"

23. WCTU

24. Anti-Saloon League

25. eugenics

26. Eugene V. Debs

27. Industrial Workers of the World

28. Louis D. Brandeis

Document 1

Read the section of the text that describes municipal government reform including the commission and city-manager forms of city government. The commission plan was pioneered in Texas by Galveston, Houston, Dallas, and other cities. People who were interested in reform in other cities and states often visited the commission pioneers. The following excerpts are from the official report of one such investigative trip to Texas. Consider the following questions: How does the report demonstrate a typical progressive-era concern for businesslike efficiency? How does the report typify the progressive faith that governmental action could solve problems and show results? If the businesslike aspects of the commission plan appealed so strongly to the Illinois senators, how do you suppose they would have regarded the city-manager innovation a few years later? Does the report evince any concern for social justice reforms in the cities studied?

In Galveston each of the four commissioners is assigned a particular part of the administrative function of the city; the other commissioners and the mayor merely ratifying their acts. This commission is composed of a very high class of men, most of them very wealthy, and they have the confidence of the entire people. This commission is a very practical body, each man carrying on his department in much the same manner that a business man would carry on his own individual business. . . . In every city we visited we found the almost unanimous sentiment of the citizens favoring the commission form of government. We sought the opinion of bankers, merchants, laboring men—in fact all classes of citizens. The enthusiasm of the people for this form of government is hardly describable. . . . Without doubt there has been a marked improvement in the conduct of the affairs of these cities under this plan of municipal government. Able, fearless, progressive and conscientious men are in charge of public affairs in these cities. Under the stimulus of great municipal movements, conducted in the same manner as the affairs of great private enterprises, these cities are entering upon an era of great prosperity, with the full confidence of their citizens in the integrity of their public officials and in the efficiency of the commission form of government.

Illinois General Assembly, Senate Committee on Municipalities, *Report Made to Senate, April 15, 1909, by Mr. McKenzie from Special Subcommittee (to Investigate the Operation of the Commission Form of City Government).*

Document 2

Read the section of the text under the heading "Suffrage for Women." The document below is drawn from a flyer published in 1905 by the Anti-Suffrage Association based in Albany, New York. The pamphlet was written by noted historian Francis Parkman and was issued several years after his death. Consider the following questions: Why would the emphasis on the "natural" way have been an effective argument against suffrage? To what extent was the suffrage fight a battle among women as well as between men and women? How do Parkman's arguments compare with those who opposed the Equal Rights Amendment in the 1970s?

The man is the natural head of the family, and is responsible for its maintenance and order. Hence he ought to control the social and business agencies which are essential to the successful discharge of the trust imposed upon him. . . .

Woman suffrage must have one of two effects. If, as many of its advocates complain, women are subservient to men, and do nothing but what they desire, then women suffrage will have no other result than to increase the power of the other sex; if, on the other hand, women vote as they see fit, without regarding their husbands, then unhappy marriages will be multiplied and divorces redoubled. . . .

But most women, including those of the best capacity and worth, fully consent that their father, husbands, brothers, or friends, shall be their political representatives. . . .

Nothing is more certain than that woman will have suffrage if they ever want it; for when they want it, men will give it to them regardless of consequences. . . .

Many women of sense and intelligence are influenced by the fact that the woman suffrage movement boasts itself a movement of progress, and by a wish to be on the liberal or progressive side. But the boast is unfounded. Progress, to be genuine, must be in accord with natural law. If it is not, it ends in failure and in retrogression. . . . To plunge [women] into politics, where they are not needed and for which they are unfit, would be scarcely more a movement of progress than to force them to bear arms and fight. . . .

Neither Congress, nor the States, nor the united voice of the whole people could permanently change the essential relations of the sexes. Universal female suffrage, even if decreed, would undo itself in time; but the attempt to establish it would work deplorable mischief. The question is, whether the persistency of a few agitators shall plunge us blindfold into the most reckless of all experiments; whether we shall adopt this supreme device for developing the defects of women, and demolish their real power to build an ugly mockery instead. For the sake of womanhood, let us hope not. . . . Let us save women from the barren perturbations of American politics. Let us respect them; and, that we may do so, let us pray for deliverance from female suffrage.

Francis Parkman, "Some of the Reasons Against Women's Suffrage" (Albany, N. Y.: Anti-Suffrage Association, 1905).

Map Exercise

Fill in or identify the following on the blank map provided. Use the narrative in the chapter as your source.

1. State known as "the laboratory of progressivism."
2. City in which Hull House was located.
3. Two cities that launched the commission form of municipal government.
4. Two states that did not ratify the Eighteenth Amendment, which established the prohibition of liquor.

Interpretive Questions

Based on what you have filled in, answer the following. On some of the questions you will need to consult the narrative in your text for information or explanation.

1. What led one state to be called the "laboratory of progressivism"? Who was this state's leading progressive?
2. In general, where were settlement houses located and why? What was their function? Why was Hull House the most famous U.S. settlement house?
3. What natural event in what city was the catalyst for the invention of the commission plan of municipal government?
4. What probably explains why the particular two states failed to ratify the Eighteenth Amendment?

Summary

Convinced that rapid industrialization and urbanization had created serious problems and disorder, progressives shared an optimistic vision that organized private and government action could improve society. Progressivism sought to control monopoly, build social cohesion, and promote efficiency. Muckrakers exposed social ills that Social Gospel reformers, settlement house workers, and other progressives attacked. Meanwhile, increasing standards of training and expertise were creating a new middle class of educated professionals including some women. The progressives tried to rationalize politics by reducing the influence of political parties in municipal and state affairs. Many of the nation's problems could not be solved, some progressives believed, if alcohol were banned, immigration were restricted, and women were allowed to vote. Educated African Americans teamed with sympathetic whites to form the NAACP and begin the movement that eventually wiped away Jim Crow. Other progressives stressed the need for fundamental economic transformation through socialism or through milder forms of antitrust action and regulation.

Review Questions

These questions are to be answered with essays. This will allow you to explore relationships between individuals, events, and attitudes of the period under review.

1. Explain the three "impulses" of the progressive movement. What specific programs embodied those impulses?

2. Progressives professed to believe that government at all levels should be strong, efficient, and democratic so that it could better serve the people. What changes in the structure and operation of government did progressives advocate to achieve these aims? Can the attempts at civil service reform in the nineteenth century be seen as a precursor of this type of progressive program?

3. To what extent did muckrakers, Social Gospel reformers, settlement house volunteers, social workers, and other experts reflect the central assumptions of progressivism?

4. Explain how progressivism affected women and, conversely, how women affected progressivism.

Chapter Self Test

After you have read the chapter in the text and done the exercises in the Study Guide, take the following self test to see if you understand the material you have covered. Answers appear at the end of the Study Guide.

MULTIPLE-CHOICE QUESTIONS

Circle the letter of the response that best answers the question or completes the statement.

1. Three of the following statements express general beliefs of the progressives. Which is the *exception?*
   a. An optimistic vision that society is capable of improvement.
   b. A belief that growth and progress should not occur recklessly as they had in the late nineteenth century.
   c. A conviction that direct, purposeful human intervention in social and economic affairs was needed to order and improve society and play an important role in improving and stabilizing society.
   d. A dedication to the theory that the natural law of the marketplace and the doctrines of laissez-faire and Social Darwinism would help solve societal problems.

2. Ida Tarbell and Lincoln Steffens were most closely associated with:
   a. muckraking.
   b. the Social Gospel.
   c. Social Darwinism.
   d. sociological jurisprudence.

3. One of the most significant examples of the Social Gospel at work was:
   a. Tammany Hall.
   b. the Salvation Army.
   c. the Chamber of Commerce.
   d. the General Federation of Women's Clubs.

4. The Social Gospel:
   a. helped bring to progressivism a powerful moral component.
   b. became the dominant philosophy in urban reform.
   c. was dismissed by serious reformers as irrelevant moralization.
   d. was rejected as materialistic by Pope Leo XIII.

5. One of the strongest elements of progressive thought stressed that ignorance, poverty, and even criminality resulted mainly from:
   a. a person's "fitness" for survival.
   b. inherent moral or genetic failings.
   c. the workings of divine providence.
   d. the effects of an undesirable environment.

6. Jane Addams's Hull House was established for the purpose of:
   a. treating the insane.
   b. rehabilitating drug addicts.
   c. aiding the urban poor, especially immigrants.
   d. disseminating scientific-farming information.

7. The professional roles available to women in the early twentieth century were:
   a. widely expanded by custom and law into virtually every field of work.
   b. restricted entirely to the settlement houses and social work.
   c. free of the organizational trends characterizing the male professional world.
   d. most often those involving "helping" or "domestic" activities associated with traditionally female roles.

8. The women's club movement tended to attract its membership primarily from:
   a. the rural poor.
   b. recent immigrants.
   c. the urban working classes.
   d. the urban middle and upper classes.

9. In general, the women's club movement:
   a. confined its activities to social and cultural activities.
   b. seldom adopted positions on controversial public issues.
   c. overtly challenged the prevailing assumptions about the proper role of women in society.
   d. played an important role in winning passage of state laws regulating conditions of housing and the workplace.

10. The advocates of women's suffrage significantly increased their general public support during the progressive era when they put increased emphasis on the argument that women's suffrage would:
    a. lead to full social and economic power for women within a generation.
    b. increase political power and office-holding opportunities available to women.
    c. bring more women into the industrial work force, thereby countering recession.
    d. enhance the likelihood of the successful enactment of other progressive reform causes.

11. During the first two decades of the twentieth century, before the ratification of the Nineteenth Amendment, women gained the right to vote in at least some elections in:

    a. all the states.

    b. only a few states in the Far West.

    c. the majority of the states.

    d. one of the states.

12. The most important professional opportunity open to educated African American women in the early years of the twentieth century was:

    a. law.

    b. medicine.

    c. education.

    d. journalism.

13. The secret ballot was adopted by most states:

    a. right after the Constitution was ratified.

    b. during the rise of "Jacksonian Democracy."

    c. during the Reconstruction period.

    d. during the late nineteenth century.

14. During the progressive period, a new form of city government was developed in which the elected city officials hired a professionally trained administrator to run the government. This administrator was usually known as the:

    a. strong mayor.

    b. city manager.

    c. municipal commissioner.

    d. urban administrative specialist.

15. Which of the following was *not* a progressive electoral reform measure?

    a. recall

    b. initiative

    c. referendum

    d. election by district or ward

16. Robert M. La Follette was significant in the progressive period of American history as:

    a. an investigative reporter.

    b. a reform mayor of Cleveland.

    c. a reform governor of Wisconsin.

    d. a corrupt city boss of New York.

17. Which of the following was *not* an electoral reform adopted by some states in the Progressive Era?

    a. initiative and referendum

    b. direct primary elections

    c. banning of interest groups

    d. recall of elected officials

18. Partly in response to progressive political reforms, the:
   a. power of party organizations collapsed.
   b. turnout of eligible voters increased.
   c. influence of special-interest groups increased.
   d. influence of party bosses disappeared.

19. Which of the following groups was most opposed to the ratification of the Eighteenth Amendment (alcohol prohibition)?
   a. Catholic immigrants
   b. rural fundamentalists
   c. settlement house workers
   d. The Women's Christian Temperance Union

20. The anti-immigration movement that emerged during the progressive period was fueled by three of the following arguments. Which is the *exception?*
   a. Immigrants were creating unmanageable urban problems.
   b. Unrestricted immigration was a threat to the nation's racial purity.
   c. The new immigrants were much less assimilable than were earlier immigrants.
   d. A completely open immigration policy was contrary to American tradition.

TRUE-FALSE QUESTIONS

Read each statement carefully. Mark true statements "T" and false statements "F."

1. "Muckraker" was the nickname given by progressives to politicians who were accused of bribery and corruption.

2. As a general rule, progressive reformers opposed placing governmental power in the hands of nonpartisan, nonelective officials who were insulated from electoral politics.

3. As a general rule, Social Darwinists stressed the role of inherent characteristics, and progressives stressed the role of environment in explaining why poor people failed to succeed economically.

4. In the 1920s, women tended to vote cohesively for candidates who supported isolationism, economic regulation, and prohibition.

5. During the progressive era, even urban political machines such as Tammany Hall advocated some reforms like improvement of working conditions and protection for child workers.

6. The settlement house movement provided an opportunity for educated women to get together for intellectually stimulating retreats in a rural setting.

7. Professional women who entered the work force during the progressive era tended to be concentrated in the so-called helping professions such as teaching and nursing.

8. The electoral devices of initiative, referendum, and direct primary were instituted in several states in order to give more political power to the average voter rather than to the incumbent legislators.

9. In general, the increasing influence of interest groups during the progressive era strengthened the power of the two political parties.

10. In general, the support for prohibition of alcoholic beverages was weakest in the urban areas of the northeastern states.

11. America's entry into World War I helped provide the final push for the adoption of the national prohibition of alcoholic beverages.

12. The years from 1900 to 1914 reflected a steadily declining European immigration to the United States.

13. Distinct from other reformers in the progressive era, some socialists proposed that an essential element for reform of the American economy was government ownership of some basic industries.

14. In the early years of the twentieth century, the Industrial Workers of the World (IWW) became significant as the most influential organization promoting safety in the workplace.

15. In his book *Other People's Money* (1913), Louis D. Brandeis argued that big business was inevitable and that big government was necessary to regulate it on an ongoing basis.

16. Booker T. Washington was more inclined than W. E. B. DuBois to stress the need for African Americans to seek higher education, cultural enrichment, and political equality.

17. The Niagara Movement brought together leading African Americans and supportive whites in an effort that led to the establishment of the NAACP.

18. Eugenics was an alleged science that asserted the superiority of some races due to heredity.

19. The Supreme Court case of *Eugene v. Debs* established the right of socialists to run for office.

20. "Taylorism" advocated increased labor efficiency in factories.

21. Lynching was opposed especially by southern women.

22. Progressives worked to help workers on the state level with such reforms as workmen's compensation.

CHAPTER TWENTY-TWO
THE BATTLE FOR NATIONAL REFORM

Objectives

A thorough study of Chapter 22 should enable the student to understand:

1. The nature and extent of Theodore Roosevelt's "Square Deal" progressivism.
2. The similarities and differences between the domestic progressivism of William Howard Taft and of Roosevelt.
3. The conservation issue and why it triggered the split between Taft and Roosevelt.
4. The consequences of the split in the Republican Party in 1912.
5. The differences between Roosevelt's New Nationalism and Wilson's New Freedom.
6. The differences between Woodrow Wilson's campaign platform and the measures actually implemented during his term.
7. The new direction of American foreign policy introduced by Roosevelt, especially in Asia and the Caribbean.
8. The similarities and differences between Taft's and Roosevelt's approaches to foreign policy.
9. The reasons for the continuation of American interventionism in Latin America under Wilson.

Main Themes

1. How Theodore Roosevelt's leadership helped fashion a new, expanded role for the national government.
2. That politics during the administration of William Howard Taft showed that most of the nation desired a more progressive approach.
3. How the administration of Woodrow Wilson embodied both conservative and progressive features.
4. That the United States assumed a much more assertive and interventionist foreign policy, especially toward the Caribbean region.

Glossary

1. arbitration: The settling of a labor-management dispute by submission of the issues to an impartial third party empowered to issue a binding settlement. Arbitrators often "split the difference" between competing demands, but they also have the right to choose between the competing demands.
2. national banks: Privately owned banks chartered by the national government and operated under federal regulations. State banks, also privately owned, are chartered and regulated by state governments. Most large banks are national banks.

Pertinent Questions

THEODORE ROOSEVELT AND THE MODERN PRESIDENCY (594-598)

1. How did Teddy Roosevelt come to be president?
2. What were Roosevelt's assumptions about the proper role of government, especially with regard to economic concentration? To what extent was he a "trust buster"?

3. What changes did Roosevelt initiate in the traditional role of the federal government in labor disputes?

4. What were the key elements of the "square deal" that helped propel Roosevelt to reelection and to significant accomplishments in his second term?

5. How did Roosevelt's actions in the effort to strengthen the Interstate Commerce Commission (ICC) illustrate his tendency to take a middle road of reform?

6. What were the two factions within the conservation movement? Toward which side did Roosevelt lean? Were his stands consistent with his general approach to reform? What was his lasting effect on national environmental policy?

7. What caused the panic of 1907? How did Roosevelt and J. P. Morgan respond?

THE TROUBLED SUCCESSION (598-601)

8. Contrast the personalities of Theodore Roosevelt and William Howard Taft. How did Taft's actions, and lack of action, contribute to the division of the Republican Party?

9. Describe the programs that Roosevelt unveiled at Osawatomie, Kansas. How did they go beyond the moderation he had exhibited as president?

10. In addition to his general ambitions, what two events pushed Roosevelt into open opposition to Taft? What kept Roosevelt and Robert La Follette apart?

11. How did Taft manage to secure the Republican nomination in 1912 despite Roosevelt's obvious popularity?

12. Why did Roosevelt break from the Republicans to form the Progressive Party? For what did it stand?

WOODROW WILSON AND THE NEW FREEDOM (601-604)

13. What in Woodrow Wilson's pre–White House career foreshadowed his role as president?

14. How did Roosevelt's New Nationalism and Wilson's New Freedom differ from each other?

15. What propelled Wilson to victory in 1912? What roles did Taft and Eugene Debs play in the campaign?

16. In what ways did Wilson concentrate political and executive power in his own hands and prepare himself to be a strong legislative leader?

17. What special efforts did Wilson mount to pass the Underwood-Simmons tariff? How did it fulfill longstanding Democratic pledges? Why was a graduated income tax needed in addition to the tariff reduction?

18. Describe how the nation's banking system was transformed during the Wilson Administration. What role did bankers play in shaping the new law?

19. What did Wilson's actions in pushing hard for the Federal Trade Commission Act and giving only lukewarm support to the Clayton Act demonstrate about his ironic move in the direction of the New Nationalism?

20. After the initial spate of New Freedom legislation, why did Wilson back away from reform? What led him, later in his first term, to advance reform once again?

"THE BIG STICK": AMERICA AND THE WORLD, 1901–1917 (604-610)

21. Explain Roosevelt's distinction between "civilized" and "uncivilized" nations. How did sea power fit into his vision?

22. What was the course of relations between the United States and Japan during Roosevelt's presidency?

23. What were the general and immediate motivations for the proclamation of the Roosevelt corollary? What policy did it establish?

24. How did the United States acquire rights to build the Panama Canal? Why have many observers questioned the propriety of U. S. methods? (How relevant were these methods to the Panama Canal Treaty controversy in 1978?)

25. What was the central focus of William Howard Taft's foreign policy? What nickname was it given?

26. What actions did Taft and Wilson take toward Central American and Caribbean nations? (What legacy was left for relations between the United States and these nations?)

27. Why did Wilson take sides in the Mexican governmental turmoil? Describe the two interventions and their results.

Identification

Identify each of the following, and explain why it is important within the context of the chapter.

1. Department of Commerce and Labor
2. Northern Securities Case
3. Alton B. Parker
4. Pure Food and Drug Act
5. *The Jungle*
6. Meat Inspection Act
7. National Forest Service
8. John Muir/Sierra Club
9. Julia Lathrop
10. Gifford Pinchot
11. Newlands Act
12. Yosemite National Park
13. "Bull Moose" Party
14. Louis Brandeis
15. Sixteenth Amendment
16. child labor laws
17. Great White Fleet
18. Platt Amendment
19. Pancho Villa
20. John J. Pershing

Document 1

Read the section of the text under the heading "Government, Capital, and Labor." Also review the parts of Chapter Seventeen that discuss the rise of big business and the role of corporate leadership. The following excerpts are from Theodore Roosevelt's First Annual Message, delivered only a few months after he became president. Read the selection and consider the following questions: Does this message reveal an attitude toward trusts consistent with the actions that Roosevelt would undertake as president? How might Roosevelt have reacted to those who called the great industrial leaders "robber barons"? Would this document support the contention that progressivism can best be explained as a reaction to the economic changes of the late nineteenth century? Are Roosevelt's views more consistent with those of Herbert Croly or of Louis Brandeis? Does the Republican Party of today reflect a similar outlook toward business? Could it be fairly characterized as a "trickle-down" view?

The tremendous and highly complex industrial development which went on with ever accelerated rapidity during the latter half of the nineteenth century brings us face to face, at the beginning of the twentieth, with very serious social problems. The old laws, and the old customs which had almost the binding force of law, were once quite sufficient to regulate the accumulation and distribution of wealth. Since the industrial changes which have so enormously increased the productive power of mankind, they are no longer sufficient.

The growth of cities has gone on beyond comparison faster than the growth of the country, and the upbuilding of the great industrial centers has meant a startling increase, not merely in the aggregate of wealth, but in the number of very large individual, and especially of very large corporate, fortunes. The creation of these great corporate fortunes has not been due to the tariff nor to any other governmental action, but to natural causes in the business world operating in other countries as they operate in our own.

The process has aroused much antagonism, a great part of which is wholly without warrant. It is not true that as the rich have grown richer the poor have grown poorer. On the contrary, never before has the average man, the wage-worker, the farmer, the small trader, been so well off as in this country and at the present time. There have been abuses connected with the accumulation of wealth; yet it remains true that a fortune accumulated in legitimate business can be accumulated by the person specifically benefited only on condition of conferring immense incidental benefits upon others. Successful enterprise, of the type which benefits all mankind, can only exist if the conditions are such as to offer great prizes as the rewards of success.

The captains of industry who have driven the railway systems across this continent, who have built up our commerce, who have developed our manufactures, have on the whole done great good to our people. Without them the material development of which we are so justly proud could never have taken place. Moreover, we should recognize the importance of this material development by leaving as unhampered as is compatible with the public good the strong and forceful men upon whom the success of business operations inevitably rests. The slightest study of business conditions will satisfy anyone capable of forming a judgment that the personal equation is the most important factor in a business operation; that the business ability of the man at the head of any business concern, big or little, is usually the factor which fixes the gulf between striking success and hopeless failure. . . .

Moreover, it cannot too often be pointed out that to strike with ignorant violence at the interests of one set of men almost inevitably endangers the interests of all. The fundamental rule in our national life—the rule which underlies all others—is that, on the whole, and in the long run, we shall go up or down together. There are exceptions; and in times of prosperity some will prosper far more, and in times of adversity, some will suffer far more, than others; but speaking generally, a period of good times means that all share more or less in them, and in a period of hard times all feel the stress to a greater or less degree. It surely ought not to be necessary to enter into any proof of this statement;

the memory of the lean years which began in 1893 is still vivid, and we can contrast them with the conditions in this very year which is now closing. Disaster to great business enterprises can never have its effects limited to the men at the top. It spreads throughout, and while it is bad for everybody, it is worst for those farthest down. The capitalist may be shorn of his luxuries; but the wage-worker may be deprived of even bare necessities.

The mechanism of modern business is so delicate that extreme care must be taken not to interfere with it in a spirit of rashness or ignorance. Many of those who have made it their vocation to denounce the great industrial combinations which are popularly, although with technical inaccuracy, known as "trusts," appeal especially to hatred and fear. These are precisely the two emotions, particularly when combined with ignorance, which unfit men for the exercise of cool and steady judgment. In facing new industrial conditions, the whole history of the world shows that legislation will generally be both unwise and ineffective unless undertaken after calm inquiry and with somber self-restraint. . . .

All this is true; and yet it is also true that there are real and grave evils, one of the chief being over-capitalization because of its many baleful consequences; and a resolute and practical effort must be made to correct these evils.

There is a widespread conviction in the minds of the American people that the great corporations known as trusts are in certain of their features and tendencies hurtful to the general welfare.

Document 2

Read the section of the chapter under the heading "Banking Reform," and note the reference to the "money monopoly." In 1913, while banking reform was being debated, a congressional committee chaired by Representative Arsene Pujo of Louisiana was studying economic concentration in general and banking in particular. Read the following excerpt, which is from the influential report of the Pujo committee, and consider these questions: Does the Pujo report seem to support the New Nationalism or the New Freedom? What influence might such a report have had on the passage of the Federal Reserve Act?

Far more dangerous than all that has happened to us in the past in the way of elimination of competition in industry is the control of credit through the domination of these groups over our banks and industries. . . . Whether under a different currency system the resources in our banks would be greater or less is comparatively immaterial if they continue to be controlled by a small group. . . . If the arteries of credit now clogged well-nigh to choking by the obstructions created through the control of these groups are opened so that they may be permitted freely to play their important part in the financial system, competition in large enterprises will become possible and business can be conducted on its merits instead of being subject to the tribute and the good will of this handful of self-constituted trustees of the national prosperity.

Map Exercise

Fill in or identify the following on the blank map provided. Use the map in the text as your source.

1. Mexico, Cuba, Haiti, Dominican Republic, Puerto Rico, Virgin Islands, Nicaragua, Panama, Venezuela, Colombia. (Mark * on those countries into which the United States intervened militarily. Mark *RC* on the country to which the Roosevelt corollary was first applied.)
2. The area of Pancho Villa's raids and General John J. Pershing's intervention.
3. The route of the Panama Canal.

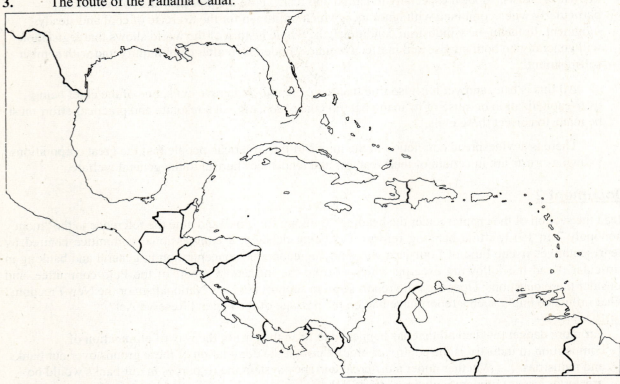

Interpretive Questions

Based on what you have filled in, answer the following. On some of the questions you will need to consult the narrative in your text for information or explanation.

1. Explain the motivation for Theodore Roosevelt's special concern with the Caribbean region. What policy did he formulate in response to his concerns?
2. What were the two possible routes for a Central American canal? What were the advantages and disadvantages of each? Why did the United States settle on the Panamanian choice? Why was Colombia upset?
3. What events inspired U.S. intervention in Nicaragua? Why was the country perceived to be important to American interests?
4. What caused the border strife between the United States and Mexico? What was its result?

Summary

Theodore Roosevelt became president as a consequence of the assassination of William McKinley, but he quickly moved to make the office his own. In many ways, Roosevelt was the preeminent progressive, yet it sometimes seemed that for him reform was more a style than a dogma. Although Roosevelt clearly envisioned a more activist national government, the shifts and contradictions embodied in his policies toward trusts, labor, and conservation reflected the complexity and diversity of progressivism. Despite being Roosevelt's hand-picked successor, President William Howard Taft managed to alienate Roosevelt and other progressive Republicans by his actions regarding tariffs, conservation, foreign policy, trusts, and other matters. In 1912, Roosevelt decided to challenge Taft for the presidency. When he failed to secure the Republican nomination, Roosevelt formed his own Progressive party. With the Republicans divided, Woodrow Wilson won the presidency. In actuality, Wilson's domestic program turned out to be much like the one Roosevelt had advocated. In the Caribbean, Wilson continued the pattern of intervention that Roosevelt and Taft had established.

Review Questions

These questions are to be answered with essays. This will allow you to explore relationships between individuals, events, and attitudes of the period under review.

1. In what ways did Theodore Roosevelt transform the role of the presidency and the national government? What specific programs resulted from his vigorous executive leadership?
2. Were the differences between the Taft administration and those of Roosevelt and Wilson more a matter of beliefs and objectives or of personalities and leadership style?
3. Considering Roosevelt's and Wilson's personalities and proposals, what do you think would have happened to domestic reform and foreign relations if Roosevelt had won the Republican nomination in 1912 and become president again?

Chapter Self Test

After you have read the chapter in the text and done the exercises in the Study Guide, take the following self test to see if you understand the material you have covered. Answers appear at the end of the Study Guide.

MULTIPLE-CHOICE QUESTIONS

Circle the letter of the response that best answers the question or completes the statement.

1. The outcome of the government's case against the Northern Securities Company in 1904 was that:
    a. Theodore Roosevelt gave up the attempt to bust the trusts.
    b. this railroad monopoly was ordered to be dissolved.
    c. the Sherman Antitrust Act was declared unconstitutional.
    d. the Sherman Antitrust Act was ruled inapplicable in this case.

2. The expression "square deal," as used by Theodore Roosevelt, meant that the federal government would:

   a. combat racial injustice.

   b. provide jobs for everyone.

   c. be favorable to labor unions.

   d. treat all interests impartially.

3. With respect to government-controlled public lands, Roosevelt generally favored:

   a. absolute preservation in their natural states.

   b. leasing for unrestricted private exploitation.

   c. conservation with carefully managed development.

   d. outright sale to private developers who could use the land in any way they wished.

4. The central issue in the Pinchot-Ballinger controversy was:

   a. the tariff.

   b. conservation.

   c. trust busting.

   d. the right of labor to bargain collectively.

5. The New Nationalism of Theodore Roosevelt called for:

   a. strengthening the regulatory powers of the federal government.

   b. returning to the laissez-faire principles of the late nineteenth century.

   c. investing the states with the largest responsibility for controlling the trusts and regulating industry.

   d. a vigorous program of trust busting to restore free competition and thus obviate the need for government regulation.

6. The New Freedom of Woodrow Wilson called for:

   a. strengthening regulatory powers of the federal government.

   b. returning to laissez-faire principles of the late nineteenth century.

   c. investing the states with large responsibility for controlling trusts and regulating industry.

   d. a vigorous program of trust busting to restore free competition.

7. In the election of 1912, the Progressive party was known by the nickname:

   a. Bull Moose.

   b. Half-breed.

   c. Mugwump.

   d. teddy bear.

8. The effect of the Progressive Party's entrance into the presidential election of 1912 was to:

   a. make no difference whatsoever in the outcome.

   b. split the Republican vote and allow the Democrat to win.

   c. split the Democratic vote and allow the Republican to win.

   d. prevent any of the three parties from gaining a majority in the electoral college.

9. The Underwood-Simmons tariff, one of the first major pieces of legislation passed in Wilson's administration, was significant in that it:

   a. was passed over the president's veto.

   b. caused a major split in the Democratic party.

   c. substantially lowered the tariff and enacted an income tax.

   d. actually raised average rates, although called a reform measure.

10. An important feature of the Federal Reserve Act of 1913 was that it:

    a. made the recurrence of a major depression impossible.

    b. provided for a more elastic currency in the form of Federal Reserve notes.

    c. required all banks in the nation to become members of the Federal Reserve system.

    d. established a central bank in which individuals could safely deposit their savings.

11. One of the most important functions of the Federal Trade Commission was to:

    a. bust trusts.

    b. promote American exports.

    c. guarantee the rights of labor.

    d. regulate businesses and prevent unfair trade practices.

12. Although Wilson had campaigned in 1912 on the principles of the New Freedom, in practice his first term went far toward enacting key principles of the:

    a. New Deal.

    b. New Nationalism.

    c. western conservationists.

    d. Republican Old Guard.

13. In 1916, Congress passed the Keating-Owen Act to regulate child labor. Congress attempted to justify this legislation under its power to:

    a. tax.

    b. promote the general welfare.

    c. regulate interstate commerce.

    d. protect the health and safety of all citizens.

14. Theodore Roosevelt's mediation was important at the Portsmouth peace conference of 1905, which:

    a. ended the Sino-Japanese War.

    b. ended the Russo-Japanese War.

    c. settled the Franco-German dispute over Morocco.

    d. settled the Venezuela boundary dispute with Great Britain.

15. The aphorism "Speak softly and carry a big stick" was used by Roosevelt in reference to his:

    a. foreign policy.

    b. policy toward labor unions.

    c. technique when on safari in Africa.

    d. political strategy toward the Democrats.

16. The main purpose of the Roosevelt corollary to the Monroe Doctrine was to:
   a. renounce the use of military force in Latin America.
   b. provide legal grounds for the extension of America's colonial empire in Latin America.
   c. justify U.S. military intervention in Latin America if necessary to forestall interference by European nations.
   d. provide a timetable for the withdrawal of U.S. troops from Caribbean islands.

17. When Panamanian rebels started a revolt against the government of Colombia in 1903, the United States:
   a. remained strictly neutral.
   b. intervened on the side of Colombia.
   c. intervened on the side of the rebels.
   d. called for a meeting of the Pan-American Union.

18. William Howard Taft's policy of encouraging private American investments in underdeveloped regions of the world was given what label by some commentators?
   a. Dollar Diplomacy
   b. Missionary Diplomacy
   c. The White Man's Burden
   d. The Good Neighbor Policy

19. Wilson refused to recognize the regime of Victoriano Huerta in Mexico because:
   a. he disapproved of its action in murdering political opponents.
   b. it would have been politically unpopular in the United States.
   c. he feared it was too leftist and would nationalize U.S. investments.
   d. he considered it a rebel government in exile, not the legitimate government.

20. The result of the American military expeditions into Mexico in 1914 and 1916 was to:
   a. drive out German influence.
   b. remove a dictator and restore democracy.
   c. embitter U.S.-Mexican relations for several years.
   d. lead to more than a decade of occupation by the U.S. Army.

TRUE-FALSE QUESTIONS

Read each statement carefully. Mark true statements "T" and false statements "F."

1. Theodore Roosevelt became president as a result of the assassination of William McKinley.

2. As president, Roosevelt contended that big businesses or trusts were an unnatural occurrence in the economy and that the federal government had the obligation to "bust" them down to a more natural size.

3. By offering to mediate a major coal strike, Roosevelt was moving to take the federal government away from an anti-labor stance toward a more neutral approach.

4. Roosevelt opposed the Pure Food and Drug Act and the Meat Inspection Act because they interfered with the laissez-faire rights of business.

5. The novel *The Jungle* helped inspire Congress to pass the bill authorizing the building of the Panama Canal.

6. The conservation movement was internally divided between those who stressed preservation and those who stressed managed exploitation of natural resources.

7. The founder of the Sierra Club was John Muir.

8. Roosevelt blamed the panic of 1907 on bankers and financiers and refused to cooperate with them in any efforts to revive the economy.

9. Roosevelt and William Howard Taft had been long-time rivals in the Republican Party before Taft became Roosevelt's vice president.

10. In the period between the time he left the White House and the outbreak of World War I, Roosevelt drifted away from progressivism and became more and more conservative in his approach to national policy issues.

11. Woodrow Wilson's so-called New Freedom program called for more effort to break up big-business combinations than Roosevelt's New Nationalism did.

12. The Federal Reserve Act made individual bank failures less likely but had little effect on the nation's basic circulating currency.

13. The Clayton Act significantly increased the power of the Justice Department to initiate antitrust lawsuits.

14. After the initial spate of action, Wilson seemed to back away from promoting reform legislation.

15. Theodore Roosevelt believed that the United States should reduce its world commitments and concentrate instead on domestic reform.

16. Roosevelt's closest adviser was Louis Brandeis.

17. "Yellow Peril" referred to the increasing isolationism among the American people who feared the cost of sending troops abroad.

18. The "Great White Fleet" was the nickname given to the naval flotilla that Roosevelt dispatched on a round-the-world tour to display American power.

19. General John J. Pershing led American troops into northern Mexico in pursuit of Pancho Villa.

20. Woodrow Wilson's greatest strength was foreign affairs, which had always been a topic of great interest to him.

CHAPTER TWENTY-THREE
AMERICA AND THE GREAT WAR

Objectives

A thorough study of Chapter 23 should enable the student to understand:

1. The background factors and immediate sequence of events that caused the United States to declare war on Germany in 1917.
2. The contributions of the American military to Allied victory in World War I.
3. The extent of government control of the economy during World War I.
4. Propaganda and the extent of war hysteria in the United States during World War I.
5. The role technology played in the war and the new technologies developed during the conflict.
6. The announced American objectives in fighting the war and Woodrow Wilson's successes and failures at Versailles.
7. The circumstances that led the United States to reject the Treaty of Versailles.
8. The economic problems the United States faced immediately after the war.
9. The reasons for the Red Scare and the resurgence of racial unrest in postwar America.

Main Themes

1. How the United States, which had leaned toward the Allies since the outbreak of World War I, was eventually drawn into full participation in the war.
2. That the American intervention on land and sea provided the balance of victory for the beleaguered Allied forces.
3. How the Wilson administration financed the war, managed the economy, and encouraged public support of the war effort.
4. That Woodrow Wilson tried to apply his lofty war aims to the realities of world politics and that he substantially failed.
5. That the American war effort had profound economic, social, and racial significance.

Glossary

1. belligerent: Any nation involved in a war.
2. Bolsheviks: The most radical and organizationally the strongest of the contending socialist groups in Russia in 1917. Also known as Reds, or simply as communists. Led by Lenin, in November 1917 the Bolsheviks won control of the central government of Russia from a moderate coalition that had taken charge provisionally after the March 1917 popular revolution which deposed the czar.

Pertinent Questions

THE ROAD TO WAR (614-616)

1. What "may have been" the most important underlying source of the tensions that led to World War I? What sparked the conflict? Which nations were referred to as the Allies? The Central Powers?

2. What considerations forced the United States out of its professed stance of true neutrality? To what degree was this decision based on economics?

3. Why did Germany rely on U-boats (submarines)? Why did it back off early in the war from the unrestricted use of U-boats?

4. Before 1917, how did Wilson balance the demands for preparedness and the cries for peace? What effect did his position have on the 1916 election?

5. What key events early in 1917 combined to finally bring the United States fully into World War I? How much resistance remained?

"WAR WITHOUT STINT" (616-621)

6. On what aspect of the war did American entry have the most immediate effect?

7. How did the United States raise the troops necessary for the massive war effort?

8. What roles did women and African Americans play in the military? How were African-American troops treated?

9. What impact did the American Expeditionary Force (AEF) have on the ground war in Europe?

10. Describe the new military technologies that the two sides employed in World War I. What were the consequences of this new killing power?

THE WAR AND AMERICAN SOCIETY (621-624)

11. On what two methods did the Wilson administration depend to finance the war effort? How did the war cost compare with the typical peacetime budgets of that era?

12. Describe the role of the War Industries Board (WIB) and the National War Labor Board. How successful were they? What implications did they have for the future of American politics?

13. On balance, what was the economic impact of the World War I era?

14. What was the "Great Migration" inspired by World War I? What was its impact?

THE SEARCH FOR SOCIAL UNITY (624-628)

15. What groups made up the peace movement prior to and, to a lesser extent, during World War I?

16. What tactics did the Committee on Public Information employ to propagandize the American people into unquestioning support of the war effort? In what other ways did the government suppress criticism? Who suffered most?

17. How did private acts of oppression supplement the official campaign to suppress diversity and promote unity? Who suffered most?

18. What was the Women in Industry Board? What did it evolve into? Does it exist today?

THE SEARCH FOR A NEW WORLD ORDER (628-632)

19. Into what three major categories did the Fourteen Points fall? How did the points reflect the ideas of progressivism?

20. What obstacles did Wilson face in getting the European leaders to accept his approach to peace? What domestic development weakened his position?

21. How did Wilson structure the American negotiating team in Paris?

22. Which of Wilson's ideals were most directly challenged at Versailles? Why were the allies so insistent on reparations?

23. What consequences did American intervention in the Russian Civil War have on the course of the Russian Revolution and the future of Soviet-American relations?

24. What victories for his ideals was Wilson able to salvage? What, in Wilson's view, was his key victory in the negotiations?

25. What were the arguments and motives of domestic opponents to the League of Nations? Who was the leading opponent in the Senate? How much of the blame for the treaty's defeat should be laid on Wilson himself?

A SOCIETY IN TURMOIL (632-639)

26. What happened to the American economy in the postwar years? Why?

27. What inspired the labor unrest of 1919? What were the most important strikes? What did the wave of strikes reveal about the labor movement?

28. Describe the nation's postwar racial climate and its causes. Why did some black soldiers feel a sense of betrayal?

29. What inspired the Red Scare of 1919 to 1920? Was the threat real or imagined?

30. What did the results of the election of 1920 indicate about the mood of the American people?

31. Explain the impact of the 19th amendment to the Constitution? What was the Shepard Tower Maternity and Infancy Act? The 1922 Cable Act?

PATTERNS OF POPULAR CULTURE (626-627)

32. How did Billy Sunday combine fundamentalism with showmanship? What effect did World War I have on the revival movement?

Identification

Identify each of the following, and explain why it is important within the context of the chapter.

1. Triple Entente
2. Triple Alliance
3. Bosnia and Serbia
4. Ottoman Empire
5. *Lusitania*
6. Charles Evans Hughes
7. Nikolai Lenin
8. Selective Service Act
9. John J. Pershing
10. Meuse-Argonne offensive
11. mustard gas
12. Liberty Bonds
13. Herbert Hoover
14. Bernard Baruch
15. Ludlow Massacre
16. Women's Peace Party
17. Eugene V. Debs

18. Bolshevik

19. David Lloyd George

20. George Clemenceau

21. "White" Russians

22. "irreconcilables"

23. Henry Cabot Lodge

24. Marcus Garvey

25. Comintern

26. Sacco-Vanzetti trial

27. James M. Cox

28. "normalcy"

Document 1

Read the section in the text entitled "A War for Democracy," paying careful attention to the discussion of the Zimmermann note. The following document is the official dispatch in which Walter Hines Page, the American ambassador to Great Britain, informed the State Department that the British had intercepted Germany's invitation to Mexico to join in the war against the United States. Unknown to the Germans, the British had broken the German diplomatic code. Read the dispatch and consider the following questions: How did the Zimmermann communication combine with other events early in 1917 to impel the United States to declare war? Why did Germany have reason to believe that Mexico might be receptive to a proposal to wage war against the United States? Why did the British government give a copy of the Zimmermann note to the United States? How does Zimmermann's note reveal that Germany expected the United States to enter the war soon?

The Ambassador of Great Britain [Walter Hines Page] to the Secretary of State [Robert Lansing]

LONDON, February 24, 1917, 1 P.M.

[Received 8:30 P.M.]

. . .[British Foreign Secretary Arthur] Balfour has handed me the text of a cipher telegram from [Arthur] Zimmermann, German Secretary of State for Foreign Affairs, to the German Minister to Mexico. . . . I give you the English translation as follows:

We intend to begin on the 1st of February unrestricted submarine warfare. We shall endeavor in spite of this to keep the United States of America neutral. In the event of this not succeeding, we make Mexico a proposal of alliance on the following basis: make war together, make peace together, generous financial support and an understanding on our part that Mexico is to reconquer the lost territory in Texas, New Mexico, and Arizona. The settlement in detail is left to you. You will inform the President [of Mexico, Venustiano Carranza] of the above most secretly as soon as the outbreak of war with the United States of America is certain and add the suggestion that he should, on his own initiative, invite Japan to immediate adherence and at the same time mediate between Japan and ourselves. Please call the President's attention to the fact that the ruthless employment of our submarines now offers the prospect of compelling England in a few months to make peace. Signed, Zimmermann.

The receipt of this information has so greatly exercised the British Government that they have lost no time in communicating it to me to transmit to you, in order that our Government may be able without delay to make such disposition as may be necessary in view of the threatened invasion of our territory. . . .

U.S. Department of State, *Papers Relating to the Foreign Relations of the U.S.,* 1917, Supplement 1, The World War (Washington, D.C.: Government Printing Office, 1931), p. 147.

Document 2

Read the section in the text under the heading "Selling the War and Suppressing Dissent." The following excerpts are from the official opinions of the United States Supreme Court in two cases involving the Espionage Act of June 15, 1917. In the first—*Schenck v. United States*—Justice Oliver Wendell Holmes formulated the famous "clear and present danger" test, and in the second—*Debs v. United States*—he applied it to the specific case of *Eugene v. Debs*, the nation's most prominent socialist. Read the opinions and consider the following questions: Why did Schenck and Debs oppose the war and, particularly, the draft? Was theirs a widespread view? Is Holmes saying that the First Amendment means one thing in peacetime and quite another in wartime? If the staid Supreme Court found that speeches and pamphlets opposing the war effort could be declared illegal, how might the general public be expected to react to such dissent? Later in the year, Holmes used the "clear and present danger" reasoning to dissent from the Court's upholding of another espionage conviction (*Abrams v. United States,* 250 U.S. 616). In this case, the leaflet was equally inflammatory. But only 5,000 were printed, they were casually distributed, and they were aimed more at American intervention in Russia than at the war against Germany. Holmes argued that there was no "present danger of immediate evil." In light of this, does it appear that the potential success of opposition can be as important as the precise words?

MR. JUSTICE HOLMES delivered the opinion of the Court:

This is an indictment in three counts. The first charges a conspiracy to violate the Espionage Act of June 15, 1917, . . . by causing and attempting to cause insubordination, &c., in the military and naval forces of the United States, and to obstruct the recruiting and enlistment service of the United States, when the United States was at war with the German Empire, to-wit, that the defendant willfully conspired to have printed and circulated to men who had been called and accepted for military service under the Act of May 18, 1917 . . . a document set forth and alleged to be calculated to cause such insubordination and obstruction. The count alleges overt acts in pursuance of the conspiracy, ending in the distribution of the document set forth. The second count alleges a conspiracy to commit an offense against the United States, to-wit, to use the mails for the transmission of matter declared to be non-mailable by title 12, 2, of the Act of June 15, 1917 . . . , to-wit, the above mentioned document, with an averment of the same overt acts. The third count charges an unlawful use of the mails for the transmission of the same matter and otherwise as above. The defendants were found guilty on all the counts. They set up the First Amendment to the Constitution forbidding Congress to make any law abridging the freedom of speech, or of the press, and bringing the case here on that ground have argued some other points also. . . .

The document in question upon its first printed side recited the first section of the Thirteenth Amendment, said that the idea embodied in it was violated by the conscription act and that a conscript is little better than a convict. In impassioned language it intimated that conscription was despotism in its worst form and a monstrous wrong against humanity in the interest of Wall Street's chosen few. It said, "Do not submit to intimidation," but in form at least confined itself to peaceful measures such as a petition for the repeal of the act. The other and later printed side of the sheet was headed, "Assert Your Rights." It stated reasons for alleging that any one violated the Constitution when he refused to recognize "your right to assert your opposition to the draft," and went on, "If you do not assert and support your rights, you are helping to deny or disparage rights which it is the solemn duty of all citizens and residents of the United States to retain." It described the arguments on the other side as coming from cunning politicians and a mercenary capitalist press, and even silent consent to the conscription law as helping to support an infamous conspiracy. It denied the power to send our citizens away to foreign shores to shoot up the people of other lands, and added that words could not express the condemnation such cold-blooded ruthlessness deserves, &c., &c., winding up, "You must do your share to maintain, support and uphold the rights of the people of this country." Of course the document would not have been sent unless it had been intended to have some effect, and we do not see what effect is could be expected to have upon persons subject to the draft except to influence them to obstruct the carrying of it out. The defendants do not deny that the jury might find against them on this point.

But it is said, suppose that that was the tendency of this circular, it is protected by the First Amendment to the Constitution. . . . We admit that in many places and in ordinary times the defendants in saying all that was said in the circular would have been within their constitutional rights. But the character of every act depends upon the circumstances in which it is done. . . . The most stringent protection of free speech would not protect a man in falsely shouting fire in a theater and causing a panic. It does not even protect a man from an injunction against uttering words that may have all the effect of force. . . . The question in every case is whether the words used are used in such circumstances and are of such a nature as to create a clear and present danger that they will bring about the substantive evils that Congress has a right to prevent. It is a question of proximity and degree. When a nation is at war many things that might be said in time of peace are such a hindrance to its effort that their utterance will not be endured so long as men fight and that no Court could regard them as protected by any constitutional right.

Schenck v. United States, 249 U.S. 47; 39 S. Ct. 247; 63 L. Ed. 470 (1919).

* * *

MR. JUSTICE HOLMES delivered the opinion of the Court:

This is an indictment under the Espionage Act of June 15, 1917. . . . The defendant was found guilty and was sentenced to ten years' imprisonment on each of the two counts, the punishment to run concurrently on both.

The main theme of the speech was Socialism, its growth, and a prophecy of its ultimate success. With that we have nothing to do, but if a part or the manifest intent of the more general utterances was to encourage those present to obstruct the recruiting service and if in passages such encouragement was directly given, the immunity of the general theme may not be enough to protect the speech. The speaker began by saying that he had just returned from a visit to the workhouse in the neighborhood where three of their most loyal comrades were paying the penalty for their devotion to the working class—these being Wagenknecht, Baker and Ruthenberg, who had been convicted of aiding and abetting another in failing to register for the draft. . . .

There followed personal experiences and illustrations of the growth of Socialism, a glorification of minorities, and a prophecy of the success of the international Socialist crusade, with the interjection that "you need to know that you are fit for something better than slavery and cannon fodder." The rest of the discourse had only the indirect thought not necessarily ineffective bearing on the offenses alleged that is to be found in the usual contrasts between capitalists and laboring men, sneers at the advice to cultivate war gardens, attribution to plutocrats of the high price of coal, &c., with the implications running through it all that the working men in are not concerned with the war, and a final exhortation, "Don't worry about the charge of treason to your masters; but be concerned about the treason that involves yourselves." The defendant addressed the jury himself, and while contending that his speech did not warrant the charges said, "I have been accused of obstructing the war. I admit it. Gentlemen, I abhor war. I would oppose the war if I stood alone." The statement was not necessary to warrant the jury in finding that one purpose of the speech, whether incidental or not does not matter, was to oppose not only war in general but this war, and that the opposition was so expressed that its natural and intended effect would be to obstruct recruiting. If that was intended and if, in all the circumstances, that would be its probable effect, it would not be protected by reason of its being part of a general program and expressions of a general and conscientious belief.

Debs v. United States, 249 U.S. 211; 39 S. Ct. 252; 63 L. Ed. 566 (1919).

Map Exercise

Fill in or identify the following on the blank map provided. Use the map in the text as your source.

1. The Allies, the Central Powers, the occupied nations, and the neutrals.
2. Paris, Berlin, Rome, London, and Moscow.
3. The principal area of submarine warfare.
4. The approximate location of Germany's deepest penetration of France.
5. The approximate location of Germany's deepest penetration of Russia.
6. The approximate location of the armistice line.

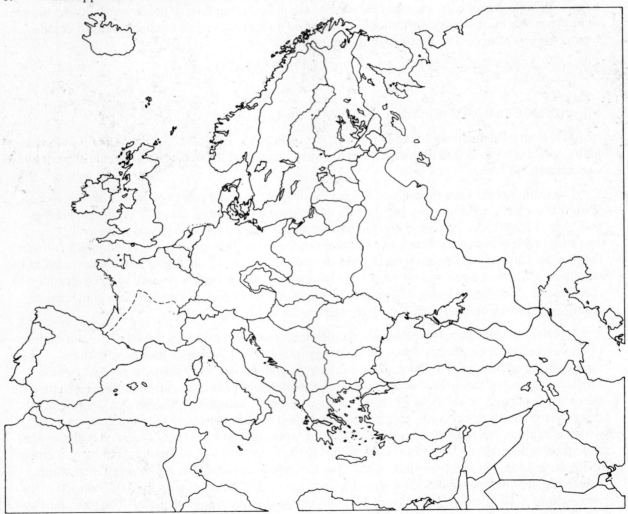

Interpretive Questions

Based on what you have filled in, answer the following. On some of the questions you will need to consult the narrative in your text for information or explanation.

1. What two nations bore the brunt of the western front fighting within their borders? What nation suffered the most on the east? How did this affect the peace negotiations?

2. Why was the ocean war so crucial in bringing the United States into the war?

3. What geographic and naval advantages did Great Britain have in sea warfare? How did Germany try to counter these advantages and how successful was it?

Summary

Following two and a half years of pro-Allied "neutrality," the United States entered World War I because of economic and cultural factors as well as German submarine warfare. The armies and civilians of Europe had already suffered mightily by the time the United States finally entered. American forces, initially at sea and then on land, provided the margin of victory for the Allies. To mount its total effort, the United States turned to an array of unprecedented measures: sharply graduated taxes, conscription for a foreign war, bureaucratic management of the economy, and a massive propaganda and anti-sedition campaign. Women entered the work force in record numbers and the hopes of African Americans were raised by military service and war-related jobs in the North. President Woodrow Wilson formulated American war aims in his famous Fourteen Points, but he was unable to convince either Europe or the United States fully to accept his tenets as the basis for peace. By 1920, the American people, tired from nearly three decades of turmoil, had repudiated Wilson's precious League of Nations in favor of an illusion called "normalcy."

Review Questions

These questions are to be answered with essays. This will allow you to explore relationships between individuals, events, and attitudes of the period under review.

1. Was American involvement in World War I inevitable? What forces worked to maintain neutrality? What forces propelled the country away from neutrality and into full belligerency?

2. Describe the suffering that the Great War visited on Europe. Why is it said that the United States emerged from the war as "the only real victor"?

3. How did World War I transform the technology and thereby the horror of modern warfare? What were the implications for wars to come?

4. What surprises did America face as the reality of "war without stint" unfolded? How did the American people respond to them? What long-term legacies came from these responses?

5. Despite his tumultuous reception by the peoples of Europe and the generally favorable response he received on his tour in the western United States, Wilson faced troublesome opposition from both European statesmen and the United States senators. Why did he encounter such intransigence? Did he respond in a rational and politically effective way?

6. Explain how the war and the demographic shifts accompanying the war effort raised the aspirations of African Americans. How were their hopes dashed? What conflicts arose?

Chapter Self Test

After you have read the chapter in the text and done the exercises in the Study Guide, take the following self test to see if you understand the material you have covered. Answers appear at the end of the Study Guide.

MULTIPLE-CHOICE QUESTIONS

Circle the letter of the response that best answers the question or completes the statement.

1. The first two countries to begin fighting in the conflict that later became known as World War I were:
   a. Austria-Hungary and Serbia.
   b. Belgium and Germany.
   c. France and Italy.
   d. Russia and Poland.

2. In the early years of World War I, from 1914 to 1916, the United States:
   a. became an arsenal for the Allies.
   b. maintained a genuinely neutral stance.
   c. remained politically and economically isolated from European affairs.
   d. became sympathetic toward the Central Powers because of the English blockade of Germany.

3. President Wilson protested German violations of American neutrality more harshly than British violations because:
   a. he admired the British and favored their cause.
   b. a profitable trade was resulting between the United States and the Allies.
   c. German actions cost some American lives.
   d. all of the above.

4. Woodrow Wilson's reaction to the sinking of the *Lusitania* was to:
   a. ask Congress for a declaration of war.
   b. break diplomatic relations with Germany.
   c. impose a complete embargo on exports to both sides.
   d. demand assurances from Germany that such outrages would not recur.

5. How did Wilson react to the question of military preparedness versus pacifism from 1914 to 1916?
   a. He was among the first leading Americans to urge a rapid military buildup.
   b. He was a consistent pacifist right up to the eve of the declaration of war.
   c. Initially opposed to a military buildup, by the end of 1915 he came to support preparedness.
   d. Initially a staunch militarist, early in 1915 he backed off from this bellicose posture for fear of antagonizing the Central Powers.

6. In the presidential election of 1916, the Democrats emphasized:

   a. that Wilson had managed so far to keep the nation out of the European war.

   b. domestic issues strongly and almost ignored the European war as an issue.

   c. a belligerent stand against German violations of American neutral rights and that a Democratic victory for president and Congress would lead to immediate military intervention on the Allied side.

   d. that the United States should take a firm stand against both German and British violations of American neutral rights and should not support or trade with either nation.

7. The significance of the Zimmermann telegram was that it:

   a. induced Mexico to join Germany as an ally.

   b. inflamed American public opinion against Germany.

   c. showed that England was not negotiating in good faith.

   d. gave encouragement to the peace faction in the United States.

8. The key immediate cause of the American declaration of war against Germany in the spring of 1917 was the:

   a. sinking of the *Sussex*.

   b. Bolshevik revolution in Russia.

   c. reports of German atrocities against civilians.

   d. German resumption of unrestricted submarine warfare.

9. Which of the following statements concerning the American Expeditionary Force (AEF) is true?

   a. The AEF broke the stalemate in favor of the Allies.

   b. Due to its inexperience, the AEF proved largely ineffective in actual combat.

   c. Due to the lateness of its arrival in Europe, the AEF saw relatively little significant combat.

   d. Casualties among the AEF were proportionately larger than among any of the other Allied armies.

10. Which were the *two* principal methods that the U.S. government used to finance the war effort? (Mark two letters.)

    a. Deficit spending and printing more Federal Reserve notes.

    b. Loans in the form of "Liberty Bonds."

    c. Increased taxes on corporations, incomes, and inheritances.

    d. Cutting most forms of federal domestic spending including education and welfare.

11. Herbert Hoover was significant to the American effort in World War I as head of the:

    a. Rationing Board.

    b. Food Administration.

    c. War Industries Board.

    d. Industrial Workers of the World.

12. Such expressions as "liberty cabbage" and "liberty sausage," as used during World War I, were an indication of:

    a. food shortages in America.

    b. American food relief to Belgium.

    c. American hostile reaction to things German.

    d. American patriotic fervor to increase the food supply by planting home "victory gardens."

13. As used in reference to the period of the Great War, the expression "Great Migration" means:

    a. blacks moving from the South to northern industrial cities.

    b. urban easterners moving west to agricultural jobs to meet the great demand for food.

    c. rural dwellers moving to big cities all over the country.

    d. desperate refugees fleeing war-torn Europe for America.

14. The main purpose of the Committee on Public Information during World War I was to:

    a. inform American consumers about wartime regulations and restrictions on food, gasoline, nylon, and the like.

    b. infiltrate behind German lines and distribute flyers to the German and occupied citizens urging them to undermine the war effort.

    c. gather data about troop movements and plans of the Central Powers.

    d. disseminate pro-war propaganda and promote public support of the war in the United States.

15. Which of the following was not one of the principal figures along with Wilson in the Versailles negotiations?

    a. Lloyd Georgia

    b. Bernard Baruch

    c. Vittorio Orlando

    d. Georges Clemenceau

16. Which of the following was *not* included in Wilson's Fourteen Points?

    a. freedom of the seas

    b. reduction in armaments

    c. reparations from those guilty of starting the war

    d. removal of economic barriers to trade between nations

17. Which of the following nations was *not* represented at the Paris Peace Conference?

    a. France

    b. Italy

    c. Britain

    d. Russia

18. In the Senate debate on ratification of the Treaty of Versailles, the so-called irreconcilables were those who were adamantly opposed to:

    a. isolationism.

    b. United States membership in the League of Nations.

    c. interjecting partisan politics into foreign relations.

    d. any modification of the treaty as it was originally drafted.

19. Both the Palmer Raids and the Sacco and Vanzetti case may be cited as evidence in the aftermath of World War I of the depth of feeling in America against:

   a. radicalism.

   b. German-Americans.

   c. Italian-Americans.

   d. internationalism.

20. In the first few years after World War I, relations between blacks and whites in America were generally characterized by:

   a. grudging acceptance due to common economic distress.

   b. extreme resentment, race riots, and numerous lynchings.

   c. relative cordiality due to the blacks' gallant service in the war.

   d. notable improvement due to new legal safeguards for blacks, which had been enacted during the progressive period.

TRUE-FALSE QUESTIONS

Read each statement carefully. Mark true statements "T" and false statements "F."

1. The "Central Powers" of World War I included Germany, the Ottoman Empire (Turkey), and the Austro-Hungarian Empire.

2. At the time of its sinking by a German submarine, the British ocean liner *Lusitania* was carrying munitions as well as passengers.

3. Woodrow Wilson's victorious presidential campaign in 1916 was significantly aided by his pledge that the United States would immediately enter World War I on the Allied side if he were reelected.

4. In World War I, Russia started out on the Allied side but joined Germany in fighting against the Allies after the communists took over.

5. After the sinking of the *Lusitania,* popular support for World War I was so great that the military draft authorized by Congress never had to be implemented.

6. Most African-American soldiers in World War I were confined to noncombat roles, but some did fight in the offensives of 1918.

7. The principal commander of German military forces was John Pershing.

8. The biggest defeat of American ground forces in World War I was in the Argonne Forest.

9. Bernard Baruch headed the War Industries Board.

10. Government actions during World War I resulted in a significant increase in labor union membership between 1917 and 1919.

11. Unlike in France and Great Britain where opposition to the Great War was treated harshly, the United States allowed antiwar dissidents to speak and operate freely without supervision or harassment.

12. In the Ludlow Massacre, German officers killed several hundred Russian prisoners of war suspected of being communists.

13. During and shortly after World War I, there were several race riots in southern cities, but race relations remained relatively harmonious in northern cities such as Chicago, Detroit, and the St. Louis area.

14. The limited U.S. military intervention in Russia was designed to help the so-called White Russians.

15. British Prime Minister David Lloyd George supported all of Wilson's Fourteen Points, but Georges Clemenceau of France resisted because of severe damage to his nation.

16. The Fourteen Points contained a proposal for an alliance of western European and north Atlantic powers against the newly created Soviet Union.

17. On his way to Paris for the peace conference, Wilson visited several European cities and encountered considerable public acclaim for his idealistic ideas.

18. Senator Henry Cabot Lodge was a key figure in the Senate's refusal to ratify the Treaty of Versailles and the League of Nations.

19. The Comintern was a consortium of western European nations to oppose the spread of communism.

20. Marcus Garvey promoted the ideology of black nationalism.

CHAPTER TWENTY-FOUR
THE NEW ERA

Objectives

A thorough study of Chapter 24 should enable the student to understand:

1. The reasons for the industrial boom in the 1920s after the initial period of economic readjustment following World War I.
2. The nature and extent of labor's problems.
3. The plight of the American farmer.
4. The changes in the American way of life and American values in the 1920s in the areas of consumerism, communications, religion, and the role of women.
5. The reflection of these changed values in American literature and art.
6. The effects of prohibition on American politics and society.
7. The reasons for xenophobia and racial unrest in the 1920s.
8. The debacle of the Harding administration.
9. The pro-business tendencies of the Republican administration in the 1920s.

Main Themes

1. How the automobile boom and new technology led to the economic expansion of the 1920s.
2. That most workers and farmers failed to share equitably in the decade's prosperity.
3. How a nationwide consumer-oriented culture began to shape society and how the "new woman" emerged.
4. How the changing society disenchanted some artists and intellectuals and led to broad cultural conflict over ethnic and religious concerns.
5. That Warren Harding and Calvin Coolidge, despite their dissimilar personalities, presided over ardently pro-business administrations.

Glossary

1. behaviorists: Those who adhere to the basic tenet of behaviorism as promulgated by John B. Watson: That psychology should become a science by using the techniques of objective observation and measurement characteristic of natural sciences such as biology.
2. "Bohemian": The term that came to be generally applied to artists, writers, and others who chose to live unconventional lifestyles that often shocked traditional society. Bohemia is a region of the Czech Republic associated with gypsies.

Pertinent Questions

THE NEW ECONOMY (642-647)

1. Outline the causes of the economic boom of the 1920s. What impact did the spectacular growth of the automobile industry have on related business activities?

2. What was the New Era trend in business organization? What types of firms were less likely to consolidate?

3. What were the elements of "welfare capitalism"? To what extent did the average worker benefit from welfare capitalism and from rising production and profits?

4. To what extent was the lag in union membership due to the unions themselves? What were the other causal factors? How did the unions serve African Americans and other ethnic minorities?

5. What was the largest immigrant group during the 1920s? Where did they concentrate? What was their economic status?

6. What caused the big drop in farm prices and income in the 1920s? Explain how parity was designed to solve the problem. What happened to parity?

THE NEW CULTURE (647-657)

7. Describe the new urban mass consumer culture. How did advertising help shape it?

8. How did newspaper chains, mass-circulation magazines, movies, and radio serve as unifying and nationalizing forces in America? What was unique about radio?

9. What new attitudes toward work, motherhood, sex, and leisure developed in the 1920s, especially among middle-class women? Was the new woman mostly a figure of myth?

10. What effect did women's suffrage have on the politics of the 1920s?

11. What changes in high-school and college attendance occurred during the 1920s? How did these changes contribute to the recognition of the distinct stage of adolescence? What else helped change attitudes toward youth?

12. How did the adoration of Thomas Edison, Henry Ford, and, especially, Charles Lindbergh illustrate the ambivalence with which many Americans regarded the decline of the "self-made man"?

13. What social forces combined to alienate the members of the so-called Lost Generation? What did these people attack? Who were the main attackers?

14. What was the Harlem Renaissance? What was its effect?

A CONFLICT OF CULTURES (657-661)

15. What more basic conflict in society did the controversy over the "noble experiment" of prohibition come to symbolize? What were the results of prohibition?

16. Explain the changes in immigration laws brought about by the National Origins Act and subsequent legislation. What ethnic groups were favored?

17. How did the resurrected Ku Klux Klan of the 1920s differ from the Reconstruction-era Klan? How influential was the new Klan?

18. Compare and contrast the views of the modernists and the fundamentalists. How did Darwinism and the Scopes trial symbolize the conflict between the two? How has the conflict persisted?

19. How were the cultural tensions of the 1920s reflected in the Democratic Party?

REPUBLICAN GOVERNMENT (661-665)

20. What features of President Warren G. Harding's personal background led to his political repudiation? What was the biggest of the various Harding-era scandals?

21. Contrast the personal lives of Harding and Calvin Coolidge. Did their politics and policies differ as much as their personalities?

22. Why did Herbert Hoover push so strongly for the creation of trade associations?

AMERICA IN THE WORLD: THE CINEMA (649)

23. Why has America dominated the filmmaking industry?

PATTERNS OF POPULAR CULTURE: DANCE HALLS (652-653)

24. What led to the dance craze of the 1920s and 30s? To what extent did the dance halls threaten traditional values?

Identification

Identify each of the following, and explain why it is important within the context of the chapter.

1. "normalcy"
2. General Motors
3. "pink collar" jobs
4. Brotherhood of Sleeping Car Porters
5. "American Plan"
6. *The Man Nobody Knows*
7. *Time* magazine
8. *The Jazz Singer*
9. Harry Emerson Fosdick
10. Margaret Sanger
11. "flapper"
12. Alice Paul
13. League of Women Voters
14. Charles Lindbergh
15. H. L. Mencken
16. Sinclair Lewis
17. Langston Hughes
18. the "noble experiment"
19. Al Capone
20. "wets" and "drys"
21. *The Birth of a Nation*
22. American Civil Liberties Union (ACLU)
23. Alfred E. Smith
24. John W. Davis
25. Andrew Mellon

Document

Read H. L. Mencken's obituary for Calvin Coolidge, noting Mencken's contempt for politics and his sarcasm concerning Coolidge's lack of aggressiveness. Mencken's iconoclastic style was extremely popular with young intellectuals; but, in fact, his *American Mercury* was not a mass-circulation magazine, and Mencken's comments reached a relatively small portion of the general public. In contrast to the often vicious and biting satire of Mencken, humorist Will Rogers poked gentle fun at American life, including politics. Rogers's "daily telegrams" appeared in hundreds of newspapers, including the *New York Times*. Read Rogers's obituary for Calvin Coolidge, and consider the following questions: How do Mencken's and Rogers's contrasting views of Coolidge reflect their differing attitudes toward American politics in general? Which column probably came closer to reflecting the American people's feelings toward Coolidge? How do both selections show how politics in 1933 was defined in terms of the Great Depression?

In what manner he would have performed himself if the holy angels had shoved the Depression forward a couple of years—this we can only guess, and one man's hazard is as good as another's. My own is that he would have responded to bad times precisely as he responded to good ones—that is, by pulling down the blinds, stretching his legs upon his desk, and snoozing away the lazy afternoons. . . . He slept more than any other President, whether by day or by night. Nero fiddled, but Coolidge only snored. . . . Counting out Harding as a cipher only, Dr. Coolidge was preceded by one World Saver and followed by two more. What enlightened American, having to choose between any of them and another Coolidge, would hesitate for an instant? There were no thrills while he reigned, but neither were there any headaches. He had no ideas, and he was not a nuisance.

H. L. Mencken, *American Mercury,* April 1933.

Beverly Hills, January 5:

Mr. Coolidge, you didn't have to die for me to throw flowers on your grave. I have told a million jokes about you but every one was based on some of your splendid qualities. You had a hold on the American people regardless of politics. They knew you were honest, economical and had a native common sense. History generally records a place for a man that is ahead of his time. But we that lived with you will always remember you because you was "with" your times. By golly, you little red-headed New Englander, I liked you. You put horse sense into statesmanship and Mrs. Coolidge's admiration for you is an American trait.

January 7:

Did Coolidge Know the Bust was Coming?

Well we just cant hardly get over the shock of the death of Mr. Coolidge.

I have had many Republican politicians tell me, "Will, you are one of Mr. Coolidge's best boosters." Well I did like him. I could get a laugh out of almost all the little things he said, but at the same time they were wise. He could put more in a line than any public man could in a whole speech.

Here is a thing do you reckon Mr. Coolidge worried over in late years? Now he could see further than any of these politicians. Things were going so fast and everybody was so cuckoo during his term in office, that lots of them just couldn't possibly see how it could ever do otherwise than go up. Now Mr. Coolidge didn't think that. He knew that it couldn't. He knew that we couldn't just keep running stocks and everything else up and up and them paying no dividends in comparison to the price. His whole fundamental training was against all that inflation. Now there was times when he casually in a speech did give some warning but he really never did come right out and say, "Hold on there, this thing cant go on! You people are crazy. This thing has got to bust."

But how could he have said or done that? What would have been the effect? Everybody would have said, "Ha, what's the idea of butting into our prosperity? Here we are going good, and you our President try to crab it. Let us alone. We know our business."

There is a thousand things they would have said to him or about him. He would have come in for a raft of criticism. The Republican Party, the party of big business, would have done their best to have stopped him, for they couldn't see it like he did, and they never could have understood until a year later.

Later in his own heart did Calvin Coolidge ever wish that he had preached it from the housetops regardless of what big business, his party, or what anybody would have said?

Now here is another thing too in Mr. Coolidge's favor in not doing it. He no doubt ever dreamed of the magnitude of this depression. That is he knew the thing had to bust, but he didn't think it would bust so big, or be such a permanent bust. Had he known of the tremendous extent of it, I'll bet he would have defied hell and damnation and told and warned the people about it. Now in these after years as he saw the thing overwhelm everybody, he naturally thought back to those hectic days when as President the country was paying a dollar down on everything on earth.

But all this is what they call in baseball a "Second Guess." Its easy to see now what might have helped lighten or prolong the shock, but put yourself in his place and I guess 99 out of a 100 would have done as he did.

Now on the other hand in saying he saw the thing coming, might be doing him an injustice. He might not. He may not have known any more about it than all our other prominent men. But we always felt he was two jumps ahead of any of them on thinking ahead.

Excerpt from *The Autobiography of Will Rogers,* edited by Donald Day. Copyright 1949 by Rogers Company. Copyright renewed 1977 by Donald Day and Beth Day.

Map Exercise

Fill in or identify the following on the blank map provided. Use the map in the text as your source.

1. Ignoring small enclaves, circle the general areas that had fifty percent or more farm tenancy in both 1910 and 1930.
2. Again ignoring small enclaves, circle the general areas that had less than fifty percent tenancy in both 1910 and 1930.

Interpretive Questions

Based on what you have filled in, answer the following. On some of the questions you will need to consult the narrative in your text for information or explanation.

1. What forces caused farmers to go from ownership to tenancy?
2. Compare this map with the discussion of southern agriculture in the Reconstruction era. What persistent pattern of tenancy is evident in the South?

Summary

Through the mid-1920s, America enjoyed unparalleled prosperity fueled by a great boom in automobile production and related businesses. Many people believed that the progressive ideal of an efficient, ordered society was at hand. The boom, however, masked problems. The prosperity was not equitably distributed through society; many workers and farmers, including most minorities, were excluded. The new ways forged by economic and technological advancement brought an unprecedented cultural nationalism, but they also aroused serious conflicts as both intellectuals and traditionalists attacked elements of the New Era culture. Presidents Harding and Coolidge, despite their contrasting styles, personified the pro-business policies of the Republican Party, which dominated American politics throughout the 1920s.

Review Questions

These questions are to be answered with essays. This will allow you to explore relationships between individuals, events, and attitudes of the period under review.

1. Many people gained from the boom of the New Era, and others fell through the economic cracks. But the prosperity was widespread enough to usher in a modern consumer society. Who gained? Who did not? What were the main elements of the national consumer-based society?
2. One of the questions that has troubled historians concerns the legacy of progressivism. Looking at the 1920s, would you argue that progressive thought had died or triumphed? Why?
3. Impressions of the 1920s vary, according to which vision one accepts—that of members of the ruling elite, such as Andrew Mellon and Herbert Hoover; of self-made men, such as Charles Lindbergh; of the disenchanted, such as H. L. Mencken and Ernest Hemingway; of provincial traditionalists, such as William Jennings Bryan; or of the blacks in the Harlem Renaissance. Briefly describe each of those visions, and tell how one or several capture the real significance of the decade.

Chapter Self Test

After you have read the chapter in the text and done the exercises in the Study Guide, take the following self test to see if you understand the material you have covered. Answers appear at the end of the Study Guide.

MULTIPLE-CHOICE QUESTIONS

Circle the letter of the response that best answers the question or completes the statement.

1. There was a dramatic increase in three of the following economic indicators during the mid 1920s. Which is the *exception?*
   a. output per worker
   b. per capita income
   c. rate of inflation
   d. gross national product

2. America's economic boom in the 1920s resulted from:
   a. the debilitation of Europe after World War I.
   b. the rapid pace of technological innovations.
   c. the expansion of the automobile industry.
   d. all of the above.

3. Which of the following industries seemed *least* affected by the trend toward consolidation in the 1920s?
   a. steel
   b. automobiles
   c. cotton textiles
   d. public utilities

4. The "welfare capitalism" of the 1920s did *not* provide American workers any:
   a. tangible economic gains.
   b. real control over their own fates.
   c. psychological comfort.
   d. opportunities for organization.

5. The essence of welfare capitalism was:
   a. company-provided benefits for workers.
   b. company-provided bonuses for management.
   c. government-provided unemployment benefits for workers.
   d. government-provided financial aid for troubled industries.

6. Which of the following did *not* contribute to the weakness of the organized labor movement in America in the 1920s?
   a. The radical leadership of the AFL.
   b. Hostility of the courts and the Justice Department to union activities.
   c. The propaganda promoted by corporate leaders that unionism was un-American.
   d. The large numbers of unskilled workers who found no place in the craft orientation of the AFL.

7. In the 1920s and after, the term "parity" was used to refer to:
   a. a fair exchange price for farm crops.
   b. equal pay for union and non-union workers.
   c. equal pay for equal work for males and females.
   d. equal employment opportunities for blacks and whites.

8. Which of the following industries was most closely associated with the rise of consumerism in America in the 1920s?
   a. banking
   b. insurance
   c. advertising
   d. fast-food chains

9. Margaret Sanger was significant to American social and cultural life in the 1920s as a promoter of:
   a. temperance.
   b. the "debunkers."
   c. progressive education.
   d. the birth-control movement.

10. Three of the following were manifestations of changing cultural values among Americans in the 1920s. Which is the *exception?*
    a. There was an increase in secularism.
    b. Many women enjoyed a less inhibited lifestyle.
    c. The national divorce rate climbed dramatically.
    d. Birth-control devices were legalized in all states, and abortion was legalized in some states.

11. According to the text, which of the following had the greatest influence in producing the sense of disillusionment characteristic of the Lost Generation?
    a. The decline of organized religion.
    b. The moral relativism of pragmatism.
    c. The widespread acceptance of evolution.
    d. The traumatic experience of World War I.

12. H. L. Mencken was significant to American social and cultural life in the 1920s as:
    a. a leading advocate of temperance.
    b. a sarcastic debunker of traditional culture.
    c. an influential proponent of progressive education.
    d. a prominent opponent of the birth-control movement.

13. A principal theme of Sinclair Lewis's novels in the 1920s was:
    a. utopian optimism for the future.
    b. romantic idealization of the past.
    c. contempt for modern American society.
    d. acceptance of modern American society as the best of all possible worlds.

14. The Harlem Renaissance referred to:

    a. a movement in black literature, art, and music.

    b. the spread of jazz to the cites of the North.

    c. a movement in New York to improve the conditions of recent immigrants to the United States.

    d. a back-to-Africa movement among black intellectuals who had repudiated American values.

15. Three of the following statements accurately describe the "noble experiment" of prohibition. Which is the *exception?*

    a. Enforcement was ludicrously ineffective in some areas.

    b. It stimulated the growth of organized crime.

    c. The Great Depression hindered efforts to repeal prohibition.

    d. Begun as a middle-class progressive reform, prohibition was later supported largely by rural Protestant Americans.

16. Which of the following was *not* a provision of the immigration laws passed in 1921 and 1924?

    a. The number of immigrants allowed into the country was reduced.

    b. Restrictions on Japanese, Chinese, and Korean immigration were eased.

    c. The number of immigrants allowed to enter the United States was expressed as quotas based on a percentage of the number of each national group already in the country at a base year.

    d. The provisions favored immigration from northwestern Europe.

17. Which of the following does *not* describe the new Ku Klux Klan (1915)?

    a. Extended its membership outside the old Confederate states.

    b. Confined its activities to protests and symbolism rather than violence.

    c. Extended its attack to include immigrants, Catholics, and Jews.

    d. Assumed the role of self-appointed guardian of traditional values.

18. A Christian fundamentalist is one who:

    a. believes in the fundamental inerrancy of the New Testament.

    b. wishes to base morality on secular rather than religious fundamentals.

    c. accepts the basic or fundamental truths of all the world's religions in the spirit of ecumenicism.

    d. believes in the basic or fundamental general ideas of the Bible but not in the literal truth of every statement.

19. John T. Scopes was accused of the "crime" of teaching:

    a. the advantages of labor union membership.

    b. that Christianity should dominate America.

    c. that communism had advantages in some societies.

    d. that Darwinian evolution best explains the origins of humans.

20. The most important problem faced by the Democratic Party in the 1920s was:

    a. a serious split between urban and rural wings of the party.

    b. the party was losing its traditional strength in the South.

    c. the fact that recent immigrants no longer tended to support the party.

    d. the restriction of immigration reduced the number of recruits to the party.

TRUE-FALSE QUESTIONS

Read each statement carefully. Mark true statements "T" and false statements "F."

1. The phrase, return to "normalcy" was used by Republicans to capitalize on public discontent with the diplomatic, racial, and economic disruptions associated with World War I and its aftermath.

2. The "American Plan" was a nickname given by corporate leaders to the open-shop concept, which held that no worker could be required to join a union to get or keep a job.

3. The economic sector most responsible for the prosperity of the 1920s was agriculture.

4. The trend toward business consolidation that had begun in the 1890s began to slow during the 1920s.

5. During the 1920s, membership in labor unions declined significantly compared to the World War I years.

6. During the 1920s, advertising expanded rapidly and advertisers were increasingly trying to identify their products with a modern lifestyle.

7. The "flapper" nickname was given to women who tried to hold on to traditional female roles and who criticized the wild ways of the youth of the decade.

8. H. L. Mencken and Sinclair Lewis were among the authors whose writings were critical of the dominant middle-class values of the 1920s.

9. The New York City-based flourishing of African American culture in the 1920s was given the nickname "Gotham Revival."

10. Support for the prohibition of liquor was strongest in the provincial, largely rural, Protestant-dominated areas of the country.

11. The effect of the immigration laws of 1921 and 1924 was to increase foreign, especially Asian, immigration following the restrictive period around World War I.

12. In the 1920s, the Ku Klux Klan grew rapidly in some Midwestern states as well as in the South.

13. Within American Protestantism, the so-called modernists tended to be urban, middle-class people who attempted to adapt religion to the teachings of modern science.

14. The Republican administrations of the 1920s accomplished notable reductions in taxes on corporate profits, personal incomes, and inheritances.

15. During most of the 1920s, the Democrats controlled Congress and the Republicans controlled the presidency.

16. The nickname "Ohio Gang" was given to several advisors of Calvin Coolidge.

17. The Teapot Dome Scandal in the 1920s involved corrupt leasing of government oil reserves to private business.

18. The scandals during the Harding administration caused little if any political harm to the Republican Party in the 1920s.

19. Calvin Coolidge was more popular than Warren Harding because he was more personable and gregarious.

CHAPTER TWENTY-FIVE
THE GREAT DEPRESSION

Objectives

A thorough study of Chapter 25 should enable the student to understand:

1. The relationship between the stock market crash and subsequent Great Depression.
2. The causes of the depression and how it became a global disaster.
3. The effects of the depression on business and industry.
4. The problems of unemployment and the inadequacy of relief.
5. The particular problems of farmers in the Dust Bowl.
6. The impact of the depression on minorities.
7. The impact of the depression on working women and the American family.
8. The reflection of the economic crisis in American culture.
9. President Herbert Hoover's policies for fighting the depression.

Main Themes

1. How weaknesses underlying the apparent prosperity of the 1920s led to the Great Depression and how the stock market crash touched it off in the United States and around the world.
2. That neither the efforts of local and private relief agencies nor the early volunteerism of Herbert Hoover were able to halt the spiral of rising unemployment and declining production.
3. How the economic pressures of the depression affected the American people, especially minorities.
4. How the misery of those affected by the depression swept Franklin Delano Roosevelt into the presidency.

Glossary

1. bull market: A situation in which stock market prices are rising and investors are optimistic about continued gains.
2. bear market: A situation in which stock market prices are falling and investors are pessimistic.

Pertinent Questions

THE COMING OF THE GREAT DEPRESSION (668-672)

1. What caused the stock market boom to get so out of hand that stock prices outran company values?
2. The decline of what previously prospering industries contributed especially to the economic decline?
3. How did the weakness of consumer demand contribute to the severity of the depression?
4. What impact did domestic debt factors have on the American economy?
5. What role did U.S. policies on trade and international debt play in worsening economic conditions?

293

6. What weaknesses in banking helped lead to the Great Depression and what happened to the banking system early in the Depression?

7. What happened to the banking system and GNP in the three years after the stock market crash of 1929? What economic statistic best represents the human costs of the depression?

THE AMERICAN PEOPLE IN HARD TIMES (672-678)

8. Describe the extent of unemployment, especially in industrial cities. What mental burdens often came with the loss of jobs?

9. How effective were local, state, and private relief agencies in meeting the ravages of widespread unemployment?

10. What special problems were faced by rural America?

11. Compare and contrast the impact of the Great Depression on blacks, Hispanics, and Asians with the impact on Americans of European heritage. What demographic shifts occurred?

12. What effect did the Depression have on the work-force role of women in general and African American women in particular? What happened to the women's movement?

13. How did families adjust to the pressures of life during the Depression?

THE DEPRESSION AND AMERICAN CULTURE (678-685)

14. How did American values, especially individualism and the success ethic, fare during the hard times?

15. In what ways did photographers and writers chronicle the impact of the depression?

16. What sort of fare dominated radio programming? How did it shape American culture?

17. What was the tone and focus of most movies of the 1930s? How were women and minorities portrayed?

18. How did popular literature of the 1930s compare and contrast with popular radio and movies?

19. What allure did such radical movements as communism and socialism have for Americans in the 1930s? What role did artistic work, film and books play in portraying social ills?

THE UNHAPPY PRESIDENCY OF HERBERT HOOVER (685-690)

20. What were Herbert Hoover's first approaches to combating the economic downturn? How effective were they?

21. In the spring of 1931 what was Hoover's new approach to the Depression? What caused his shift in emphasis?

22. What impact did Hoover's handling of the "Bonus Army" have on his popularity?

23. What made Franklin Roosevelt such an attractive presidential candidate for the Democrats? Why did he win the 1932 election?

24. What happened in the months between Roosevelt's election and his inauguration?

WHERE HISTORIANS DISAGREE: CAUSES OF THE GREAT DEPRESSION (670-671)

25. Briefly explain the "monetary," "spending" (fiscal), and "timing" explanations of the causes for the beginning and/or duration of the Great Depression. What are the implications of each for public policy?

AMERICAN IN THE WORLD: THE GLOBAL DEPRESSION (673)

26. Why could the depression be called "a major factor—maybe the single most important factor—in the coming of World War II"?

27. What caused the Dust Bowl? What solved, or at least partially solved, the problem? Who were the Okies? Where did they go?

PATTERNS OF POPULAR CULTURE: THE FILMS OF FRANK CAPRA (682-683)

28. What was Frank Capra's vision of society and politics? Why did it resonate so clearly with American audiences in the 1930s and 40s?

Identification

Identify each of the following and explain why it is important within the context of the chapter.

1. Dow Jones Industrial Average

2. "Black Tuesday"

3. soup kitchen

4. "Okies"

5. Scottsboro case

6. Dale Carnegie

7. Erskine Caldwell

8. Richard Wright

9. John Steinbeck

10. Walt Disney

11. *Gone with the Wind*

12. *Life* Magazine

13. Abraham Lincoln brigade

14. "Popular Front"

15. Norman Thomas

16. Southern Tenant Farmers Union

17. Hawley-Smoot Tariff

18. "Hooverville"

19. Farmers Holiday Association

20. Reconstruction Finance Corporation

Document

The years 1932 and 1933 were the hardest of the Great Depression. Even normally conservative, business-oriented *Fortune* magazine was convinced that extraordinary measures were necessary in the face of the collapse of existing relief agencies and the inadequacy of the $300 million Emergency Relief Act. The excerpt below is from *Fortune's* September 1932 issue. Consider the following questions: Why were existing relief programs so inadequate? Why is it especially significant that a business-minded publication like *Fortune* would, in the autumn of 1932, stress the magnitude of the crisis and the failure of the response? What do you suppose the writer meant by the statement "One does not talk architecture while the house is on fire . . ."?

There can be no serious question of the failure of those methods. For the methods were never seriously capable of success. They were diffuse, unrelated, and unplanned. The theory was that

295

private charitable organizations and semi-public welfare groups, established to care for the old and the sick and the indigent, were capable of caring for the casuals of a worldwide economic disaster. And the theory in application meant that social agencies manned for the service of a few hundred families, and city shelters set up to house and feed a handful of homeless men, were compelled by the brutal necessities of hunger to care for hundreds of thousands of families and whole armies of the displaced and the jobless. And to depend for their resources upon the contributions of communities no longer able to contribute, and upon the irresolution and vacillation of state legislatures and municipal assemblies long since in the red on their annual budgets. The result was the picture now presented in city after city and state after state—heterogeneous groups of official and semiofficial and unofficial relief agencies struggling under the earnest and untrained leadership of the local men of affairs against an inertia of misery and suffering and want they are powerless to overcome. . . .

One does not talk architecture while the house is on fire and the tenants are still inside. The question at this moment is the pure question of fact. Having decided at last to face reality and do something about it, what is reality? How many men are unemployed in the U.S.? How many are in want? *What are the facts?*

The following minimal statements may be accepted as true—with the certainty that they underestimate the real situation:

1. Unemployment has steadily increased in the U.S. since the beginning of the depression and the rate of increase during the first part of 1932 was more rapid than in any other depression year.

2. The number of persons totally unemployed is now at least 10 million.

3. The number of persons totally unemployed next winter will, at the present rate of increase, be 11 million.

4. Eleven million unemployed means better than one man out of every four employable workers.

5. This percentage is higher than the percentage of unemployed British workers registered under the compulsory insurance laws (17.1 percent in May 1932, as against 17.3 percent in April and 18.4 percent in Jan.) and higher than the French, the Italian, and the Canadian percentages, but lower than the German (43.9 percent of trade unionists in April 1932) and the Norwegian.

6. Eleven million unemployed means 27,500,000 whose regular source of livelihood has been cut off.

7. Twenty-seven and a half million without regular income includes the families of totally unemployed workers alone. Taking account of the numbers of workers on part time, the total of those without adequate income becomes 34 million, or better than a quarter of the entire population of the country.

8. Thirty-four million persons without adequate income does not mean 34 million in present want. Many families have savings. But savings are eventually dissipated and the number in actual want tends to approximate the number without adequate income. How nearly it approximates it now or will next winter no man can say. But it is conservative to estimate that the problem of next winter's relief is a problem of caring for approximately 25 million souls. . . .

Such, broadly speaking, are the facts of unemployment relief in the late summer of 1932. Ahead, whether the depression "ends" this fall or not, is the problem of caring for some 25 million souls through what may prove to be one of the most difficult winters of the republic's history. Behind are three years of muddled purpose, insufficient funds, and unscientific direction. Across the threshold lies a new federal policy and a formal acceptance of the issue.

From "No One Has Starved," *Fortune,* September 1932. © 1932 Time Inc. All rights reserved.

Map Exercise

Fill in or identify the following on the blank map provided. Use the map in the text as your source.

1. States carried by Hoover.
2. States carried by Roosevelt.

Interpretive Questions

Based on what you have filled in, answer the following. On some of the questions you will need to consult the narrative in your text for information or explanation.

1. Why did the nation so thoroughly reject Herbert Hoover? What was expected from Roosevelt?
2. What parts of the country that were normally reliably Republican voted for Roosevelt in 1932? What does that signify about the seriousness of the Depression?

Summary

In October 1929, the stock market's overinflated values collapsed and the Great Depression began. Its causes were complex and its consequences were enormous. In a few short years, the 2 percent unemployment rate of the 1920s had become the 25 percent rate of 1932. The nation's political institutions were not equipped to respond. The task overwhelmed local and private relief efforts. President Herbert Hoover's tentative program of voluntary cooperation, big-business loans, and limited public works was activist by old standards but inadequate to the challenge. American tariffs and war-debt policy aggravated international economic problems and thereby added to domestic woes. Although the suffering of Americans, especially blacks and Hispanics, was great, most citizens clung to traditional values and resisted radical solutions. With veterans marching, farmers protesting, and millions not working, Franklin Delano Roosevelt won the presidency.

Review Questions

These questions are to be answered with essays. This will allow you to explore relationships between individuals, events, and attitudes of the period under review.

1. List and explain the five factors that the text identifies as having been principally responsible for making the Great Depression severe. How did these factors interrelate with each other?

2. On what causes of the Depression did Herbert Hoover place emphasis? How did that shape his response?

3. What did the Depression mean to typical Americans in terms of standard of living and lifestyle? Who suffered most? How did basic American social and political values stand up to the economic crisis?

Chapter Self Test

After you have read the chapter in the text and done the exercises in the Study Guide, take the following self test to see if you understand the material you have covered. Answers appear at the end of the Study Guide.

MULTIPLE-CHOICE QUESTIONS

Circle the letter of the response that best answers the question or completes the statement.

1. Three of the following statements correctly describe conditions in the stock market during the year and a half preceding the Great Crash of 1929. Which is the *exception*?
   a. There was a widespread speculative fever.
   b. The average price of most stock increased dramatically.
   c. The daily volume of stock traded increased dramatically.
   d. Most brokers required cash payment in full for stock purchases.

2. In the several months preceding the Great Crash of 1929, three of the following economic indicators decreased dramatically. Which one *increased?*
   a. automobile sales
   b. wholesale prices
   c. freight-car loadings
   d. business inventories

3. One of the most important causes of the Great Depression was the fact that during the 1920s:
   a. government regulation and trust busting had stifled free enterprise.
   b. there was a fundamental maldistribution of purchasing power.
   c. not enough profits were plowed back into business as new capital investment.
   d. low tariff policies had benefited foreign competitors and seriously damaged domestic industry.

4. In much of the 1920s, European nations were able to make their war-debt payments to the United States, and Germany and Austria were able to continue reparation payments by:
   a. inflating their currencies.
   b. draining their gold reserves.
   c. expanding exports to the United States.
   d. getting new loans from the United States.

5. At the worst of the Depression in 1932, the unemployment rate in the United States was estimated to have been:

    a. 50 percent.

    b. 75 percent.

    c. 25 percent.

    d. 10 percent.

6. In the early 1930s, the term "Okies" referred to:

    a. moonshiners trying to make a living in Appalacia.

    b. oil speculators losing money in the Southwest.

    c. swamp dwellers out of the mainstream in the Deep South.

    d. dispossessed farmers fleeing the Dust Bowl.

7. Three of the following statements accurately describe the condition of blacks during the Great Depression. Which is the *exception?*

    a. The migration of blacks to the North ended abruptly.

    b. Blacks suffered a higher unemployment rate than whites.

    c. Discrimination against blacks increased, particularly in competition for jobs.

    d. Local government and private relief benefits for blacks were smaller than for whites.

8. In the 1920s, the great majority of Hispanics in California and the American Southwest originally migrated from:

    a. Cuba.

    b. Mexico.

    c. Puerto Rico.

    d. none of these, for Hispanics were specifically excluded by the immigration laws of the early 1920s.

9. One effect of the Great Depression on women was to:

    a. open up new opportunities for women in the professions.

    b. strengthen the belief that a woman's place was in the home.

    c. drive most women out of the labor force by the time the economic crisis was over.

    d. gain increased public support for such feminist organizations as the National Woman's Party.

10. Three of the following were effects of the Great Depression on the American family. Which is the *exception?*

    a. The birth rate declined.

    b. The marriage rate declined.

    c. The divorce rate increased.

    d. Middle-class families as well as working-class families suffered great traumatic impact.

11. Popular culture during the Depression era, as manifested by radio, movies, and literature, was generally characterized by:

    a. upbeat and romantic messages as a sort of escapism.

    b. appeals to prurient interests in sex and crime.

    c. a return to traditional religious values.

    d. a deep social concern to portray the human consequences of the national economic disaster.

12. Three of the following novels manifest an implicit protest against social injustices in then-contemporary American society. Which is the *exception?*
    a. Erskine Caldwell's *Tobacco Road* (1932)
    b. Margaret Mitchell's *Gone with the Wind* (1936)
    c. John Steinbeck's *Grapes of Wrath* (1939)
    d. Richard Wright's *Native Son* (1940)

13. The Abraham Lincoln brigade was most closely associated with:
    a. Coxey's Army.
    b. the Bonus Army.
    c. the Spanish Civil War.
    d. veterans of the American Expeditionary Force in World War I.

14. The Popular Front tactics pursued by the American Communist Party between 1935 and 1939 were aimed at developing a broad alliance against:
    a. fascism.
    b. Franklin Delano Roosevelt.
    c. racial injustice.
    d. nonpolitical unionism.

15. For the eight years immediately before becoming president, Herbert Hoover had been the:
    a. vice president.
    b. secretary of state.
    c. secretary of commerce.
    d. Speaker of the House of Representatives.

16. The purpose of the Agricultural Marketing Act, proposed by Hoover even before the Great Crash of 1929, was to:
    a. keep farm prices up.
    b. impose government regulation on the commodities exchange market.
    c. establish quotas for the importation of foreign agricultural products.
    d. promote reciprocal trade agreements with foreign countries for agricultural products.

17. After the effects of the Depression spread to Europe, in an attempt to restore international economic stability, Hoover proposed:
    a. a cancellation of war debts owed to the United States.
    b. a moratorium on war debts, reparations, and private international debts.
    c. that the United States follow Europe's lead in going off the gold standard.
    d. that the United States, by means of massive loans, help the European countries to maintain the gold standard.

18. Hoover's measures to deal with the Depression included support for three of the following. Which is the *exception?*
    a. A large-scale federal program of direct relief to the unemployed.
    b. A system of government home-loan banks to assist mortgage holders.
    c. The Reconstruction Finance Corporation to make loans to businesses.
    d. The Hawley-Smoot Tariff to protect agriculture from foreign competition.

19. The Reconstruction Finance Corporation was largely ineffective in promoting recovery from the Depression because:

    a. the Supreme Court declared it unconstitutional.

    b. its activities did not gain the support of President Hoover.

    c. its programs benefited primarily the small banks and family corporations.

    d. it was underfunded and overcautious in the use of the funds it did have.

20. When it was first organized, how did the Farmers' Holiday Association seek to gain higher prices for farm products?

    a. by lobbying in Washington

    b. by withholding crops from the market

    c. by running its own candidates for state legislatures

    d. by establishing its own cooperative marketing facilities

TRUE-FALSE QUESTIONS

Read each statement carefully. Mark true statements "T" and false statements "F."

1. When the stock market began to decline in October 1929, large financial institutions such as J. P. Morgan and Company tried to stem the drop.

2. The prosperity of the American economy in the mid-1920s was largely dependent on the construction and automobile industries.

3. During the 1920s, corporate profits went disproportionately to the producers rather than potential consumers.

4. The stock market reached its lowest point of the depression era in late 1929 and then gradually inched back up, finally reaching 1929 levels by mid-1932.

5. Most economic historians believe that one important cause of the Great Depression was the United States' decision early in the 1920s to forgive the debts that France and Great Britain owed to U.S. banks for loans taken out during World War I.

6. During the Great Depression, several hundred thousand African Americans left the industrial cities of the North to return to their agriculturally based families in the South.

7. Black women in the South suffered massive unemployment partly because many white families cut back on domestic help during the Depression.

8. In general, American social values apparently changed relatively little in response to the Depression.

9. The Scottsboro case illustrated the corrupt practices of many stock brokers and securities dealers.

10. In response to the economic crisis, membership in the American Communist Party grew into a significant political force and the party obtained virtual autonomy from Soviet control.

11. Norman Thomas's columns in the *New York Times* warned Americans to resist the rising strength of socialism and political radicalism.

12. The Southern Tenant Farmers Union tried to build an economic coalition between black and white sharecroppers and cash renters.

13. Herbert Hoover's public response to the Depression in 1929 and 1930 was to deny that the nation was even in a recession or depression.

14. The Hawley-Smoot Tariff tried to counter the economic downturn by slashing rates to encourage more trade.

15. The Bonus Army, organized by the NAACP, demanded that the Hoover administration provide more relief for the unemployed.

16. The Farmers' Holiday Association, fearing a loss in prestige for agricultural pursuits, demanded that October 15 be designated as Harvest Day in honor of their contributions.

17. Realizing that Hoover had been discredited, the Republicans nominated former President William Howard Taft to run against Franklin Roosevelt in 1932.

18. Despite a physical handicap due to polio, Roosevelt exuded a confident and buoyant personality.

19. "New Deal" was the nickname given to Roosevelt's depression-fighting plans by journalists even though he never used the term himself.

20. During the period from the November 1932 election and the March 1933 inauguration, Roosevelt and Hoover put aside partisan differences and worked on immediate relief projects.

CHAPTER TWENTY-SIX
THE NEW DEAL

Objectives

A thorough study of Chapter 26 should enable the student to understand:

1. The series of emergency measures designed to restore confidence and enacted during the first 100 days.
2. The New Deal programs for raising farm prices and promoting industrial recovery.
3. The first federal efforts at regional planning.
4. The New Deal program for reforming the financial system.
5. The federal relief programs and Social Security.
6. The political pressures from both the left and the right that caused Franklin Roosevelt to move in new directions from 1935 on.
7. The changes in organized labor during the New Deal period.
8. The effects of the court-packing scheme, and of the recession of 1937 and 1938 on Roosevelt and the New Deal.
9. The impact of the New Deal on minorities and women.
10. The lasting significance of the New Deal to the American economy and political system.

Main Themes

1. How Franklin Roosevelt, although limited by his basically traditional economic views, pushed through programs of economic planning and depression relief.
2. How popular protests against New Deal policies, protests from rightists, leftists, and those who defied categorization, inspired Roosevelt to launch a new burst of action known as the Second New Deal.
3. That despite Roosevelt's overwhelming reelection in 1936, the New Deal was virtually moribund by 1938, thanks to increasing conservative opposition, his own political blunders, and continuing hard times.
4. That the New Deal helped give rise to a new role for the national government as a "broker state" among various organized interests.

Glossary

1. refinance: To renew or reorganize financing—often achieved in a process whereby an existing loan or mortgage is paid off with the proceeds of a new loan secured by the same collateral. Refinancing is often undertaken to avoid foreclosure. The new loan is usually at a lower interest rate for a longer term and with lower payments.

Pertinent Questions

LAUNCHING THE NEW DEAL (694-699)

1. What sort of relationship did President Roosevelt develop with the press and the public?

2. Why was banking the new president's number one order of business? What was done immediately and in 1934 and 1935?

3. What did the Economy Act of 1933 reveal about Roosevelt's fundamental economic philosophy?

4. What was the principal feature of New Deal farm policy? How well did it work? Which farmers were served best?

5. Describe the goals and concepts of the National Recovery Administration (NRA). Why was it less than fully successful? How did it end?

6. What were the goals of the Tennessee Valley Authority (TVA)? How well did it meet them?

7. What effect did taking the nation off the gold standard have on the economy?

8. How did the New Deal try to reform the banking and securities industries?

9. How did the Federal Emergency Relief Administration (FERA) help the states?

10. What assumption about relief was reflected in the Civil Works Administration (CWA) and the Civilian Conservation Corps (CCC)? What was unique about the CCC?

11. What was done for mortgage relief?

THE NEW DEAL IN TRANSITION (699-707)

12. Who led the conservative attack on Roosevelt in 1934 and 1935? How did the president react?

13. How successful were the socialists and communists in exploiting the unrest caused by the depression?

14. Briefly explain the ideas of Huey Long, Francis Townsend, and Charles E. Coughlin and how they exploited popular apprehension. Who was probably most important among them? How did Roosevelt respond?

15. What 1935 legislative initiatives by Roosevelt and others indicated Roosevelt's changing attitude toward big business and the emergence of the Second New Deal?

16. Compare and contrast craft unionism and industrial unionism. What organization emerged to represent industrial unions?

17. Why did organized labor become more militant in the 1930s? How did the Wagner Act (National Labor Relations Act) help? In what industries did unions make especially significant gains?

18. How did the Social Security Act try to maintain a distinction between "insurance" and "public assistance"? What programs did the act establish?

19. Describe the Works Progress Administration (WPA) and its accomplishments. How did it go beyond traditional public-works programs?

20. What were the elements of the New Deal-Democratic political coalition that Roosevelt built?

THE NEW DEAL IN DISARRAY (707-709)

21. What was Roosevelt's objective in the "Court-packing" plan? How was the objective substantially accomplished? What were the political repercussions of the episode?

22. What seems to have been the main cause of the 1937 recession? What economic theory appeared to have been supported by the recession and the administration's response to it?

LIMITS AND LEGACIES OF THE NEW DEAL (709-715)

23. What is meant by "broker state"? How did the New Deal create it?

24. What did the New Deal offer to black Americans? What role did Eleanor Roosevelt play, and what political change resulted?

25. What new direction in Indian policy was the objective of Commissioner of Indian Affairs John Collier? What were the results of the new policy?

26. What pushed the New Deal toward a greater role for women? What held it back?

27. Why was the New Deal's impact greater in the West?

PATTERNS OF POPULAR CULTURE: THE GOLDEN AGE OF COMIC BOOKS (706-707)

28. What did the popularity of superheroes, particularly Superman, reveal about American culture in the late 1930s and early 1940s?

WHERE HISTORIANS DISAGREE (712-713)

29. Why did one leading historian call the New Deal a "halfway revolution"? Does this characterization still ring true in light of the work of later historians?

Identification

Identify each of the following, and explain why it is important within the context of the chapter.

1. "fireside chats"
2. "bank holiday"
3. Twenty-first Amendment
4. Blue Eagle
5. Harry Hopkins
6. American Liberty League
7. John L. Lewis
8. sit-down strike
9. Alf M. Landon
10. Federal Arts/Music/Theater Projects
11. Union party
12. Keynesian economics
13. Marian Anderson
14. "Black Cabinet"
15. John Collier
16. Frances Perkins

The New Deal created many so-called "alphabet agencies." Explain the purpose of each of the following.

1. Agricultural Adjustment Administration (AAA)
2. Rural Electrification Administration (REA)
3. National Recovery Administration (NRA)
4. Public Works Administration (PWA)
5. Tennessee Valley Authority (TVA)
6. Federal Deposit Insurance Corporation (FDIC)
7. Securities and Exchange Commission (SEC)
8. Federal Emergency Relief Administration (FERA)

9. Civil Works Administration (CWA)

10. Civilian Conservation Corps (CCC)

11. Federal Housing Administration (FHA)

12. National Labor Relations Board (NLRB)

13. Works Progress Administration (WPA)

14. National Youth Administration (NYA)

15. Aid to Dependent Children (ADC)

Document 1

In the campaign of 1932, Franklin Roosevelt revealed little of what would become the New Deal. And during the interregnum of 1932 and 1933, he refused to announce the specifics of his program. In fact, some of his campaign speeches were so conservative the New Dealer Marriner Eccles later commented that they sometimes "read like a giant misprint in which Roosevelt and Hoover speak each other's lines." By March 1933, however, although he may not yet have known where he was headed, Roosevelt knew where he was going to start. The most quoted line of his first inaugural address was his famous dictum that "the only thing we have to fear is fear itself." The following excerpts are from later in the speech where he acknowledged the severity of the crisis and outlined his proposed course of action. Read the selection, and consider the following questions: How were Roosevelt's experiences as a member of the wartime Wilson administration reflected in his approach to the Depression? What values of the progressive era did the Roosevelt program embody? How many of the promised programs were implemented during the first two years of the New Deal? How many worked as intended?

In such a spirit on my part and on yours, we face our common difficulties. They concern, thank God, only material things. Values have shrunken to fantastic levels; taxes have risen; our ability to pay has fallen; government of all kinds is faced by serious curtailment of income; the means of exchange are frozen in the currents of trade; the withered leaves of industrial enterprise lie on every side; farmers find no market for their produce; the savings of many years in thousands of families are gone.

More important, a host of unemployed citizens face the grim problem of existence, and an equally great number toil with little return. Only a foolish optimist can deny the dark realities of the moment. . . .

There must be an end to a conduct in banking and in business which too often has given to a sacred trust the likeness of callous and selfish wrongdoing.

Small wonder that confidence languishes, for it thrives only on honesty, on honor, on the sacredness of obligations, on faithful protection, on unselfish performance; without them it cannot live.

Restoration calls, however, not for changes in ethics alone. This nation asks for action, and action now.

Our greatest primary task is to put people to work. This is no unsolvable problem if we face it wisely and courageously.

It can be accomplished in part by direct recruiting by the government itself, treating the task as we would treat the emergency of a war, but at the same time, through this employment, accomplishing greatly needed projects to stimulate and reorganize the use of our natural resources.

Hand in hand with this, we must frankly recognize the overbalance of population in our industrial centers and, by engaging on a national scale in a redistribution, endeavor to provide a better use of the land for those best fitted for the land.

The task can be helped by definite efforts to raise the values of agricultural products and with this the power to purchase the output of our cities.

It can be helped by preventing realistically the tragedy of the growing loss, through foreclosure, of our small homes and our farms.

It can be helped by insistence that the Federal, State and local governments act forthwith on the demand that their cost be drastically reduced.

It can be helped by the unifying of relief activities which today are often scattered, uneconomical and unequal. It can be helped by national planning for and supervision of all forms of transportation and of communication and other utilities which have a definitely public character.

There are many ways in which it can be helped, but it can never be helped merely by talking about it. We must act, and act quickly.

Finally, in our progress toward a resumption of work we require two safeguards against a return of the evils of the old order; there must be a strict supervision of all banking and credits and investments; there must be an end to speculation with other people's money, and there must be provision for an adequate but sound currency.

These are the lines of attack. I shall presently urge upon a new Congress in special session detailed measures for their fulfillment, and I shall seek the immediate assistance of the several States.

Through this program of action we address ourselves to putting our own national house in order and making income balance outgo.

Our international trade relations, though vastly important, are, in point of time and necessity, secondary to the establishment of a sound national economy.

I favor as a practical policy the putting of first things first. I shall spare no effort to restore world trade by international economic readjustment, but the emergency at home cannot wait on that accomplishment.

Document 2

Read the section in the text entitled "Attacks from the Right and the Left," and pay careful attention to the discussion of the American Liberty League. The following documents are newspaper reports on various Liberty League attacks on Roosevelt and the New Deal. Read these articles, and consider the following questions: Did the TVA in fact embody some aspects of socialism? Was it fair to imply that Senator George W. Norris and other TVA backers wanted to build a "socialistic State"? How did Wendell Willkie's business-oriented opposition to the New Deal put him in a position to become the Republican presidential nominee in 1940? What was Roosevelt proposing in 1935 that inspired the comparison to George III, Hitler, and Mussolini? Was the economic planning proposed by Roosevelt stringent enough to justify the charges by the Liberty League, and later by such historians as Edgar E. Robinson (see "Where Historians Disagree" in this chapter), that the New Deal shared many objectives with communism?

TVA 'Socialism' Hit by Liberty League

WASHINGTON, May 26—Sponsors of the Tennessee Valley Authority are interested primarily in building up a socialistic State, the American Liberty League charged today in attacking the Norris bill to enlarge and clarify the powers of the TVA. . . .

"Never have the dreams of bureaucrats flowered so perfectly as in the Tennessee Valley," the League said in a statement. "Bureaucracy thrives on interference in the affairs of individuals and in the conduct of business."

"Unless the courts intervene, the TVA may become more potent than the government of any of the seven States in which it exerts its influence." . . .

Wendell L. Willkie, president of the Commonwealth & Southern Corporation [and the 1940 Republican nominee for president], joined in the attack on TVA by sending a letter to 200,000 security holders of his company today.

From *The New York Times,* May 27, 1935. Copyright □ 1935 by The New York Times Company. Reprinted by permission.

* * *

Warns of New George III

WASHINGTON, Nov. 10 (AP) —President Roosevelt was likened to King George III of England in a pamphlet issued today by the American Liberty League.

The pamphlet, entitled "Economic Planning—Mistaken But Not New," also asserted that the New Deal's "economic planning" carries "points of similarity" with both Soviet communism and fascism, closely resembling "in many regards the Five-Year Plans of the Soviet Government."

"King George III," it said, "was the symbol of autocratic power against which the Colonies revolted. The twenty-seven grievances enumerated in the Declaration of Independence were directed specifically against him.

"Under New Deal laws and usurpations of authority, autocratic power to plan the course of economic affairs has become centered in the President of the United States. In Italy Mussolini and in Germany Hitler typify autocracy and a planned economic order."

New York Times, 11 November, 1935. Dispatch to the *New York Times,* from the Associated Press, 10 November, 1935. Reprinted by permission of the Associated Press.

Map Exercise

Fill in or identify the following on the blank map provided. Use the map in the text as your source.

1.   Approximate route of the Tennessee River from source to the Ohio River.
2.   Knoxville and Chattanooga.
3.   Approximate extent of the Tennessee Valley basin, noting the states affected.
4.   Muscle-Shoals.

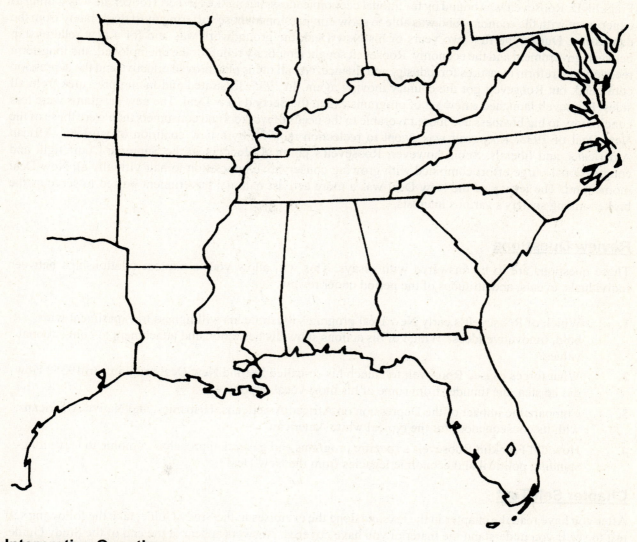

Interpretive Questions

Based on what you have filled in, answer the following. On some of the questions you will need to consult the narrative in your text for information or explanation.

1. What development in the utility industry sparked the final approval of the TVA concept? What impact did the TVA have on the industry?
2. How did the TVA benefit the region? What were its limitations?
3. Why did the New Deal fail to embark on any other regional projects of the magnitude of the TVA?

Summary

Franklin D. Roosevelt was bound by traditional economic ideas, but unlike Herbert Hoover, he was willing to experiment with the economy and was able to show compassion to those suffering most desperately from the depression. During the first two years of his New Deal, the groundwork was laid for a new relationship between government and the economy. Roosevelt sought temporary relief for the unemployed, and long-term recovery and reform measures for industry and finance. Not all of his plan proved effective and the depression continued, but Roosevelt got the country moving again. In 1935, frustrated and facing pressures from all sides, Roosevelt launched a new set of programs called the Second New Deal. The new programs were less conciliatory to big business and more favorable to the needs of workers and consumers than were those of the New Deal of 1933. Roosevelt was swept to reelection in 1936 by a new coalition of workers, African Americans, and liberals. Soon, however, Roosevelt's political blunders in the Supreme Court fight and congressional purge effort combined with growing conservative opposition to halt virtually all New Deal momentum. The legacy of the New Deal was a more activist national government poised to serve as the broker among society's various interests.

Review Questions

These questions are to be answered with essays. This will allow you to explore relationships between individuals, events, and attitudes of the period under review.

1. Which of Roosevelt's early New Deal programs illustrate his willingness to experiment with bold, innovative ideas? Which of his actions show his hesitation and attachment to conventional values?

2. What forces caused Roosevelt to launch his so-called Second New Deal programs in 1935? How did he steal the thunder from some of his most vocal opponents?

3. Compare the impact of the Depression on African Americans, Hispanics, and Native Americans with its consequences for the typical white American.

4. How did Franklin Roosevelt's specific programs and general approaches combine to leave long-standing political and economic legacies from the New Deal?

Chapter Self Test

After you have read the chapter in the text and done the exercises in the Study Guide, take the following self test to see if you understand the material you have covered. Answers appear at the end of the Study Guide.

MULTIPLE-CHOICE QUESTIONS

Circle the letter of the response that best answers the question or completes the statement.

1. Much of Roosevelt's success in restoring public confidence in government might be attributed to his:
    a. consistent application of clear-cut philosophies to social and economic problems.
    b. optimistic and ebullient personality.
    c. refusal to engage in tedious and politically charged press conferences.
    d. public demonstration of how a man could overcome physical paralysis.

2. Roosevelt's first concern as president was the:
   a. public panic caused by the bank failures.
   b. collapse of agriculture.
   c. problem of widespread unemployment.
   d. deflationary spiral that had crippled business.

3. The Twenty-first Amendment, ratified in 1933, repealed the:
   a. progressive income tax.
   b. poll tax, literacy test, and other discriminatory voting restrictions.
   c. prohibition on the manufacture and sale of alcoholic beverages.
   d. "quota system" of immigration limitations.

4. Initial implementation of the Agricultural Adjustment Act in 1933 was controversial because it:
   a. involved large-scale destruction of existing crops and livestock to reduce surpluses.
   b. required farmers to boost agricultural production.
   c. outlawed the practices of farm tenancy and sharecropping.
   d. favored the interests of small farmers over those of large farmers.

5. Of greatest impact on large numbers of poor farmers was a New Deal program to:
   a. provide payments for reduced production in the interest of soil conservation.
   b. help irrigate and reclaim marginal lands for cultivation.
   c. provide loans for resettlement.
   d. make electric power available through utility cooperatives.

6. Which of the following provisions was *not* included in the National Industrial Recovery Act of 1933?
   a. Trade association agreements on pricing and production.
   b. Loans by the national government to railroads, banks, and insurance companies.
   c. Legal protection to the right of workers to form unions and engage in collective bargaining.
   d. A major program of public works designed to pump needed funds into the economy.

7. The Supreme Court declared the National Industrial Recovery Act unconstitutional partly because it:
   a. used an overbroad definition of interstate commerce.
   b. waived antitrust laws for cooperating businesses.
   c. granted public money to private corporations.
   d. applied only to corporations, not partnerships and sole proprietors.

8. The Tennessee Valley Authority (TVA):
   a. received strong support from the nation's utility companies.
   b. suffered as a result of the collapse of the electrical utility empire of Samuel Insull.
   c. was intended to serve as an agent for comprehensive redevelopment of the entire region.
   d. converted the Tennessee Valley into one of the most prosperous regions of the country.

9. The Roosevelt administration instituted all of the following financial reforms *except* to:
   a. take the country off the gold standard.
   b. establish the Federal Deposit Insurance Corporation (FDIC).
   c. transfer control over interest rates from the Federal Reserve Board to Congress.
   d. establish the Securities and Exchange Commission (SEC) to police the stock market.

10. To provide assistance to those in need, Roosevelt and his adviser Harry Hopkins regarded which of the following as best?
    a. cash grants to states
    b. work relief
    c. a government dole for individuals
    d. private charity

11. The relief efforts of the early New Deal were intended to:
    a. stimulate a broad recovery of the economy.
    b. be limited in scope and temporary in duration.
    c. create a permanent welfare system.
    d. apply the principles of Keynesian economics.

12. Franklin Roosevelt's political philosophy could most accurately be described or characterized as:
    a. pragmatic.
    b. laissez-faire.
    c. doctrinaire liberal.
    d. democratic socialist.

13. During his first few days in office, Roosevelt achieved three of the following either by proclamation or by congressional enactment. Which is the *exception?*
    a. All banks were closed temporarily.
    b. The manufacture and sale of 3.2 percent beer was legalized.
    c. The nation's commitment to the gold standard was explicitly reaffirmed.
    d. Government salaries and veterans' pensions were reduced in an attempt to balance the budget.

14. Section 7(a) of the National Industrial Recovery Act represented a significant gain for:
    a. organized labor.
    b. ethnic minorities.
    c. trade associations.
    d. the great mass of consumers.

15. Three of the following were purposes behind the establishment of the Tennessee Valley Authority. Which is the *exception?*
    a. Flood control.
    b. Experimentation with regional planning and rehabilitation.
    c. The establishment of a standard of comparison for measuring private power rates.
    d. The establishment of a precedent for full government ownership and operation of all utilities.

16. In addition to putting young men back to work, a principal purpose of the Civilian Conservation Corps was to:
    a. limit population growth.
    b. promote reforestation and land conservation.
    c. help young married couples buy homes on easy mortgage terms.
    d. provide an interracial living experience to promote harmony.

17. The American Liberty League was dedicated to:
    a. strong conservative opposition to the New Deal.
    b. promoting civil rights for blacks and other minorities.
    c. promoting popular support for the spirit of the New Deal.
    d. a desire among intellectuals to adopt more radical solutions to the nation's economic ills.

18. The significance of the Wagner Act (National Labor Relations Act) to organized labor was that it:
    a. abolished the remnants of the National War Labor Board.
    b. provided unemployment benefits for workers on strike.
    c. provided strong government protection for unions.
    d. explicitly repudiated the right of collective bargaining.

19. The Congress of Industrial Organizations (CIO) was organized on the principle that all workers in a particular industry should be included in one union. This principle is referred to as:
    a. union shop.
    b. closed shop.
    c. craft unionism.
    d. industrial unionism.

20. The 1935 Social Security Act provided for three of the following. Which is the *exception?*
    a. retirement benefits
    b. unemployment benefits
    c. health insurance benefits
    d. benefits to dependent children of impoverished parents

TRUE-FALSE QUESTIONS

Read each statement carefully. Mark true statements "T" and false statements "F."

1. The term "fireside chat" was used during the Depression to indicate that most Americans could not afford any entertainment other than sitting around the stove and visiting with friends.

2. The principal feature of New Deal agricultural policy was that it provided direct income supplements to farmers rather than trying to increase prices and thereby indirectly raising farm income.

3. The Agricultural Adjustment Act turned out to be more beneficial to sharecroppers and tenant farmers than it was to landowning farmers.

4. The National Recovery Administration was just beginning to show positive results in industrial recovery at the time that it was ruled to be unconstitutional.

5. The Tennessee Valley Authority was popular with private utility corporations because it sold them inexpensive hydroelectric-generated power, which they could distribute to their customers.

6. Taking the United States off the gold standard in 1933 had relatively little effect on the economy.

7. Francis E. Townsend based his depression recovery program on giving parents a cash stipend for each child, with the requirement that all of the money be spent on consumer goods.

8. Huey Long wanted to use his "Share-Our-Wealth" program as a basis for a run for president.

9. Roosevelt's response to Townsend, Long, Charles Coughlin, and other critics was to become noticeably more conservative in 1935 and 1936.

10. The Liberty League used the Blue Eagle as the symbol of its opposition to the New Deal.

11. In combating the vast problem of unemployment during the Depression, federally funded work projects under the WPA were extended to include artists, musicians, and writers, as well as basic unskilled and semiskilled laborers.

12. In the election of 1936, the Republican platform emphasized adopting economic measures more radical than those of the New Deal.

13. The ultimate outcome of Roosevelt's plan to pack the Supreme Court was that although the plan was defeated, the Court became more favorable to New Deal legislation.

14. According to Keynesian economics, during a depression the government should balance the budget.

15. The Roosevelt administration finally came to accept the implications of Keynesian economics as a result of the recession of 1937 and 1938.

16. Harry Hopkins was significant to the New Deal as for heading several projects including the WPA.

17. The idea of the broker state means that the government should become supervisor of the competition between contending interest groups.

18. John L. Lewis was the most influential member of Roosevelt's so-called Black Cabinet.

19. Many blacks shifted their political support to the Democrats as a consequence of the New Deal.

20. Frances Perkins was Secretary of Labor and the first woman ever appointed to the cabinet.

CHAPTER TWENTY-SEVEN
THE GLOBAL CRISIS, 1921–1941

Objectives

A thorough study of Chapter 27 should enable the student to understand:

1. The new directions of American foreign policy in the 1920s.
2. The effects of the Great Depression on foreign relations.
3. The pattern of Japanese, Italian, and German aggression that eventually led to World War II.
4. The factors that led to the passage of neutrality legislation in the 1930s.
5. The sequence of events that brought the United States into the war.

Main Themes

1. That in the 1920s, the United States tried to increase its role in world affairs, especially economically, while avoiding commitments.
2. How America, in the face of growing world crises in the 1930s turned increasingly toward isolationism and legislated neutrality.
3. How war in Europe and Asia gradually drew the United States closer and closer to war until the attack on Pearl Harbor finally sparked American entry into World War II.

Glossary

1. fascism: A political system that glorifies the nation, minimizes individual rights, and operates through an autocratic central government that tightly controls all economics, political, and social behavior. In the 1930s and 1940s, the term applied to governments under Benito Mussolini in Italy, Adolf Hitler in Germany, and Francisco Franco in Spain.
2. blitzkrieg: A quick, coordinated military attack utilizing armored ground vehicles and intensive air support. The word is German for "lightning war."

Pertinent Questions

THE DIPLOMACY OF THE NEW ERA (720-723)

1. Why did the United States negotiate separate treaties after World War I?
2. What was accomplished by the Washington Conference and subsequent naval and disarmament conferences?
3. How did American loans and investments work at cross purposes with United States tariff policy? What was the result?
4. What did Hoover do to improve relations with Latin America?
5. What happened to the international efforts at economic stability and disarmament in Europe in the late 1920s and early 1930s?
6. How did the Hoover administration deal with Japanese expansionism? How effective was the approach?

ISOLATIONISM AND INTERNATIONALISM (723-728)

7. To what extent did Roosevelt change the U.S. approach to international debt and currency issues?

8. In what ways did U.S. relations with the U.S.S.R. change in the early 1930s?

9. Compare and contrast the Latin American policy of Herbert Hoover with the "Good Neighbor Policy" of Franklin D. Roosevelt. What resulted?

10. What ideas and developments fed isolationist sentiment in the first half of the 1930s? What was Roosevelt's position?

11. Taken as a whole, what were the basic provisions and central purpose of the Neutrality Acts of 1935, 1936, and 1937? What European and Asian developments put strains on American neutrality?

12. What aggressive German moves finally started World War II in Europe? How did Britain, France, and the Soviet Union react to the series of aggressive actions?

FROM NEUTRALITY TO INTERVENTION (728-736)

13. How did Roosevelt manage to get aid to Great Britain in 1939 and 1940 despite the limitations imposed by the Neutrality Acts? What changes in American public opinion coincided with the worsening situation for France and Britain?

14. What were the two principal positions in the domestic debate over the degree to which the United States should participate in the European war?

15. How did the lend-lease program and the concept of "hemispheric defense" manage to circumvent isolationist arguments about the alleged mistakes of World War I? Why did the U.S. support the Soviet Union in the war?

16. What actions by Hitler and Germany in 1941 led the United States to the brink of war in Europe?

17. What Japanese moves in Asia brought Japan into conflict with the United States?

18. Why could the attack on Pearl Harbor be considered a tactical victory but a political blunder by the Japanese? How have historians treated the attack?

AMERICA IN THE WORLD: THE SINO-JAPANESE WAR, 1931-1941 (726)

19. What basic motivation lay behind the Japanese desire to conquer China and build an empire? What role did oil play?

PATTERNS OF POPULAR CULTURE: ORSON WELLES (728-729)

20. What did the public reaction to the *War of the Worlds* broadcast reveal about the power of radio and the anxieties of the American people in 1938?

WHERE HISTORIANS DISAGREE: THE QUESTION OF PEARL HARBOR (734-735)

21. What are the differences between historians who argue that the attack on Pearl Harbor was a result of blunders by the Roosevelt administration and those who postulate deliberate provocation? Which view is more convincing?

Identification

Identify each of the following and explain why it is important within the context of the chapter.

1. Henry Cabot Lodge
2. isolation
3. Charles Evans Hughes
4. Kellogg-Briand Pact
5. Dawes Plan
6. Benito Mussolini
7. Nazi Party
8. Aryan people
9. Chiang Kai-shek
10. Reciprocal Trade Act
11. Nye investigation
12. Axis
13. Francisco Franco
14. *Panay* incident
15. Munich and "appeasement"
16. America First Committee
17. Henry A. Wallace
18. Wendell Willkie
19. Atlantic Charter
20. Tripartite Pact
21. Hideki Tojo
22. Jeanette Rankin

Document

Read the section in the text entitled "The Rise of Isolationism," paying careful attention to the discussion of the investigations chaired by Senator Gerald P. Nye (R-N.D.). The following statements were made in May 1935 by Nye and Senator Bennett Champ Clark (D-Mo.), a member of Nye's committee, before a "Keep America Out of War" meeting at Carnegie Hall in New York City. Also on the program was Representative Maury Maverick (D-Tex.), another isolationist. Read the statements and consider the following questions: Was it really the sale of munitions that led America into World War I? Why might a 1935 audience have been especially receptive to charges that bankers were responsible for war? How successful were Nye, Clark, and others in enlisting the "overwhelming body of public sentiment" for neutrality legislation? If Roosevelt had strictly followed the spirit of the neutrality legislation, could American entry into World War II have been avoided?

SENATOR GERALD P. NYE (R.-N.D.)

[The investigations of the Senate Munitions Committee have not been in vain;] truly worthwhile legislation will be forthcoming to meet the frightful challenge.

Out of this year of study has come tremendous conviction that our American welfare requires that great importance be given to the subject of our neutrality when others are at war.

Let us be frank before the next war comes as Wilson was frank after the last war was over. Let us know that it is sales and shipments of munitions and contraband, and the lure of profits in them, that will get us into another war.

If Morgan and the other bankers must get into another war, let them do it by enlisting in the Foreign Legion. That's always open.

SENATOR BENNETT CHAMP CLARK (D-Mo.)

In these resolutions [calling for neutrality legislation] we propose that American citizens who want to profit from other people's war shall not be allowed again to entangle the United States.

We appeal to you to lend your efforts to the creation of an overwhelming body of public sentiment to bring about the firm establishment of that policy. The time for action is due and past due.

From *The New York Times,* May 28, 1935. Copyright © 1935 by The New York Times Company. Reprinted by permission.

Map Exercise

The Map Exercise in Chapter Twenty-Eight covers this chapter also.

Summary

After World War I, the United States avoided international commitments but not international contact. Relations with Latin America improved, but in Asia and Europe, crises were brewing. The initial American reaction to the aggressive moves of Italy, Germany, and Japan was one of isolationism. Anxious to avoid involvement in another world war, the United States passed a series of Neutrality Acts; but as the Axis aggressors became bolder, Roosevelt eased the nation closer and closer to war. The attack on Pearl Harbor blew away all isolationist remnants and the nation entered World War II determined and unified.

Review Questions

These questions are to be answered with essays. This will allow you to explore relationships between individuals, events, and attitudes of the period under review.

1. How isolationist was the United States in the 1920s? Was the dual policy of economic penetration and arms limitation an effective approach?

2. Compare and contrast the American reactions to World Wars I and II. Explain the relationship between attitudes toward World War I and the isolationist sentiment and neutrality legislation of the 1930s.

Chapter Self Test

After you have read the chapter in the text and done the exercises in the Study Guide, take the following self-test to see if you understand the material you have covered. Answers appear at the end of the Study Guide.

MULTIPLE-CHOICE QUESTIONS

Circle the letter of the response that best answers the question or completes the statement.

1. The series of treaties signed at the Washington Conference of 1921 to 1922 dealt with three of the following. Which is the *exception?*
    a. The limitation of land forces.
    b. The limitation of naval armaments.
    c. The reaffirmation of the Open Door in China.
    d. Mutual respect between the four major powers for territorial possessions in the Pacific.

2. The Kellogg-Briand Pact of 1928 pledged the signatory nations to:
    a. join the League of Nations.
    b. respect the Open Door policy in China.
    c. renounce war as an instrument of national policy.
    d. establish a binding regional-security military alliance with one another.

3. How did the Hoover administration respond to the Japanese conquest of Manchuria?
    a. It supported the Japanese action.
    b. It imposed economic sanctions on the Japanese.
    c. It refused to grant diplomatic recognition to the new Japanese territories.
    d. It ordered the Pacific fleet to stand by off the China coast.

4. In 1933, the United States finally recognized the government of communist Russia in part because the:
    a. United States hoped for substantial trade with Russia.
    b. United States felt it needed a new ally against Hitler.
    c. Soviet Union completely abandoned support of the Comintern.
    d. communists had established their legitimacy through free elections.

5. Official recognition of the Soviet regime in Russia by the American government in 1933 resulted in:
    a. increased understanding and appreciation of the theories of communism by most Americans.
    b. plans by which the Soviet Union and the United States intended to contain expansion by fascist governments.
    c. significantly increased sales of American manufactured goods inside the Soviet Union.
    d. relatively little change in the mutual mistrust which had characterized Soviet-American relations in the past.

6. According to the Dawes Plan of 1924, the United States would:
    a. provide economic assistance to rebuild the economies of Poland and Russia.
    b. provide loans to Germany, enabling it to pay reparations to Britain and France.
    c. reduce tariff rates, allowing trading partners to increase exports and thus earn needed funds to repay debts.
    d. double its investments in Latin America, providing modern facilities to weaken the appeal of revolutionary groups in that region.

7. With regard to Latin America, Herbert Hoover:

    a. relied on "dollar diplomacy" as William H. Taft had.

    b. returned to military intervention as Woodrow Wilson had.

    c. renounced the Monroe Doctrine and encouraged western European intervention.

    d. repudiated the Roosevelt corollary and refused to send in U.S. troops when Caribbean nations got into debt problems and political instability.

8. The Good Neighbor policy of Franklin D. Roosevelt applied specifically to:

    a. Canada.

    b. Great Britain.

    c. Latin America.

    d. the Philippines.

9. The Nye committee reached the conclusion that an important factor leading the United States into war in 1917 was the:

    a. threat to the balance of power in Europe.

    b. power vacuum created by the decline of Turkey.

    c. need to protect American bank loans to the Allies.

    d. need to protect American overseas colonial possessions.

10. The Neutrality Acts of the 1930s were based on the assumption that the United States could stay out of war by:

    a. ending the Depression.

    b. freeing all American colonies.

    c. staying out of the League of Nations.

    d. banning arms sales to countries at war.

11. Which of the following place names most readily brings to mind appeasement of the Nazis?

    a. Dunkirk

    b. Munich

    c. Stockholm

    d. Warsaw

12. World War II in Europe began when Hitler:

    a. invaded Poland.

    b. annexed Austria.

    c. occupied Czechoslovakia.

    d. signed a nonaggression pact with Stalin.

13. The Lend-Lease bill in 1941 empowered the president to:

    a. grant government loans to the Allies.

    b. lend physical goods rather than money to the Allies.

    c. authorize private American loans to the Allies.

    d. abrogate the Neutrality Act of 1939 by executive order.

14. Although not yet officially involved in World War II, by the autumn of 1941, the United States was:

    a. supplying war material to Great Britain.

    b. supplying war material to the Soviet Union.

    c. escorting convoys of merchant ships in the Atlantic.

    d. doing all of the above.

15. Which of the following most seriously threatened the Japanese war effort and forced Japan to choose between conciliating the United States and enlarging the scope of the war?

    a. the Stimson Doctrine

    b. the League of Nations

    c. world reaction to the *Panay* incident

    d. the freezing of Japanese assets in the United States

16. The quiet lull in World War II in Europe in the winter and early spring of 1940 gave rise to the term:

    a. "phony war."

    b. "phantom enemy."

    c. "peace at any cost."

    d. "missing military."

17. The American First Committee advocated:

    a. immediate U.S. entry into the war to defend France.

    b. concentrating U.S. power in the Pacific.

    c. keeping the United States out of the war.

    d. significantly increasing American assistance to the Allies short of actual entry into the war.

18. In the August 1941 Atlantic Charter, President Roosevelt and Prime Minister Winston Churchill:

    a. decided that as soon as Nazi submarines were controlled in the Atlantic, military forces should make the defeat of Japan in the Pacific the "highest priority."

    b. announced a set of *de facto* war aims with "common principles" that called for the "final destruction of Nazi tyranny."

    c. resolved to defeat Germany as quickly as possible because they both regarded the Soviet Union as "a greater threat to world self determination."

    d. agreed that the British would have principal responsibility for "command and control" in the European theater and that the United States would have it in Asia.

19. The militant Japanese Prime Minister and leader of the so-called war party was General:

    a. Hirohito.

    b. Yamamoto.

    c. Kamikaze.

    d. Tojo.

20. Militarily, the most significant U.S. loss in the attack on Pearl Harbor was the:

   a. sinking of eight battleships.

   b. sinking or disabling of four aircraft carriers.

   c. delay in obtaining a congressional declaration of war because of the demoralizing of the American public.

   d. delay in declaring war on Germany because of all the immediate anger focusing on Japan.

TRUE-FALSE QUESTIONS

Read each statement carefully. Mark true statements "T" and false statements "F."

1. Rather than being a pure isolationist, Senator Henry Cabot Lodge wanted the United States to exert its influence internationally but in a way that reflected U.S. interests and virtues and avoided obligations to other nations.

2. Even though many people characterized American foreign policy during the 1920s as "isolationism," in fact the United States played a more active role in world affairs than at almost any other peacetime period.

3. Secretary of State Charles Evans Hughes was the key figure in resisting efforts to reduce significantly the size of the American naval establishment after World War I.

4. The Dawes Plan of international finance granted France and Britain a moratorium on payment of war debts to the United States as long as Germany remained unable to make timely war-reparation payments to them.

5. American tariff policy in the 1920s was designed to encourage the sort of trade that would allow European nations to acquire foreign exchange credits so that they could pay their war debts to the United States.

6. When Japan invaded northern Manchuria and further into China in 1931–1932, President Hoover cooperated with the League of Nations in imposing economic sanctions against Japanese aggression.

7. Benito Mussolini was the leader of the Spanish Nazi party.

8. The Reciprocal Trade Agreement Act was designed to raise tariffs and protect American industry during the Depression.

9. The improved diplomatic climate resulting from U.S. diplomatic recognition of the Soviet Union in 1933 proved short-lived and mutual distrust returned by 1934.

10. The provisions of the Neutrality Acts of 1935–1937 were based, to a great extent, on the assumption that the United States should avoid activities that had led the nation into World War I.

11. In the Spanish Civil War, the forces of General Francisco Franco were supported by Hitler and Mussolini.

12. The *Panay* incident involved last-minute diplomatic efforts to keep Italy from making an alliance with Germany.

13. In the 1940 election between Franklin Roosevelt and Wendell Willkie, the voters were presented with a clear choice between an advocate of strong but nonmilitary support for Great Britain and an advocate of immediate military intervention.

14. The term "appeasement" referred to the fact that the United States was not willing to join the war against Germany as long as the Soviet Union maintained its nonaggression pact with the Nazi regime.

15. President Roosevelt circumvented the provisions of the Neutrality Acts by trading fifty American destroyers to Britain in exchange for the right to establish bases on British territory in the Western Hemisphere.

16. The America First Committee was led by several prominent citizens including Charles Lindbergh.

17. Even before the United States officially entered the war in December 1941, German submarines were firing at American vessels and American destroyers were authorized to shoot "on sight" if they spotted U-boats.

18. In the summer of 1941, Japanese forces invaded French Indochina and threatened the Dutch East Indies.

19. Before the attack on Pearl Harbor, the United States had already brought pressure on Japan by first terminating the long-standing commercial treaty and then freezing assets and establishing a complete trade embargo.

20. After the Pearl Harbor attack the U.S. Congress unanimously declared war on Japan with even Representative Jeanette Rankin, who had opposed World War I, voting for war.

CHAPTER TWENTY-EIGHT
AMERICA IN A WORLD AT WAR

Objectives

A thorough study of Chapter 28 should enable the student to understand:

1. The efforts of the federal government to mobilize the nation's economy for war production.
2. The effects of American participation in the war on the depression and on New Deal reformism.
3. The changes that the wartime involvement brought for women and racial and ethnic minorities.
4. The contributions of the United States military to victory in North Africa and Europe.
5. The contributions of the United States military to victory in the Pacific.

Main Themes

1. That the vast productive capacity of the United States was the key to the defeat of the Axis.
2. That the war had a profound effect on the home front.
3. How three major western offensives combined with an ongoing Russian effort to defeat Germany.
4. How sea power contained the Japanese, and how Allied forces moved steadily closer to Japan and prepared for an invasion until the atomic bomb ended the war.

Glossary

1. Free French: French military forces that refused to recognize the legitimacy of the German puppet French government at Vichy. Under the principal leadership of Charles de Gaulle, Free French forces fought on the side of the Allies.

Pertinent Questions

WAR ON TWO FRONTS (740-743)

1. What were the two broad offensives that the U.S. planned against Japan? What two naval victories stemmed the Japanese tide? What was the situation by mid-1943?
2. What did the North African offensive accomplish?
3. Why did Roosevelt and Churchill decide to invade Italy? What impact did the Italian campaign have on other war plans?
4. What was happening on the eastern front during the North African and Italian offensives? How did the Soviet Union react to American and British decisions?
5. How did the United States react to the Holocaust? Why did the United States not do more to save the European Jews?

THE AMERICAN PEOPLE IN WARTIME (743-756)

6. What region of the country benefited most from the enormous government spending for the war effort? Why?
7. What impact did the war have on organized labor?
8. What efforts did the national government make to regulate production, labor, and prices during the war? How successful were they?

9. How did scientific and technological advances help the Allies win the war? What were the peacetime implications of these developments?

10. Describe the demographic, social, and military changes for African Americans and Mexican Americans during the war. What tensions resulted?

11. How did World War II challenge traditional Indian life and redirect federal Indian policy?

12. How were the women who filled war jobs treated? What obstacles did they face? What long-term consequences for the role of women in society and the work force were foreshadowed by the wartime experience?

13. Describe popular culture on the homefront. What efforts were made to make life less disruptive for the service members themselves?

14. How were Japanese Americans treated? Why did they suffer more than German Americans? How did their treatment contrast with Chinese Americans? What was done to atone for the internment of Japanese Americans?

15. What impact did the war effort have on the various programs of the New Deal?

THE DEFEAT OF THE AXIS (756-765)

16. Describe the Normandy invasion and the liberation of France. What role did air power play in preparing for the assault?

17. Describe how Allied forces closed in on Germany and Berlin from east and west. What role did air power play? Who actually captured Berlin?

18. Describe the gradual advance toward Japan in the Pacific. What was the condition of the Japanese war machine by July 1945?

19. Why did the United States decide to use the atomic bomb against Japan? Was it a wise decision?

PATTERNS OF POPULAR CULTURE: THE AGE OF SWING (752-753)

20. Why were some Americans worried by the great popularity of swing music?

WHERE HISTORIANS DISAGREE: THE DECISION TO DROP THE ATOMIC BOMB (762-763)

21. The principal biographers of Harry S Truman and many other historians contend that the President's decision to use the atomic bomb was based purely on the motivation to end the war quickly and save lives. Why do some historians dispute that view? Why is the issue so politically volatile as evidenced by the *Enola Gay* controversy at the Smithsonian Institution?

Identification

Identify each of the following, and explain why it is important within the context of the chapter.

1. Douglas MacArthur
2. Chester Nimitz
3. George S. Patton
4. George C. Marshall
5. Dwight D. Eisenhower
6. Mussolini
7. siege of Stalingrad
8. radar and sonar
9. Ultra and Magic
10. A. Philip Randolph

11.   Fair Employment Practices Commission (FEPC)

12.   Congress of Racial Equality (CORE)

13.   *braceros*

14.   "zoot suit"

15.   "Rosie the Riveter"

16.   WACs and WAVEs

17.   "baby boom"

18.   pinup

19.   USO

20.   Issei and Nisei

21.   Thomas E. Dewey

22.   Harry S Truman

23.   Battle of the Bulge

24.   *Luftwaffe*

25.   Joseph W. Stilwell

26.   Chiang Kai-shek

27.   Battle of Leyte Gulf

28.   Okinawa

29.   Emperor Hirohito

30.   kamikaze

31.   Manhattan Project

32.   J. Robert Oppenheimer

33.   Hiroshima and Nagasaki

Document

Read the section of the text under the heading "African Americans and the War," paying careful attention to the discussion of the march on Washington, the establishment of the Fair Employment Practices Commission (FEPC), and the formation of the Congress of Racial Equality (CORE). The following excerpt is from a magazine article that A. Philip Randolph wrote after the FEPC was organized but before CORE was born. Consider the following questions: Could Randolph's remarks be interpreted as a threat that American blacks might not support the war effort unless they received assurances of better treatment? Was his description of the plight of blacks in the military and in defense plants accurate? Was Randolph right in saying that racial tension in America was worth "many divisions to Hitler and Hirohito"?

Though I have found no Negroes who want to see the United Nations[1] lose this war, I have found many who, before the war ends, want to see the stuffing knocked out of white supremacy and of empire over subject peoples. American Negroes, involved as we are in the general issues of the conflict, are confronted not with a choice but with the challenge both to win democracy for ourselves at home and to help win the war for democracy the world over.

There is no escape from the horns of this dilemma. There ought not to be escape. For if the war for democracy is not won abroad, the fight for democracy cannot be won at home. If this war cannot be won for the white peoples, it will not be won for the darker races.

Conversely, if freedom and equality are not vouchsafed the peoples of color, the war for democracy will not be won. Unless this double-barreled thesis is accepted and applied, the darker

326

races will never whole-heartedly fight for the victory of the United Nations. That is why those familiar with the thinking of the American Negro have sensed his lack of enthusiasm, whether among the educated or uneducated, rich or poor, professional or nonprofessional, religious or secular, rural or urban, North, South, East, or West.

That is why questions are being raised by Negroes in church, labor union, and fraternal society; in poolroom, barbershop, schoolroom, hospital, hairdressing parlor; on college campus, railroad, and bus. One can hear such questions asked as these: What have Negroes to fight for? What's the difference between Hitler and that "cracker" Talmadge of Georgia?[2] Why has a man got to be Jim-Crowed to die for democracy? If you haven't got democracy yourself, how can you carry it to somebody else?

What are the reasons for this state of mind? The answer is: discrimination, segregation, Jim Crow. Witness the Navy, the Army, the Air Corps; and also government services at Washington. In many parts of the South, Negroes in Uncle Sam's uniform are being put upon, mobbed, sometimes even shot down by civilian and military police, and, on occasion, lynched. Vested political interests in race prejudice are so deeply entrenched that to them winning the war against Hitler is secondary to preventing Negroes from winning democracy for themselves. This is worth many divisions to Hitler and Hirohito.[3] While labor, business, and farm are subjected to ceilings and floors and not allowed to carry on as usual, these interests trade in the dangerous business of race hate as usual.

When the defense program began and billions of the taxpayers' money were appropriated for guns, ships, tanks, and bombs, Negroes presented themselves for work only to be given the cold shoulder. North as well as South, and despite their qualifications, Negroes were denied skilled employment. Not until their wrath and indignation took the form of a proposed protest march on Washington, scheduled for July 1, 1941, did things begin to move in the form of defense jobs for Negroes. The march was postponed by the timely issuance (June 25, 1941) of the famous Executive Order No. 8802 by President Roosevelt. But this order and the President's Committee on Fair Employment Practice, established thereunder, have as yet only scratched the surface by way of eliminating discriminations on account of race or color in war industry. Both management and labor unions in too many places and in too many ways are still drawing the color line.

[1]The United Nations was the official name of the Allies. After the war, the name was used for the new international organization.

[2]Eugene Talmadge, racist governor of Georgia.

[3]Emperor of Japan.

Survey Graphic, November 1942.

Map Exercise

Fill in or identify the following on the blank maps provided. Use the maps in the text as your sources.

1. Label the major belligerents, and indicate after the name whether the nation was Axis (AX) or Allied (AL). Circle the areas under Axis control.
2. Indicate by arrows the main American (AM) and British (GB) thrusts against the enemy in North Africa.
3. Label Normandy, Paris, Rome, and Berlin, and draw an arrow indicating the approximate line of advance of the Allied forces on the western fronts.
4. Label Stalingrad, and draw an arrow indicating the approximate line of advance of the Russian forces on the eastern front.
5. Label Japan, China, Manchuria, Burma, Indochina, Australia, Hawaii, the Philippines, Iwo Jima, and Okinawa.
6. Draw a light circle to indicate the approximate extent of the Japanese advance at its peak. Draw a darker circle around the area under Japanese control at the time the first atomic bomb was dropped.

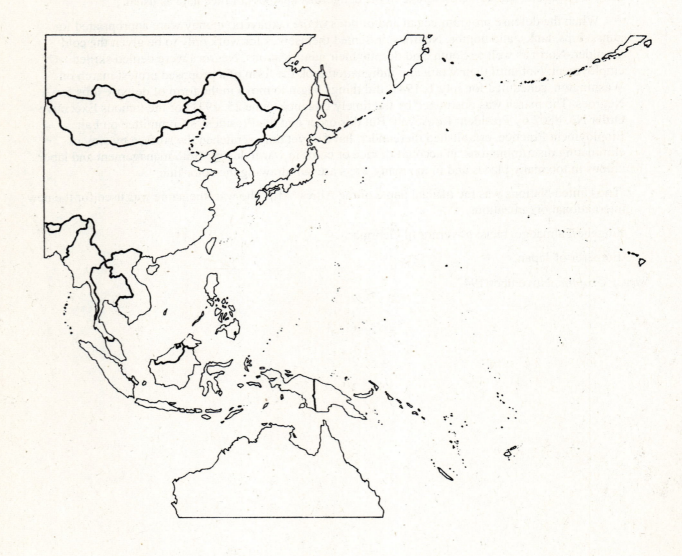

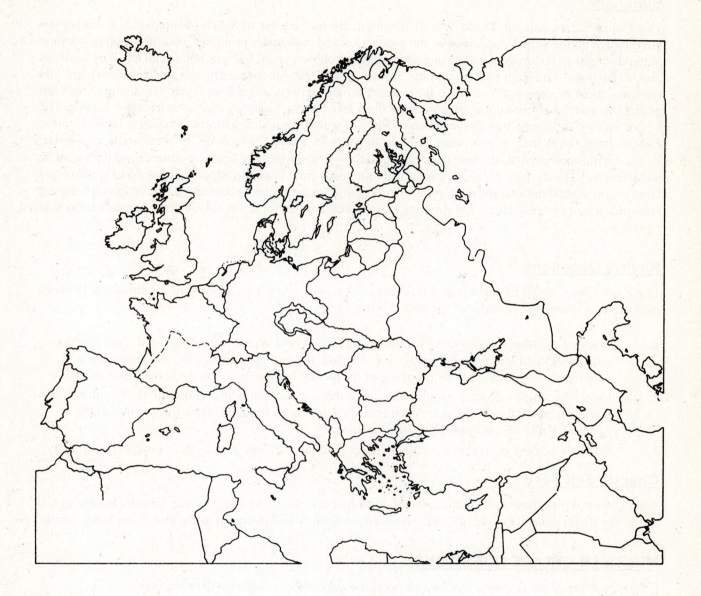

Interpretive Questions

Based on what you have filled in, answer the following. On some of the questions you will need to consult the narrative in your text for information or explanation.

1. How was Great Britain isolated during the height of Axis conquest?
2. Why was Allied control of North Africa considered important?
3. Compare the Allied advance in World War II with that in World War I. (See the Map Exercise in Chapter Twenty-Three.) Why did France and Russia suffer the most in both wars?
4. Why was "island hopping" the most effective strategy for the Allies in the Pacific?

Summary

The United States entered World War II ideologically unified but militarily ill-prepared. A corporate-government partnership solved most of the production and manpower problems, and the massive wartime output brought an end to the Great Depression. Labor troubles, racial friction, and social tensions were not absent, but they were kept to a minimum. Roosevelt and the American generals made the decision that Germany must be defeated first, since it presented a more serious threat than Japan. Gradually, American production and American military might turned the tide in the Pacific and on the western front in Europe. The key to victory in Europe was the invasion of France, which coincided with the Russian offensive on the eastern front. Less than a year after D-Day, the war in Europe was over. In the Pacific, American forces—with some aid from the British and Australians—first stopped the Japanese advance and then went on the offensive. The strategy for victory involved long leaps from island to island that bypassed and isolated large enemy concentrations and drew progressively closer to the Japanese homeland. Conventional bombing raids pulverized Japanese cities, and American forces were readied for an invasion that the atomic bomb made unnecessary.

Review Questions

These questions are to be answered with essays. This will allow you to explore relationships between individuals, events, and attitudes of the period under review.

1. Many of the broad strategy and social decisions of World War II are still debated. Describe the key issues involved in the Germany-first decision, the second-front debate, the Japanese-American internment, and the dropping of the atomic bombs. Were the right decisions made?
2. United States-Soviet relationships were tense throughout World War II despite the fact that the Soviets were on the Allied side. What issues caused those tensions? How important was the eastern front to the outcome of the war in Europe?
3. Which was more critical to the Allied victory, military strategy or American productive capacity?

Chapter Self Test

After you have read the chapter in the text and done the exercises in the Study Guide, take the following self test to see if you understand the material you have covered. Answers appear at the end of the Study Guide.

MULTIPLE-CHOICE QUESTIONS

Circle the letter of the response that best answers the question or completes the statement.

1. During the first few months following American entry into World War II:
    a. national opinion was sharply divided about the war.
    b. national opinion was remarkably unified even though the war was going badly.
    c. national opinion was initially divided but soon unified by a string of impressive victories.
    d. national opinion was ambivalent and fairly uninvolved due to the so-called phony war.
2. The Battles of the Coral Sea and of Midway were significant in:
    a. saving the Philippines from being invaded.
    b. thwarting the Japanese army's drive through Burma.
    c. stemming the tide of Japanese advances in the Pacific.
    d. driving the last vestiges of American sea power from the Pacific.

3. The first area to be liberated from Axis occupation by the Allies was:

    a. France.

    b. Sicily.

    c. the Balkans.

    d. North Africa.

4. The Soviet Union's position regarding the American and British campaigns in North Africa and Italy was to:

    a. favor both because they tied down Axis forces.

    b. oppose both because they delayed the cross-channel invasion of France.

    c. oppose North Africa but favor Italy since it was closer to Germany.

    d. favor North Africa but oppose Italy because it was after the Stalingrad victory.

5. With reference to World War II, the term "Holocaust" refers to:

    a. Hitler's "blitzkrieg" against Poland.

    b. Hitler's campaign to exterminate the Jews.

    c. the American nuclear destruction of Hiroshima and Nagasaki.

    d. the American effort to prevent Hitler's extermination of the Jews.

6. Which region of the United States benefited most from wartime spending?

    a. Northeast

    b. Midwest

    c. Plains

    d. West

7. Three of the following statements accurately describe conditions of organized labor during World War II. Which is the *exception?*

    a. Union membership increased.

    b. There were no strikes, thanks to the "no-strike" pledge.

    c. Congress gave the president power to seize a struck war plant.

    d. The Little Steel formula set a 15 percent limit on wage increases.

8. Government efforts to raise revenue and control inflation during World War II included three of the following. Which is the *exception?*

    a. selling war bonds

    b. imposing direct price controls

    c. balancing the federal budget

    d. levying higher taxes on personal incomes

9. Three of the following statements accurately describe or characterize black experiences during World War II. Which is the *exception?*

    a. Racial segregation was abolished in the military.

    b. The black migration from the rural South to industrial cities increased.

    c. Black organizations displayed greater militancy in putting forth their demands.

    d. Blacks had some success in influencing the federal government to reduce racial inequities.

10. Which does *not* describe the internment of Japanese Americans during World War II?

   a. The Supreme Court upheld their evacuation from the West Coast.

   b. Reparations were finally paid to evacuees about forty years after the war.

   c. Many of the evacuees were United States citizens.

   d. Outside California, there was widespread public opposition to the internment policy.

11. The objective of the Manhattan Project was to develop:

   a. the atomic bomb.

   b. synthetic rubber.

   c. a system of coastal defenses.

   d. a system for dispersion of civilian urban populations.

12. Harry S Truman came to national prominence and the vice presidency through:

   a. chairing an investigative committee that exposed waste and corruption in wartime production.

   b. leading the southern conservative wing in Congress.

   c. managing Roosevelt's renomination campaign at the Democratic convention.

   d. coordinating the planning of the D-Day invasion.

13. In the final months of World War II in Europe, American and British forces:

   a. pushed into the heart of Germany while Soviet troops bogged down in Poland.

   b. entered Germany from the west and Soviet troops entered Germany from the east and occupied Berlin.

   c. stalled along the Rhine River just outside Germany until they linked with Soviet forces.

   d. rushed toward Berlin to gain a "knock-out punch" on Hitler before the Soviet troops could arrive in the capital city.

14. Chinese-American relations were seriously strained during World War II because Chiang Kai-shek:

   a. ordered General Joseph Stilwell to leave the country.

   b. would not commit his full strength against the Japanese.

   c. would not allow United States bombers to operate from Chinese soil.

   d. had too-close ties with the Chinese communist forces under Mao Zedong.

15. During World War II, the Japanese word "kamikaze" referred to:

   a. atomic fallout.

   b. ritual disembowelment.

   c. the lightning speed with which the Japanese armies swept through Southeast Asia.

   d. a suicide mission in which a Japanese pilot purposely crashed his plane into an enemy ship.

16. The Battle of Leyte Gulf:

   a. demonstrated that the Japanese fleet was still strong enough to slow the potential American invasion force.

   b. brought the Soviet Union into the Pacific war.

   c. all but destroyed Japan's ability to continue serious naval warfare.

   d. stopped Japanese advance in the central Pacific near Guam and Midway.

17. In the weeks before the dropping of the atomic bombs on Japan, Japanese political and military leaders:
   a. were united in their determination to continue the war.
   b. were united in their decision to seek peace.
   c. were split with some wishing to seek peace and others wishing to continue the fight.
   d. offered to surrender if they could keep control of Okinawa and Korea.

18. The key facilities for development and production of the American atomic bomb were located in:
   a. New York City and Chicago.
   b. Tennessee, Washington, and New Mexico.
   c. Wyoming and Pennsylvania.
   d. Southern California, Georgia, and Oklahoma.

19. The two cities on which the United States dropped atomic bombs were (Mark *two* letters):
   a. Hiroshima.
   b. Yokohama.
   c. Tokyo.
   d. Nagasaki.

20. When did the Soviet Union enter the Pacific war against Japan?
   a. in June 1941, right after Hitler attacked the Soviet Union
   b. in December 1941, right after the bombing of Pearl Harbor
   c. in February 1945, right after the Yalta Conference
   d. in August 1945, about a week before the Japanese surrendered

TRUE-FALSE QUESTIONS

Read each statement carefully. Mark true statements "T" and false statements "F."

1. Japanese forces attacked American bases in the Philippines soon after the attack on Pearl Harbor.
2. Douglas MacArthur commanded U.S. troops in Europe.
3. The Battles of Coral Sea and Midway Island were both victories for the United States.
4. The U.S. Army Chief of Staff during World War II was General George C. Patton.
5. The Soviet Union complained about the North African campaign because they believed that it had delayed a major second front in Europe.
6. Because of the horror of the Holocaust, the American and British command officers decided to make the liberation of Nazi concentration camps a higher priority than achieving the quickest possible end to the war.
7. The economic buildup for the war virtually wiped out unemployment and finally ended the Great Depression.
8. Labor union membership declined during World War II.
9. The major unions gave "no-strike" pledges during the war, but many work stoppages occurred despite the pledges.
10. Because of the general popularity of the war effort, price controls and rationing were cheerfully accepted and black-market activities were inconsequential.
11. A. Philip Randolph was the principal planner of a civil rights march on Washington that was cancelled only after Roosevelt agreed to establish the Fair Employment Practices Commission.

12. *Braceros* was the nickname given to Mexican-American gangs that became powerful in Los Angeles during the war.

13. In order not to slow down the economic recovery, President Roosevelt and Congress decided to finance the war effort almost entirely from war bond proceeds rather than raising taxes.

14. The nickname often applied to women who took wartime industrial jobs was "Homefront Hannah."

15. The domestic Japanese internment program moved virtually all Issei to camps but did not move Nisei unless they were the minor children of Issei.

16. During World War II President Roosevelt indicated that the political emphasis should shift away from domestic reform, declaring that "Dr. New Deal" should give way to "Dr. Win the War."

17. The Normandy invasion came in the spring of 1944, and Paris was liberated from Nazi control by the end of that summer.

18. In January of 1945, the Soviet Union captured Poland and made peace with Nazi Germany, so the United States and the British had to carry the bulk of the burden of conquering Berlin.

19. The relatively easy conquest of Iwo Jima and Okinawa by naval and marine forces indicated that the Japanese military had nearly lost the means and will to resist.

20. President Harry Truman's decision to drop atomic bombs on Japan was probably inevitable since as U.S. senator he had been chairman of the top secret congressional committee that oversaw the atomic bomb development project.

CHAPTER TWENTY-NINE
THE COLD WAR

Objectives

A thorough study of Chapter 29 should enable the student to understand:

1. The background of United States relations with the Soviet Union before World War II.
2. The extent of collaboration between the United States and the Soviet Union during World War II and the differences of view that developed between the two nations concerning the nature of the postwar world.
3. The meaning of the doctrine of containment and the specific programs that implemented containment.
4. The problems of postwar readjustment in the United States, especially controlling inflation.
5. The nature of the Fair Deal—its successes and failures.
6. The significance of China's becoming communist to American foreign policy in Asia.
7. The circumstances that led to United States participation in a "limited" war in Korea.
8. The reaction of American public opinion to President Harry Truman's handling of the "police action" in Korea including his firing of General Douglas MacArthur.
9. The nature and extent of American fears of internal communist subversion during the early Cold War years.

Main Themes

1. How a legacy of mistrust between the United States and the Soviet Union combined with the events of World War II to cause the Cold War.
2. How the policy of containment led to an increasing United States involvement in crises around the world.
3. How World War II ended the Depression and ushered in an era of nervous prosperity.
4. That the turbulent postwar era climaxed in a period of hysterical anticommunism.

Glossary

1. "right-to-work": Nickname given by antiunion forces to section 14(b) of the Taft-Hartley Act which allows states to prohibit union shops. In right-to-work states, a person cannot be required to join a union even if the majority of workers at the site are union members and have a collective bargaining agreement with management.
2. filibuster: A parliamentary practice that, in effect, allows a minority of United States senators to kill a bill that the majority favors by tying up the business of the chamber with continuous speech making. In the 1950s, a vote of two-thirds (now three-fifths) of the senators was needed to end a filibuster by cloture. Opponents of civil rights legislation were the main users of the filibuster in the decade and a half after World War II.

335

Pertinent Questions

ORIGINS OF THE COLD WAR (768-770)

1. What had led to the deep mutual mistrust and tension between the Soviet Union and the United States before World War II?

2. At the time of World War II, how did the vision of the postwar world held by the United States differ from that of the Soviets and the British?

3. What was accomplished at the Casablanca and Teheran Conferences? What was left unresolved?

4. How did the Yalta Conference deal with the Polish and German questions?

5. Explain the basic structure of the United Nations and contrast its reception in the United States with that of the League of Nations.

THE COLLAPSE OF THE PEACE (770-775)

6. Contrast the attitudes of Franklin Roosevelt and Harry Truman toward Stalin and the Russians. How did this difference play out at Potsdam?

7. Why did the U.S. continue to support Chiang Kai-shek even as his control of mainland China slipped away? How did events in China impact on United States attitudes toward Japan?

8. Explain the Truman Doctrine and containment. What new approach did these concepts substitute for Roosevelt's "one world" vision?

9. In what ways was the Marshall Plan the economic component of containment? How well did it work?

10. How did the National Security Act of 1947 reorganize national-security administration? What agencies were created?

11. Why did Stalin blockade Berlin? How did the United States respond and what resulted?

12. What was the basic commitment of NATO? How did the Soviets respond?

13. What events of 1949 thrust the Cold War into a new and seemingly more dangerous stage?

AMERICAN POLITICS AND SOCIETY AFTER THE WAR (775-779)

14. What kept the United States from experiencing another depression after the war? What economic challenges did the nation face?

15. How did reconversion affect the many women and minorities who had taken war-related jobs?

16. What was the Fair Deal? How did Congress react during President Truman's first term? Which of his goals was Truman able to accomplish through Congress or executive order after his surprising reelection in 1948?

17. Why did the Democratic Party split into factions in 1948? How did Truman manage to win the presidential election despite the problems within the party?

18. What were the Truman administration's domestic successes and failures after the 1948 election?

19. Describe how Americans were torn between pessimistic and optimistic views of the "Nuclear Age." Which view seemed to predominate in national opinion?

THE KOREAN WAR (779-782)

20. What caused the Korean War? What was the role of the United Nations?

21. How did the war's objectives change and how did the war turn into a stalemate?

22. Why did Truman dismiss Douglas MacArthur? Why was the decision so controversial?

23. What social and economic effects did the Korean War have in America?

THE CRUSADE AGAINST SUBVERSION (782-787)

24. What factors combined to create the anticommunist paranoia that led to the national mood that allowed the rise to prominence of Sen. Joseph McCarthy?

25. How did McCarthy exploit the existing mood of hysteria? What sorts of tactics did he use in his attacks on alleged subversion?

26. What personalities and policies led to the Republican victory in the presidential election of 1952?

WHERE HISTORIANS DISAGREE: ORIGINS OF THE COLD WAR (770-771)

27. What is the "post-revisionist" view of the origins and nature of the Cold War?

WHERE HISTORIANS DISAGREE: MCCARTHYISM (784-785)

28. Most historians agree that the anti-communist mood of the late 1940s and early 1950s led to excessive governmental actions, but was it an episode of paranoid and politically motivated response to an insignificant radical few or an overly hysterical reaction to a legitimate threat to American security?

Identification

Identify each of the following and explain why it is important within the context of the chapter.

1. Mao Zedong

2. George F. Kennan

3. Czechoslovakian coup

4. Selective Service System

5. Atomic Energy Commission (AEC)

6. Warsaw Pact

7. Formosa (Taiwan)

8. NSC-68

9. GI Bill of Rights

10. Taft-Hartley Act

11. "right-to-work" laws

12. Strom Thurmond and the "Dixiecrats"

13. Americans for Democratic Action (ADA)

14. Thomas E. Dewey

15. *film noir*

16. Syngman Rhee

17. 38th parallel

18. House Un-American Activities Committee (HUAC)

19. Hollywood blacklist

20. Alger Hiss

21. J. Edgar Hoover

22. McCarran Internal Security Act

23. Julius and Ethel Rosenberg

24. Adlai E. Stevenson

25. Dwight D. Eisenhower

26. Richard M. Nixon

Document 1

Read the section of the chapter under the heading "The Containment Doctrine," paying special attention to the discussion of the Truman Doctrine. The following is an excerpt from the March 12, 1947 speech in which Truman proclaimed the doctrine. He later remembered this program as "the turning point in America's foreign policy." Consider the following questions: What were the implications of a president unilaterally issuing what was, in essence, a treaty-like commitment? Was the speech based on a false dichotomy between communist and "free" peoples? What in the speech foreshadows the economic containment approach of the Marshall Plan? Does American foreign policy continue to be based on the assumptions of containment and the Truman Doctrine?

I am fully aware of the broad implications involved if the United States extends assistance to Greece and Turkey, and I shall discuss these implications with you at this time.

One of the primary objectives of the foreign policy of the United States is the creation of conditions in which we and other nations will be able to work out a way of life free from coercion. This was a fundamental issue in the war with Germany and Japan. Our victory was won over countries which sought to impose their will, and their way of life, upon other nations. . . .

The peoples of a number of countries of the world have recently had totalitarian regimes forced upon them against their will. The Government of the United States has made frequent protests against coercion and intimidation, in violation of the Yalta Agreement, in Poland, Rumania, and Bulgaria. . . .

At the present moment in world history nearly every nation must choose between alternative ways of life. The choice is too often not a free one.

One way of life is based upon the will of the majority, and is distinguished by free institutions, representative government, free elections, guarantees of individual liberty, freedom of speech and religion, and freedom from political oppression.

The second way of life is based upon the will of a minority forcibly imposed upon the majority. It relies upon terror and oppression, a controlled press and radio, fixed elections, and the suppression of personal freedoms.

I believe that it must be the policy of the United States to support free people who are resisting attempted subjugation by armed minorities or by outside pressures.

I believe that we must assist free peoples to work out their own destinies in their own way.

I believe that our help should be primarily through economic and financial aid, which is essential to economic stability and orderly political processes.

The world is not static and the status quo is not sacred. But we cannot allow changes in the status quo in violation of the Charter of the United Nations by such methods as coercion, or by such subterfuges as political infiltration. In helping free and independent nations to maintain their freedom, the United States will be giving effect to the principles of the Charter of the United Nations.

It is necessary only to glance at a map to realize that the survival and integrity of the Greek nation are of grave importance in a much wider situation. If Greece should fall under the control of an armed minority, the effect upon its neighbor, Turkey, would be immediate and serious. Confusion and disorder might well spread throughout the entire Middle East.

Moreover, the disappearance of Greece as an independent state would have a profound effect upon those countries in Europe whose peoples are struggling against great difficulties to maintain their freedoms and their independence while they repair the damages of war.

It would be an unspeakable tragedy if these countries, which have struggled so long against overwhelming odds, should lose that victory for which they sacrificed so much. Collapse of free institutions and loss of independence would be disastrous not only for them but for the world. Discouragement and possibly failure would quickly be the lot of neighboring peoples striving to maintain their freedom and independence.

Should we fail to aid Greece and Turkey in the fateful hour, the effect will be far reaching to the West as well as to the East. We must take immediate and resolute action.

The seeds of totalitarian regimes are nurtured by misery and want. They spread and grow in the evil soil of poverty and strife. They reach their full growth when the hope of a people for a better life has died.

We must keep that hope alive.

The free peoples of the world look to us for support in maintaining their freedoms.

If we falter in our leadership, we may endanger the peace of the world—and we shall surely endanger the welfare of our own Nation.

Great responsibilities have been placed upon us by the swift movement of events.

I am confident that the Congress will face these responsibilities squarely.

Document 2

Read the section of the text headed "The Crusade Against Subversion," paying close attention to the subsection "McCarthyism." The following is a brief excerpt from Joseph McCarthy's initial "red-baiting" speech which was delivered at Wheeling, West Virginia, on February 9, 1950. Press accounts indicate that McCarthy had charged that there were 205 communists in the State Department, but the version printed in the *Congressional Record* reduced the number to 57. The senator was never very precise about specifics. After reading the excerpt, consider the following questions: How did McCarthy, a Roman Catholic, incorporate religion into his appeal? Does he seem somewhat jealous and resentful of those more sophisticated and better educated than he? What specific individual(s) might he have been alluding to? How would such charges help McCarthy's own political career and the general fortunes of the Republicans?

Today we are engaged in a final, all-out battle between communistic atheism and Christianity. The modern champions of communism have selected this as the time. And, ladies and gentlemen, the chips are down—they are truly down. . . . The reason why we find ourselves in a position of impotency is not because our only powerful potential enemy has sent men to invade our shores, but rather because of the traitorous actions of those who have been treated so well by this Nation. It has not been the less fortunate or members of minority groups who have been selling this Nation out, but rather those who have had all the benefits that the wealthiest nation on earth has had to offer—the finest homes, the finest college education, and the finest jobs in Government we can give.

This is glaringly true in the State Department. There the bright young men who are born with silver spoons in their mouths are the ones who have been worst.

. . . In my opinion the State Department, which is one of the most important government departments, is thoroughly infested with Communists.

I have in my hand 57 cases of individuals who would appear to be either card carrying members or certainly loyal to the Communist Party, but who nevertheless are still helping to shape our foreign policy.

Congressional Record, 81st Cong., 2nd sess., 1950, pp. 1594–1956.

Map Exercise

Fill in or identify the following on the blank map provided. Use the map in the text as your source.

1. All the countries.
2. Berlin on the large map; show the approximate dividing line on the inset.
3. Warsaw Pact nations.
4. NATO nations.
5. The "Iron Curtain."

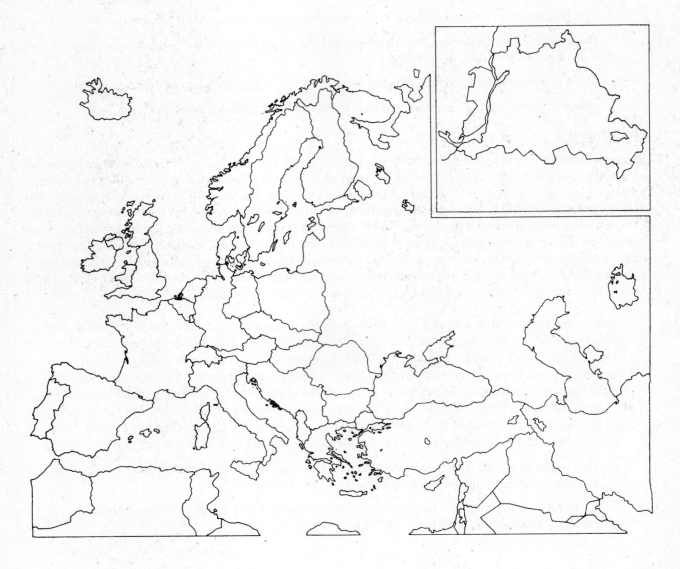

340

Interpretive Questions

Based on what you have filled in, answer the following. On some of the questions you will need to consult the narrative in your text for information or explanation.

1.   Why was the form of government in Poland such a difficult issue to resolve?

2.   Why was Germany divided and why was Berlin divided even though it lay in the Russian zone? What caused the United States, Great Britain, and France to combine their zones into a single nation?

3.   Explain the policy of the Truman Doctrine. What was to be contained? Where? What developments were the catalyst for Truman's promulgation of the policy? What was the economic manifestation of the idea?

4.   Why was the Soviet Union so suspicious of the West and so insistent on control of East Germany and the nations along the Soviet border? Were the Soviet concerns justified?

Summary

The mutual hostility between the United States and the Soviet Union grew out of ideological incompatibility and concrete actions stretching back to World War I and before. The alliance of convenience and necessity against Germany temporarily muted the tensions, but disagreement over the timing of the second front and antagonistic visions of postwar Europe pushed the two nations into a "cold war" only a few months after the victory over the Axis. The Cold War was marked by confrontation and the fear of potential military conflict. The United States vowed to contain communism by any means available.

Meanwhile, the American people, exhausted from a decade and a half of depression and war, turned away from economic reform. They were worried about the alleged Soviet threat in Europe, especially after Russia exploded its own atomic bomb in 1949. They were dismayed by the communist victory in China and perplexed by the limited war in Korea. Many Americans latched onto charges of domestic communist subversion as an explanation for the nation's inability to control world events. No one exploited this mood more effectively than did Joseph McCarthy.

Review Questions

These questions are to be answered with essays. This will allow you to explore relationships between individuals, events, and attitudes of the period under review.

1.   The United States hotly protested Stalin's actions in Poland, East Germany, and the rest of Eastern Europe as a violation of the "one world" principle of the Atlantic Charter and a departure from the agreements reached at Yalta and Potsdam. Aside from pushing for creation of the United Nations, did American policy actually abide by its own principles or was it just as much based on national self-interest as the Soviet Union's?

2.   Explain how the Truman Doctrine, the Marshall Plan, NATO, support for Chiang Kai-shek, and the Korean War were based on the policy of containment. What did that policy concede to the Soviets? How did NSC-68 refine the doctrine? What geopolitical realities limited American options in Asia and Eastern Europe?

3.   What general factors made the United States susceptible to the anticommunist paranoia of 1947 to 1953? What activities fanned the fury and paved the way for the rise of McCarthy?

Chapter Self Test

After you have read the chapter in the text and done the exercises in the Study Guide, take the following self-test to see if you understand the material you have covered. Answers appear at the end of the Study Guide.

MULTIPLE-CHOICE QUESTIONS

Circle the letter of the response that best answers the question or completes the statement.

1. Which was not a source of Soviet bitterness toward the United States in the period before the outbreak of World War II? The United States:
   a. opposed the Bolshevik revolution that created the Soviet Union.
   b. refused to have any economic contact with the Soviet Union in the 1930s.
   c. refused to extend diplomatic recognition to the Soviet Union government until 1933.
   d. sent troops into the Soviet Union toward the end of World War I.

2. Which of the following was the most important source of Soviet resentment about Allied conduct of World War II?
   a. The slowness of the Allies in opening a major second front.
   b. The fact that Russia was not invited to the Casablanca Conference.
   c. The refusal of the United States to include Russia in the lend lease program.
   d. The refusal of the United States to have any official dealing with a communist government.

3. An important reason why Franklin Roosevelt and Winston Churchill agreed at Casablanca (1943) to demand unconditional surrender of the Axis powers was to:
   a. hasten the end of the war.
   b. destroy the morale of the Axis powers.
   c. encourage the Italians to split with Germany.
   d. reassure the Russians that they would not be left abandoned to fight on alone.

4. At Yalta (1945), the Soviet Union gained territorial concessions in Asia in return for agreeing to:
   a. join the United Nations.
   b. enter the war against Japan.
   c. give up reparations from Germany.
   d. give up claims to Polish territory.

5. With respect to the countries of Europe liberated from Nazi control, the Yalta Conference provided for:
   a. permanent Soviet occupation.
   b. a system of United Nations mandates.
   c. interim governments and subsequent free elections.
   d. the withdrawal of the Red Army and immediate self-government.

6. When it became evident that Chiang Kai-shek's nationalist forces were losing the Chinese civil war to Mao Zedong's communists, the Truman administration devoted increased attention to the revitalization of what nation as a strong pro-Western force in Asia?

   a. India

   b. Indonesia

   c. Japan

   d. The Philippines

7. The concept of the policy of containment was most closely associated with:

   a. Douglas MacArthur.

   b. George F. Kennan.

   c. George C. Marshall.

   d. Henry A. Wallace.

8. The Truman Doctrine was initially promulgated in conjunction with U.S. assistance against Soviet pressures in:

   a. Egypt.

   b. Latin America.

   c. Western Europe.

   d. Greece and Turkey.

9. The result of the Marshall Plan aid to the countries of Western Europe was that:

   a. the recipient nations underwent a remarkable economic recovery.

   b. communist influence actually increased in the countries receiving the aid.

   c. the United States economy was nearly bankrupted by this giveaway program.

   d. the recipient nations engaged in bitter competition with one another to gain the largest share of the aid.

10. Three of the following were significant features of the National Security Act of 1947. Which is the *exception?*

    a. It established the CIA.

    b. It abolished the Joint Chiefs of Staff.

    c. It created the National Security Council.

    d. It combined the functions of secretary of war and secretary of navy under one secretary of defense.

11. Truman's response to the Berlin blockade was to:

    a. abandon the Western-occupied portions of Berlin.

    b. airlift all necessary supplies into Berlin for almost a year.

    c. give up plans for uniting the three Western zones of Germany.

    d. use military force to break the blockade of land routes into Berlin.

12. The NATO agreement (1949) required that every member must:

    a. consider an attack on one as an attack on all.

    b. refer all cases of armed aggression to the United Nations.

    c. confer with one another in case of an attack on any member.

    d. do none of the above.

13. Following their defeat in 1949 by the Chinese communists under Mao, Chiang Kai-shek and his nationalist followers:
    a. were executed.
    b. were imprisoned.
    c. fled to Thailand (Burma).
    d. fled to the island of Formosa (Taiwan).

14. Which of the following is *not* an accurate explanation of why the United States avoided the general economic collapse that many feared would occur in 1946–1947 following the end of World War II?
    a. A multi-billion dollar tax cut.
    b. The release of pent-up civilian consumer demand.
    c. Significant government spending for veterans' benefits.
    d. Military spending remained almost at wartime levels due to the Cold War.

15. Truman's domestic social and economic program after World War II was known as the:
    a. Fair Deal.
    b. Square Deal.
    c. New Frontier.
    d. New Deal Revisited.

16. The significance of the midterm elections of 1946 was that:
    a. Truman's domestic policy won a vote of confidence.
    b. the voting public demanded more radical governmental reforms.
    c. the Republicans won control of both the House and the Senate.
    d. in a political upset, the Democrats regained control of both the House and the Senate.

17. Truman's position on the Taft-Hartley Act was favorable to:
    a. farming.
    b. big business.
    c. organized labor.
    d. southern conservatives.

18. In 1948, Strom Thurmond and the "Dixiecrats" opposed Truman's policy on _____, whereas Henry A. Wallace and the Progressives opposed Truman's _____ policy.
    a. civil rights, confrontational Cold War
    b. the Cold War, aggressive civil rights
    c. economic reconversion, the Social Security system
    d. the Social Security system, economic reconversion

19. After the election of 1948, Truman succeeded in getting three of the following parts of his domestic program passed. Which one did Congress *not* approve?
    a. increase of the minimum wage
    b. expansion of the Social Security system
    c. federal construction of low-income housing
    d. a civil rights act including the Fair Employment Practices Commission

20. When Japanese control of Korea ended as a result of Japanese defeat in World War II, Korea was:

    a. occupied entirely by United States forces.

    b. occupied by the same four powers as in Germany.

    c. united under the nationalist government of Syngman Rhee.

    d. divided into United States and Soviet zones of occupation.

TRUE-FALSE QUESTIONS

Read each statement carefully. Mark true statements "T" and false statements "F."

1. According to "Where Historians Disagree," the new "post revisionist" literature on the Cold War tends to stress that U. S. actions were most responsible for creating the Cold War climate.

2. Franklin D. Roosevelt was committed to a "one world" vision that downplayed spheres of influence and stressed the importance of international cooperation.

3. One reason that the Soviet Union was able to obtain such favorable treatment at the Yalta Conference was the inexperience of the new President Harry Truman.

4. The plan for the postwar United Nations was agreed to by the Allies and others before the end of World War II.

5. The United States believed that the Soviet Union complied with the Yalta accords in Poland, but Great Britain argued that the Soviets had violated the spirit of Yalta.

6. By the late 1940s, the Chinese government of Chiang Kai-shek was corrupt, incompetent, and lacking in broad popular support.

7. Mao Zedong and the Communists launched their eventual conquest of China from their stronghold on the island of Formosa.

8. The Truman Doctrine declared that the United States would intervene in foreign affairs only when U.S. economic or strategic interests were directly at stake.

9. The Marshall Plan was originally offered to the Soviet Union and the Eastern European nations but they declined to participate.

10. The Atomic Energy Commission was created to promote civilian use of nuclear energy while the Department of Defense would retain authority over military nuclear research and development.

11. The major weakness of NATO was that it lacked any provisions for cooperative military command.

12. Berlin was surrounded by the Soviet occupation zone in Germany.

13. The food and supplies that reached Berlin during the blockade were brought in by air.

14. Although the United States apparently expected that it would take Soviet scientists and technicians several more years to develop an atomic weapon, the Soviet Union exploded its first atomic bomb in 1949.

15. A major problem for returning servicemen after World War II was finding industrial jobs, since a large portion of the positions were now occupied by women.

16. The "right-to-work" provision of the Taft-Hartley Act allowed individual states to pass laws banning the so-called union shop in which workers in an organized plant had to join the union after they were hired, if they were not already members.

17. The Americans for Democratic Action was politically liberal.

18. One of the most influential anticommunist crusaders of the late 1940s and early 1950s, other than Joseph McCarthy, was Alger Hiss.

19. Julius and Ethel Rosenberg led the fight against McCarthyism.

20. In 1952, the Democrats were so split by the civil rights and anticommunist issues that they could not unify on a single nominee, so Adlai Stevenson and J. Edgar Hoover split the Democratic vote.

CHAPTER THIRTY
THE AFFLUENT SOCIETY

Objectives

A thorough study of Chapter 30 should enable the student to understand:

1. The strengths and weaknesses of the economy in the 1950s and early 1960s.
2. The changes in the American lifestyle in the 1950s.
3. The significance of the Supreme Court's desegregation decision and the early civil rights movement.
4. The characteristics of Dwight Eisenhower's middle-of-the-road domestic policy.
5. The new elements of American foreign policy introduced by Secretary of State John Foster Dulles.
6. The causes and results of increasing United States involvement in the Middle East.
7. The sources of difficulties for the United States in Latin America.
8. The reasons for new tensions with the Soviet Union toward the end of the Eisenhower administration.

Main Themes

1. That the technological, consumer-oriented society of the 1950s was remarkably affluent and unified despite the persistence of a less privileged underclass and the existence of a small corps of detractors.
2. How the Supreme Court's social desegregation decision of 1954 marked the beginning of a civil-rights revolution for American blacks.
3. How President Dwight Eisenhower presided over a business-oriented "dynamic conservatism" that resisted most new reforms without significantly rolling back the activist government programs born in the 1930s.
4. That while Eisenhower continued to allow containment by building alliances, supporting anticommunist regimes, maintaining the arms race, and conducting limited interventions, he also showed an awareness of American limitations and resisted temptations for greater commitments.

Glossary

1. Third World: A convenient way to refer to all the nations of the world besides the United States, Canada, the Soviet Union, Japan, Australia, New Zealand, Israel, China, and the countries of Europe. Basically, the Third World is made up of the less industrially developed regions of Asia, Africa, and Latin America. The term sometimes also excludes Mexico, South Africa, and much of the oil-rich Middle East.
2. Zionists: Members of a militant worldwide movement dedicated to the goal of establishing a Jewish nation in Palestine. The Zionist movement took its name from a hill in Jerusalem on which Solomon's Temple had been built.
3. summit conference: A diplomatic meeting of the heads of government of major nations; that is, a conference held at the summit of power.

Pertinent Questions

THE ECONOMIC "MIRACLE" (790-793)

1. What were the causes of the great economic growth from 1945 to 1960? What was the impact on the American standard of living?

2. Why did the West grow faster than the rest of the nation in the post–World War II era?

3. Explain Keynesian economic theory. How did the developments of the 1950s and early 1960s seem to confirm the theory?

4. What was the post war trend in economic consolidation?

5. What was the nature of the "postwar contract" that developed between big labor and big business? What were "escalator clauses"?

6. How was the labor movement hampered by scandal, new government restrictions, and other factors?

THE EXPLOSION OF SCIENCE AND TECHNOLOGY (793-798)

7. Describe the major medical advances of the mid twentieth century. What was the societal result?

8. What key developments in electronics in the 1950s and 1960s transformed consumer and industrial products and paved the way for the computer revolution?

9. How did America react to the Soviet *Sputnik*? What was the result?

PEOPLE OF PLENTY (798-807)

10. Explain the expanded role of advertising and consumer credit. Why can it be said that the prosperity of the 1950s and 1960s was substantially consumer-driven?

11. What was the impact of the automobile and the super highway on metropolitan development patterns, especially the traditional downtown? What was the impact of the automobile culture on railroads, energy consumption, air pollution, and retailing?

12. What was the appeal of Levittown and similar suburban developments? How did typical suburbs transform family life and shape women's attitudes?

13. Why can it be said that television "was central to the culture of the postwar era?" How did the medium simultaneously unify and alienate Americans?

14. How did writers in the 1950s respond to the growing tension between an organized, bureaucratic society and the tradition of individualism?

15. What were the manifestations of the widespread restlessness among young Americans in the 1950s?

16. How did the music of African Americans influence the development of rock and roll? To what extent was the audience multi-racial?

THE "OTHER AMERICA" (807-809)

17. What groups in society seemed mired in "hard core" poverty largely outside the prosperity of the 1950s? Why?

18. What demographic shifts occurred in minority population during WWII and the postwar era?

19. Compare and contrast rural poverty and inner-city poverty. What was the result of the "urban renewal" program?

THE RISE OF THE CIVIL RIGHTS MOVEMENT (809-812)

20. On what reasoning did the Supreme Court base its *Brown v. Board of Education* ruling?

21. Describe the "massive resistance" pattern reflected in the Deep South. What did President Eisenhower do in response to the open defiance in Little Rock?

22. What was the importance of the Montgomery, Alabama, bus boycott?

23. What philosophy shaped the approach of Martin Luther King, Jr., to civil rights protest? Why did he become the principal leader and symbol of the movement?

24. What forces within the African American community led to the civil rights movement of the 1950s? Why was the movement able to attract notable non-southern white support?

EISENHOWER REPUBLICANISM (812-813)

25. From what segment of society did President Dwight Eisenhower draw most of the members of his administration? How did these individuals differ from their 1920s counterparts of similar background?

26. How did the domestic policies of the Eisenhower administration compare and contrast with Roosevelt and Truman administrations?

27. Even though anticommunist sentiment did not disappear, what led to the demise of Senator Joseph McCarthy?

EISENHOWER, DULLES, AND THE COLD WAR (813-818)

28. Why did John Foster Dulles move the United States toward the policy of massive retaliation?

29. How did the Korean War end?

30. Describe the background of the struggle in Southeast Asia. How did the United States respond to the French predicament at Dien Bien Phu?

31. What role did the United States play in the creation of modern Israel?

32. Why was the United States so committed to friendliness and stability in the Middle East? How was this approach implemented in Iran?

33. What led to the Suez Crisis of 1956? What position did the United States take?

34. What led to Fidel Castro's rise in Cuba? How did the United States deal with his new regime at first and why did the American position quickly change?

35. What international episodes during the Eisenhower administration illustrated that the Cold War persisted but that the U.S. would exercise restraint?

PATTERNS OF POPULAR CULTURE: LUCY AND DESI (804-805)

36. What did Lucille Ball mean when she said that the success of the show was that "We just took ordinary situations and exaggerated them."? What one thing about her situation that was a bit out of the ordinary almost kept the show from ever airing?

Identification

Identify each of the following, and explain why it is important within the context of the chapter.

1. baby boom
2. AFL-CIO
3. Salk vaccine
4. DDT
5. UNIVAC
6. IBM
7. hydrogen bomb
8. ICBM
9. NASA

10. Neil Armstrong and Edwin Aldrin

11. space shuttle

12. Disney

13. Benjamin Spock

14. Echo Park

15. Sierra Club

16. "beatniks"

17. "juvenile delinquency"

18. Elvis Presley

19. "disk jockey" and "payola"

20. Earl Warren

21. Rosa Parks

22. Jackie Robinson

23. Federal (Interstate) Highway Act of 1956

24. John Foster Dulles

25. Ho Chi Minh

26. Hungarian Revolution

27. U-2 crisis

28. Nikita Khrushchev

29. "military-industrial complex"

Documents

Read the section of the text under the heading "The Rise of the Civil Rights Movement," paying special attention to the subsection on "The Brown Decision and 'Massive Resistance.'" The documents below include excerpts from the Supreme Court decision in *Brown* and from a resolution of the all-white South Carolina State Senate defying the decision and its follow-up implementation rulings. Sentiments similar to the South Carolina resolution were expressed in other southern state legislatures and in the "Southern Manifesto" signed by nineteen U.S. senators and eighty-two congressmen. It was in this same mood that the General Assembly in Georgia changed the state flag from one based on the "stars and bars" of the Confederacy to one containing the more familiar Confederate battle flag, which had come to be a widely recognized symbol of white resistance to racial integration. Consider the following questions: Why was it important for the Court to stress that it could not "turn the clock back" in considering the impact of segregation? What is the significance of the Court's distinction between physical equality and true educational equality? Which do you think truly bothered the South Carolina legislator more, the constitutional principles or the issue of race?

Brown et al. v. Board of Education of Topeka et al. (1954)

Mr. Chief Justice Warren delivered the opinion of the Court. In each of the cases, minors of the Negro race . . . seek the aid of the courts in obtaining admission to the public schools of their community on a nonsegregated basis. In each instance, they had been denied admission to schools attended by white children under laws requiring or permitting segregation according to race. This segregation was alleged to deprive the plaintiffs of the equal protection of the laws under the Fourteenth Amendment. . . . The plaintiffs contend that segregated public schools are not "equal" and cannot be made "equal." . . . The Negro and white school involved have been equalized, or are being equalized, with respect to buildings, curricula, qualifications and salaries of teachers, and other "tangible" factors. Our decision, therefore, cannot turn on merely a comparison of these tangible factors. . . . We must look instead to the effect of segregation itself on public education.

In approaching this problem, we cannot turn the clock back to 1868 when the Amendment was adopted, or even to 1896 when *Plessy v. Ferguson* was written. We must consider public education in light of its full development and its present place in American life. . . .

We come then to the question presented: Does segregation of children in public school solely on the basis of race even though the physical facilities and other "tangible" factors may be equal, deprive the children of the minority group of equal educational opportunity? We believe that it does. . . .

To separate [children] from others of similar age and qualifications solely because of their race generates a feeling of inferiority as to their status in the community that may affect their hearts and minds in a way unlikely ever to be undone. . . .

We conclude that in the field of public education the doctrine of "separate but equal" has no place. Separate educational facilities are inherently unequal.

* * *

JOINT RESOLUTION OF THE STATE OF SOUTH CAROLINA, Feb. 14, 1956.

. . . The right of each of the States to maintain at its own expense racially separate public schools for the children of its citizens and other racially separate public facilities is not forbidden or limited by the language or the intent of the Fourteenth Amendment. . . . For almost sixty years, beginning in 1896, an unbroken line of decisions of the [U.S. Supreme] Court interpreted the Fourteenth Amendment as recognizing the right of the States to maintain racially separate public facilities for their people. . . . The Supreme Court of the United States on May 17, 1954, relying on its own views of sociology and psychology, for the first time held that the Fourteenth Amendment prohibited the States from maintaining racially separate public schools and since then the Court has enlarged this to include other public facilities. . . . Be it enacted by the General Assembly of the State of South Carolina: . . . That the States have never delegated to the central government the power to change the Constitution nor have they surrendered to the central government the power to prohibit to the States the right to maintain racially separate but equal public facilities.

Map Exercise

Fill in or identify the following on the blank map provided. Use the maps and narrative in your text as your source.

1. Shade in those states that had at least a 10 percent black population by 1980 and that had less than 10 percent in 1910. (Use the maps on pp. 645 and 804 of your text.)
2. Identify Chicago, New York, Los Angeles, and the Appalachia region.

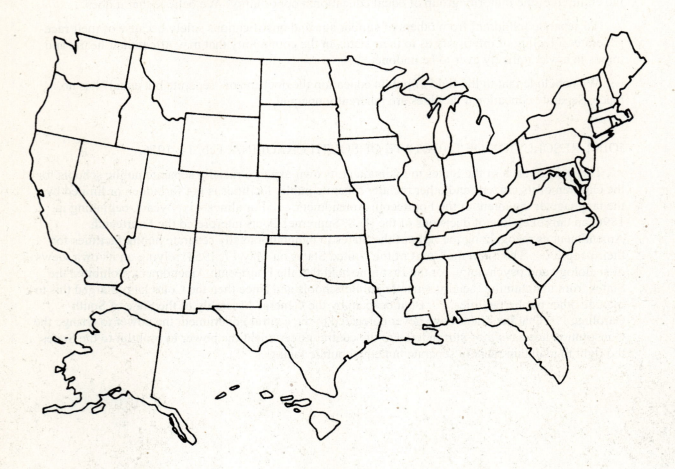

Interpretive Questions

Based on what you have filled in, answer the following. On some of the questions you will need to consult the narrative in your text for information or explanation.

1. What forces that had drawn blacks northward during the "Great Migration" continued to operate during and after World War II? (What new enticements were there?)
2. Although the focus of the civil rights movement was on the southern states, what problems did many northern blacks, especially those in the inner cities, face?

Summary

From the late 1940s through the 1950s, the United States experienced continued economic growth and low unemployment. Most of the nation participated in the prosperity and agreed about the beneficence of

American capitalism. Only a few intellectuals questioned the rampant consumerism and the values of the growing corporate bureaucracies. The politics of the period, symbolized by President Eisenhower the cautious war hero, reelected the popular contentment. African Americans, inspired by the *Brown* school desegregation decision, began the protests that would bring the civil rights revolution of the 1960s. Locked into a policy of containment and a rigidly dualistic worldview, the United States was less successful in its overseas undertakings. Despite a string of alliances, an awesome nuclear arsenal, and vigorous use of covert operations, the nation often found itself unable to shape world events to conform to American desires.

Review Questions

These questions are to be answered with essays. This will allow you to explore relationships between individuals, events, and attitudes of the period under review.

1. Analyze the causes and consequences of the economic boom of the 1950s. Were the Keynesians correct in asserting that government action could ensure both economic stability and economic growth?

2. Describe the tendency toward economic consolidation in business, agriculture, and labor. How did this change the American economy?

3. Did the assumptions of containment lead the United States into unwise commitments and actions in Southeast Asia, Latin America, and the Middle East, or was the nation acting prudently in response to hostile communist expansionism?

4. What new cultural developments accompanied the prosperity and suburbanization of the 1950s? How did intellectuals regard the highly organized and homogenized new society?

Chapter Self Test

After you have read the chapter in the text and done the exercises in the Study Guide, take the following self test to see if you understand the material you have covered. Answers appear at the end of the Study Guide.

MULTIPLE-CHOICE QUESTIONS

Circle the letter of the response that best answers the question or completes the statement.

1. America's economic prosperity in the 1950s was fueled by:
   a. increased public funding of schools, housing, veterans' benefits, welfare, and interstate highways.
   b. massive cold-war-inspired military spending.
   c. the "baby boom" and rapid expansion of the suburbs.
   d. all of the above.
   e. none of the above.

353

2. Which portion of the nation grew most rapidly during the late 1940s and 1950s?
   a. Northeast
   b. Southeast
   c. Midwest/Great Plains
   d. West

3. According to the principles of Keynesian economics, which of the following tactics should government employ to combat recession?
   a. Reduce interest rates.
   b. Cut the federal budget.
   c. Raise taxes.
   d. All of the above.

4. Keynesian economics seemed to offer government the proper theories to eliminate forever the problems of:
   a. maldistributed wealth.
   b. trade deficits.
   c. financial injustice.
   d. economic instability.

5. The prosperity of the 1950s was accompanied by:
   a. a decrease in government spending.
   b. corporate mergers and the formation of conglomerates.
   c. equitable distribution of corporate profits.
   d. the survival and renewal of the family farm.

6. All of the following trends marked the American labor movement of the 1950s *except:*
   a. merger of the AFL and CIO to create the giant federation, the AFL-CIO.
   b. fairly stable membership numbers.
   c. greater success in organizing new workers than in winning benefits for workers already organized in strong unions.
   d. signs of corruption and indifference among some labor leaders as the unions themselves became wealthy, powerful bureaucracies.

7. Which TWO of the following were major developments in allowing electronic devices to become smaller and cheaper in the 1950s and later.
   a. transistors
   b. vacuum tubes
   c. thermal fuses
   d. integrated circuits

8. According to many social observers, American culture in the 1950s seemed dominated by a(n):
   a. restless search by individuals for identity and purpose.
   b. quest for economic political justice within the United States.
   c. absorption with consumer goods by a growing middle class.
   d. isolationist desire to avoid international affairs or commitments.

9. In contrast to that of the central cities, life in suburbia became attractive to many American families in the 1950s because the suburbs seemed to provide:

   a. variety and excitement in lifestyles and entertainment.

   b. racial integration in neighborhoods and schools.

   c. greater opportunities for cultural and educational advancement.

   d. larger, safer, and more private homes.

10. According to the widely respected child-care expert of the late 1940s and 1950s, Dr. Benjamin Spock, mothers should:

   a. fulfill their career and professional goals.

   b. subordinate their activities and interests to the needs of their children.

   c. share the role of parenting equally with the fathers.

   d. work to supplement the family income.

11. According to the text, during the 1950s, television:

   a. affected only a small percentage of the total population.

   b. encouraged independent value formation among members of the white middle class.

   c. heightened the sense of alienation and powerlessness among minority groups.

   d. failed to attract significant interest from commercial advertisers.

12. According to the text, the most widely revered heroes of the United States during the early 1960s were the nation's:

   a. medical researchers.

   b. professional athletes.

   c. astronauts.

   d. industrial tycoons.

13. The United States accomplished which of the following feats *before* the Soviet Union did?

   a. launching of a satellite into outer space

   b. sending a manned flight into outer space

   c. landing a man on the surface of the moon

   d. *none* of the above

   e. *all* of the above

14. Three of the following statements accurately describe the American economic and demographic conditions in the 1950s. Which is the *exception?*

   a. The rate of population growth declined.

   b. There was a continual annual growth in GNP.

   c. Unemployment was a tolerable 5 percent or less.

   d. Inflation was in the range of a modest 3 percent per year.

15. When the governor of Arkansas and, later, an angry mob of citizens attempted to prevent the court-ordered racial integration of a high school in Little Rock, President Eisenhower responded by:

a. ordering the Governor to be arrested.

b. negotiating a settlement that delayed local integration for a three-year "cooling-off" period.

c. sending federal troops to uphold the court order.

d. refusing to involve the federal government in what he considered to be strictly a state matter.

16. The Montgomery, Alabama, bus boycott was significant in establishing a new form of racial protest and in elevating which black leader to prominence as a new leader in the civil rights movement?

a. Malcolm X

b. H. Rap Brown

c. Stokely Carmichael

d. Martin Luther King, Jr.

17. The black man who broke the race barrier in major league baseball was:

a. Henry Aaron.

b. Roy Campanella.

c. Willie Mays.

d. Jackie Robinson.

18. Joseph McCarthy's influence in the nation waned quickly mainly as a consequence of:

a. the Oppenheimer case.

b. his expulsion from the Senate.

c. the reports that he was an alcoholic.

d. his behavior in the Army-McCarthy hearings.

19. The expression "more bang for a buck" was related to Secretary of State John Foster Dulles's announced policy of:

a. liberation.

b. containment.

c. mutual security.

d. massive retaliation.

20. In his farewell address in January 1961, Eisenhower warned the American people against:

a. the rise of military pacifism.

b. the tendency to hysterical anticommunism.

c. the risk of creeping socialism.

d. the influence of the military-industrial complex.

TRUE-FALSE QUESTIONS

Read each statement carefully. Mark true statements "T" and false statements "F."

1. From 1945 to 1960 the American economy grew significantly because of rapid population growth, but the growth was misleading because the economy was actually declining in real per capita dollars.

2. Even though IBM (International Business Machines) had not been a pioneer in the invention of the computer, its superior marketing approach to business made it the world leader in the computer business of the 1950s and 1960s.

3. In 1955 the American Federation of Labor (AFL) and the Congress of Industrial Organizations (CIO) split due to philosophical differences and did not reunify until the early 1980s.

4. The effect of "escalator clauses" in union contracts was to base wages on seniority.

5. A major reason for the growth of the western United States was that the region received a disproportionate amount of federal spending, including military contracts.

6. The economic expansion that followed the Kennedy-Johnson tax cuts was an example of a successful application of Keynesian economic theory.

7. Although most middle-class families had TV by the end of the 1950s, television was not available in the majority of American homes until about 1965.

8. The major radio networks resisted television, so the emerging medium was mostly controlled by new corporations in California.

9. One result of the launching of *Sputnik* was that American schools began to give increasing emphasis to math and science.

10. The "beats," or "beatniks," argued that American life and culture was mostly sterile, conformist, and banal.

11. In the 1950s, Native Americans were the most economically deprived group, even more so than Hispanics and African Americans.

12. The term "massive resistance" was generally used to signify the widespread efforts on behalf of racial desegregation such as sit-ins, boycotts, marches, and so on.

13. The Chief Justice of the U.S. Supreme Court at the time of the *Brown v. Board of Education* ruling was Earl Warren.

14. Martin Luther King, Jr., drew much of his philosophy of nonviolent, passive opposition to segregation from the teaching of Mahatma Gandhi of India.

15. Secretary of State John Foster Dulles believed that the U.S. military had placed too much reliance on the atomic bomb and "massive retaliation" strategy, so he began to shift military spending priorities toward "flexible response."

16. Before the Eisenhower administration learned that Fidel Castro was a communist, significant military aid was funneled to his rebels who were attempting to overthrow the corrupt anti-American dictator of Cuba.

17. The Korean War ended very early in the Eisenhower administration with an armistice that left the Korean peninsula divided at approximately the 38th parallel.

18. The United States armed the rebels in the Hungarian Revolution, but refused at the last minute to provide air cover as promised by the CIA.

19. In 1948 when the Jews in Palestine proclaimed the existence of the independent nation of Israel, President Truman delayed for several months extending diplomatic recognition to the new nation because he did not want to offend the oil-rich Arab countries.

CHAPTER THIRTY-ONE
CIVIL RIGHTS, VIETNAM, AND THE ORDEAL OF LIBERALISM

Objectives

A thorough study of Chapter 31 should enable the student to understand

1. The new directions of domestic reform manifested by John Kennedy's New Frontier program.
2. The new elements added to Kennedy's program by Lyndon Johnson's Great Society proposals.
3. The reasons the African American movement became increasingly assertive in the 1960s.
4. The significance of Martin Luther King, Jr. to the civil-rights movement and the importance of other forces including the Nation of Islam.
5. The new elements that Kennedy introduced in both the nation's defense strategy and its foreign policy.
6. The background and sequence of events leading to the Cuban missile crisis.
7. How the United States became committed to defending the government in the southern part of Vietnam and the reasons that U. S. involvement in Vietnam changed both quantitatively and qualitatively in 1965.
8. The reasons the 1968 Tet Offensive had such a critical impact on both American policy toward Vietnam and domestic policies.
9. The reasons why 1968 was such a critical year in American politics and in our relationship with other nations.

Main Themes

1. How Lyndon Johnson used the legacy of John Kennedy plus his own political skill to erect his Great Society and fight the war on poverty with programs for health, education, job training, and urban development.
2. How the civil-rights movement finally generated enough sympathy among whites to accomplish the legal end of segregation, but the persistence of racism gave rise to the black power philosophy and left many problems unsolved.
3. How containment and the U. S. preoccupation with communism led the nation to use military force against leftist nationalist movements in Cuba, the Dominican Republic, and, most disastrously, Vietnam.
4. How 1968 became a critical year for American liberalism.

Chronology of the War in Indochina

Because American involvement in Indochina stretched from the 1940s through the 1970s, the material is in several chapters. This chronology will help you see the entire span of the Vietnam War.

1945–1954 Ho Chi Minh led the fight against French colonialism
1950   United States was paying for most of the French effort
1954   French defeated at Dien Bien Phu

	Geneva Conference partitioned Indochina
1956	President Diem refused to hold reunification elections
1959	National Liberation Front (NLF) (Viet Cong) organized
	About 650 American advisers in South Vietnam
1963	Diem deposed and killed
	About 15,000 American advisers in South Vietnam
1964	Gulf of Tonkin Resolution passed
1965	Thieu government established
	American bombing of North Vietnam began
	180,000 American troops in Vietnam
1966	Fulbright hearings began
	300,000 American troops in Vietnam
1967	Major antiwar protests began
	500,000 American troops in Vietnam
1968	January Tet offense
	March Johnson announced bombing pause and his withdrawal from the presidential race
1969	American troop strength peaked at 540,000
1970	May Cambodia invaded
	Kent State and Jackson State incidents
	December Gulf of Tonkin Resolution repealed
1971	Pentagon papers released
1972	Spring Hanoi and Haiphong bombed
	Fall American troop strength down to 60,000
	December "Christmas bombings"
1973	Cease-fire; Paris accords
1975	Vietnam unified by North Vietnam's victory
1978	Vietnam invaded Cambodia
	China invaded Vietnam

Glossary

1. fiscal and monetary policy: The practice of influencing the economy through manipulation of government spending (fiscal) and the money supply (monetary).

2. affirmative action: The policy of making a special effort to provide jobs, college admission, or other benefits to members of a group that was previously discriminated against, such as blacks or women.

Pertinent Questions

EXPANDING THE LIBERAL STATE (822-826)

1. Describe John F. Kennedy's background and his conception of the role of the president. How did his New Frontier fare?

2. How did Lyndon Johnson differ from Kennedy in personality and in ability to influence Congress? What did he call his program?

3.   What were the purposes of Medicare and Medicaid? What limits and what problems kept government health programs controversial?

4.   What agency was the "centerpiece" of Johnson's "war on poverty"? How successful was the war at reducing poverty?

5.   Who opposed federal aid to education? How did Johnson's legislation manage to circumvent much of the opposition?

6.   How did the Immigration Act of 1965 change the characteristics of migration to the United States?

7.   How did the effort to fund both the Great Society and a great military establishment affect the federal budget? What was the effect on the nation's poverty rate?

THE BATTLE FOR RACIAL EQUALITY (826-832)

8.   Describe the events of 1960 to 1963 that brought the civil rights movement to the forefront of national attention. How did President Kennedy respond to increasing black activism and southern white resistance?

9.   What were the results of "freedom summer" and the Selma march?

10.   Describe the shift in black population that had occurred by the mid-1960s. What implications did this shift have on the nature of the civil rights movement?

11.   Describe the race riots of 1964 to 1967, indicating which was the first major one and which was the largest. What reasons for the riots and what appropriate response to them did the Commission on Civil Disorder suggest? How did many white Americans react to the disorder?

12.   What did "black power" mean? What impact did it have on the civil rights movement and on the attitudes of American blacks in general?

WHERE HISTORIANS DISAGREE – THE CIVIL RIGHTS MOVEMENT (828-829)

13.   Compare and contrast the "leader-centered" narrative of the civil rights movement to the "rank and
file" theory. Also, how have historians looked at the following: the beginnings of the civil rights movement, leaders in the movement, the Black Power movement, and the famous *Brown* decision?
Was there one monolithic civil rights movement? Or were there many civil rights movements?

"FLEXIBLE RESPONSE" AND THE COLD WAR (832-834)

14.   What did Kennedy do to provide the United States with a more flexible response capability?

15.   What were the purpose and the result of the Bay of Pigs invasion?

16.   What precipitated the Cuban Missile crisis? How was it resolved and how did it shape future Soviet policy?

17.   Why did Lyndon Johnson send troops to the Dominican Republic? Was the action reminiscent of the interventions in the days of the Roosevelt corollary?

THE AGONY OF VIETNAM (834-843)

18.   How did the United States end up supporting the French in the First Indochina War? Was it the correct decision? What was the result?

19.   Describe the cultural and economic differences between the northern and southern parts of Vietnam. How did these differences shape the conflict between the two?

20.   Why did Ngo Dinh Diem, with U.S. support, refuse to hold the 1956 reunification elections called for by the Geneva accords?

21.   What were President Ngo Dinh Diem's political problems and what led to his demise?

22. What assumptions and advice led Lyndon Johnson to his major commitment to aid the government in southern Vietnam? What incident did he use to give the war an appearance of legality?

23. Recount Johnson's escalation of the Vietnam War. Why were the American strategies of "attrition" and "pacification" unable to achieve victory? What kept Johnson from expanding American action even further?

24. Why does the text refer to the Vietnam War in the mid 1960s as a "quagmire"? Why did the "hearts and minds" strategy fail?

25. Where did opposition to the war originate? How did it spread?

THE TRAUMAS OF 1968 (843-849)

26. What effect did the Tet Offensive have on American public opinion concerning the war and on the course of the 1968 presidential election?

27. How did the nation respond to the assassination of Martin Luther King, Jr.?

28. How did conservative Americans respond to such events as race riots, antiwar demonstrations, and the assassinations of Robert Kennedy and King? How did Richard Nixon capitalize on these anxieties? What other politician tried to ride such feelings to the White House?

WHERE HISTORIANS DISAGREE: THE VIETNAM COMMITMENT (836-837)

29. What has the work of historians revealed about the motives, assumptions, and decisions that led to prolonged American involvement in Indochina? How might events have been different if John F. Kennedy had not been assassinated?

PATTERNS OF POPULAR CULTURE: THE FOLK MUSIC REVIVAL (842-843)

30. Why did the message of folk music, "that there is a 'real' America rooted in values of sharing and community," exert such a strong appeal to many American youths in the 1960s?

AMERICA IN THE WORLD: 1968 (844-845)

31. Compare and contrast the events of 1968 in the U. S. with those in other countries. What two factors combined to create fertile ground for disruptions?

<u>Identification</u>

Identify each of the following and explain why it is important within the context of the chapter.

1. Richard Nixon

2. Lee Harvey Oswald

3. Warren Commission

4. Barry Goldwater

5. Robert Weaver

6. sit-in

7. Student Nonviolent Coordinating Committee (SNCC)

8. Congress of Racial Equality (CORE)

9. Southern Christian Leadership Conference (SCLC)

10. George Wallace

11. "affirmative action"

12. "I have a dream"

13. *de jure* and *de facto* segregation

14. Black Panthers

15. Malcolm X

16. Green Berets

17. "Alliance for Progress"

18. Agency for International Development (AID)

19. Peace Corps

20. Berlin Wall

21. Nikita Khrushchev

22. Ho Chi Minh

23. Viet Cong/National Liberation Front (NLF)

24. Dean Rusk

25. Robert McNamara

26. Gulf of Tonkin Resolution

27. Ho Chi Minh Trail

28. Eugene McCarthy

29. Hubert Humphrey

30. "silent majority"/"middle America"

Document 1

Read the sections of Chapter Thirty-One that deal with the war in Vietnam. Also review the relevant parts of earlier chapters. The first selection is from a speech given by President Lyndon Johnson on April 7, 1965 at Johns Hopkins University. The second selection was written in the early 1960s by a staff member of the Defense Department. It was prepared for the historical analysis section of the classified report that became known as the Pentagon Papers after it was leaked to the press in 1971. Consider the following questions: Which was more accurate—Johnson's public declaration of South Vietnam as a "small and brave nation" or the Pentagon Papers' characterization of it as "the creation of the United States"? Should the war in Vietnam be portrayed principally as a civil war or as a response to aggression? Despite the obvious difference in rhetoric and candor, do the two documents really differ on the question "Why are we in South Vietnam?"

> Why are we in South Vietnam? We are there because we have a promise to keep. Since 1954 every American President has offered to support the people of South Vietnam. We have helped to build and we have helped to defend. Thus, over many years, we have made a national pledge to help South Vietnam defend its independence. I intend to keep our promise. To dishonor that pledge, to abandon this small and brave nation to its enemy—and to the terror that must follow—would be an unforgivable wrong. We are there to strengthen world order. Around the globe—from Berlin to Thailand—are people whose well-being rests, in part, on the belief they can count on us if they are attacked. To leave Vietnam to its fate would shake the confidence of all these people in the value of American commitment. The result would be increased unrest and instability, or even war.

Lyndon Johnson, Speech at Johns Hopkins University, April 7, 1965.

* * *

HISTORICAL ANALYSIS: The Special American Commitment to Vietnam

Finally, in this review of factors that would affect policy-making in Vietnam, we must note that South Vietnam (unlike any of the other countries in Southeast Asia) was essentially the creation of the United States.

Without U.S. support Diem almost certainly could not have consolidated his hold on the South during 1955 and 1956.

Without the threat of U.S. intervention, South Vietnam could not have refused to even discuss the elections called for in 1956 under the Geneva settlement without being immediately overrun by the Viet Minh armies.

Without U.S. aid in the years following, the Diem regime certainly, and an independent South Vietnam almost as certainly, could not have survived.

U.S. Department of Defense, *United States-Vietnamese Relations 1945–1967* (Washington, D.C.: House Committee on Armed Services, 1971), Book 2 (IV.B.1.), pp. 6–7.

Document 2

Read the section of the chapter under the heading "Urban Violence." The document below is drawn from the 1967 report of the National Commission on Civil Disorders, often called the Kerner Commission because it was headed by Governor Otto Kerner of Illinois. Consider the following questions: Why did the riots come at a time when blacks were making legal gains? How would conservative whites react to the commission's findings? What traditional American values does the report affront? What values does it affirm? More than thirty years later, how close is America to realizing the vision of the Kerner Commission? Does the elimination of racism remain "the major unfinished business of this nation"?

This is our basic conclusion: Our nation is moving toward two societies, one black, one white—separate and unequal.

Reaction to last summer's disorders has quickened the movement and deepened the division. Discrimination and segregation have long permeated much of American life; they now threaten the future of every American.

This deepening racial division is not inevitable. The movement apart can be reversed. Choice is still possible. Our principal task is to define that choice and to press for a national resolution.

To pursue our present course will involve the continuing polarization of the American community and, ultimately, the destruction of basic democratic values.

The alternative is not blind repression or capitulation to lawlessness. It is the realization of common opportunities for all within a single society.

This alternative will require a commitment to national action—compassionate, massive and sustained, backed by the resources of the most powerful and the richest nation on this earth. From every American it will require new attitudes, new understanding, and, above all, new will.

The vital needs of the nation must be met; hard choices must be made, and, if necessary, new taxes enacted.

Violence cannot build a better society. Disruption and disorder nourish repression, not justice. They strike at the freedom of every citizen. The community cannot—it will not—tolerate coercion and mob rule.

Violence and destruction must be ended—in the streets of the ghetto and in the lives of people.

Segregation and poverty have created in the racial ghetto a destructive environment totally unknown to most white Americans.

What white Americans have never fully understood—but what the Negro can never forget—is that white society is deeply implicated in the ghetto. White institutions created it, white institutions maintain it, and white society condones it.

It is time now to turn with all the purpose at our command to the major unfinished business of this nation. It is time to adopt strategies for action that will produce quick and visible progress. It is time to make good the promises of American democracy to all citizens—urban and rural, white and black, Spanish-surname, American Indian, and every minority group.

National Commission on Civil Disorders, 1967.

Map Exercise

Fill in or identify the following on the blank map provided.

1. All countries.
2. Mekong Delta and Gulf of Tonkin.
3. Hanoi, Saigon, Haiphong, Phnom Penh, and Bangkok.
4. DMZ.

Interpretive Questions

Based on what you have filled in, answer the following. On some of the questions you will need to consult the narrative in your text for information or explanation.

1. Why did the United States oppose independence for Vietnam after World War II and get dragged into the conflicts in Indochina? How did Vietnam get temporarily divided?

2. From what internal and external sources did the Viet Cong receive their support? How did this make them so difficult to defeat?

3. What trap of competing factors kept Lyndon Johnson from either withdrawing or further escalating the war? How did the geographic position of Indochina in relation to China affect this trap?

Summary

The 1960s began with John F. Kennedy squeezing out one of the narrowest presidential victories in United States history. Three years later he was dead, and it was up to Lyndon Johnson to carry through his liberal legacy. The first three years of Johnson's presidency were legislatively one of the most productive periods ever, as Congress passed many of the civil rights, health, education, and welfare measures of the Great Society. In 1961, the nation bungled an attempt to dislodge Castro from Cuba, and a year and a half later, the world came to the brink of nuclear war during the Cuban missile crisis. By the latter half of the decade, the foreign policy focus had moved halfway around the world. By the end of 1967, the United States had 500,000 troops in Southeast Asia and the Vietnam War had become the central issue of American politics. The election year of 1968 was one of the most turbulent times in the nation's history.

Review Questions

These questions are to be answered with essays. This will allow you to explore relationships between individuals, events, and attitudes of the period under review.

1. What were the central elements of the New Frontier and the Great Society? Why was Johnson able to succeed where Kennedy had failed? What were the long-term results of the liberal legislation of 1964 to 1966?

2. How did the reaction of many southern whites to the civil rights activities ironically serve to help the blacks' cause? How did blacks respond when it became clear that the legislative victories of 1964 and 1965 were not enough to satisfy their aspirations?

3. What was the heart of the problem in Vietnam that made military victory so difficult, if not impossible? Who seemed to understand this problem better—the Johnson administration or its critics? How was the Johnson administration trapped by the war?

Chapter Self Test

After you have read the chapter in the text and done the exercises in the Study Guide, take the following self-test to see if you understand the material you have covered. Answers appear at the end of the Study Guide.

MULTIPLE-CHOICE QUESTIONS

Circle the letter of the response that best answers the question or completes the statement.

1. John F. Kennedy made an attractive presidential candidate in 1960 for all the following reasons *except* his:

   a. family wealth and prestige.

   b. past accomplishments as a handsome war hero.

   c. personal eloquence, wit, and charisma.

   d. promise to keep the nation on the course of the 1950s.

2. In contrast to Kennedy, President Lyndon B. Johnson:

   a. rejected the concept of dynamic governmental activism.

   b. possessed a shy and reticent personality.

   c. displayed remarkable skill in influencing Congress.

   d. sympathized with southern conservatives on civil rights issues.

3. Lyndon B. Johnson billed his domestic program as the:

   a. Great Society.

   b. New Frontier.

   c. Era of Equality.

   d. Alliance for Progress.

4. A significant reason that the Medicare proposal was able to overcome opposition and win congressional approval was because it:

   a. made benefits available to all elderly Americans, regardless of economic need.

   b. strictly regulated the fee structure of doctors and hospitals.

   c. established annual spending ceilings to be set by a panel of health-care professionals and economists.

   d. shifted responsibility for paying a large proportion of medical charges from the government to the patient.

5. The "centerpiece" of Lyndon Johnson's "war on poverty" was the:

   a. Department of Family Services, with an emphasis on social work.

   b. Children's Relief Fund, with an emphasis on preschooling.

   c. Office of Economic Opportunity, with an emphasis on community action.

   d. Agency for Economic Advancement, with an emphasis on job training.

6. Robert Weaver was significant as the:

   a. architect of the war on poverty.

   b. leader of conservative opposition to the welfare state.

   c. author of *The Other America*.

   d. the first African American cabinet member.

7. Civil rights activists traveled through the South on buses to protest segregation in seating on buses and in depots. These efforts were generally called:

   a. "rolling sit-ins."

   b. "freedom rides."

   c. "Greyhound diplomacy."

   d. "marches on wheels."

8. Martin Luther King, Jr., delivered his famous "I have a dream" speech:

   a. while he was in jail in Birmingham, Alabama.

   b. on the river bridge on the edge of downtown Selma, Alabama.

   c. at the Ebenezer Baptist Church in Atlanta.

   d. in front of the Lincoln Memorial as part of a march on Washington.

9. Which of the following best characterizes the level of violence associated with the civil rights activities in the South from 1960 to 1965?

   a. There was virtually no violence, thanks mainly to Martin Luther King, Jr.'s passive-resistance philosophy.

   b. White law enforcement officials beat demonstrators or condoned beatings on numerous occasions and several activists were murdered.

   c. More radical black power advocates captured the movement and assassinated several white officeholders.

   d. Major riots broke out in the larger southern cities when blacks were turned away from the polls.

10. Malcolm X was a leading member of the:

    a. Black Panthers.

    b. Student Nonviolent Coordinating Committee (SNCC).

    c. Nation of Islam (Black Muslims).

    d. Pan African Congress (PAC).

11. In response to urban racial violence, in 1968 the special Commission on Civil Disorders appointed by President Johnson recommended:

    a. massive spending on social problems in the ghettoes.

    b. the elimination of state government involvement in welfare programs.

    c. slowing the pace of racial change to allow the nation a "cooling-off" period.

    d. a return to segregated housing patterns to lessen the emotional outbursts that sparked violence in mixed neighborhoods.

12. The first major race riot of the mid-1960s occurred in the Watts section of what major city?

    a. New York

    b. Los Angeles

    c. Detroit

    d. Atlanta

13. The most important and lasting impact of the black power movement was the:
    a. stress on the ideal of interracial cooperation rather than self-reliance.
    b. unification of previously feuding black political groups.
    c. instilling of racial pride and identity in black Americans.
    d. reduced emphasis on the importance of African heritage and an emphasis on blacks' rightful place in American history.

14. John Kennedy's "Alliance for Progress" was intended to provide:
    a. mutual reduction of missiles and warheads by the United States and the Soviet Union.
    b. additional aid to the pro-American forces in South Vietnam.
    c. young American volunteers to work in health and education facilities in developing nations.
    d. better relations between the United States and the nations of Latin America.

15. In the aftermath of the Cuban missile crisis:
    a. Kennedy traveled to Vienna for his first meeting with the Soviet Premier.
    b. the Soviets ordered construction of the Berlin Wall to stop the exodus of East Germans.
    c. a large CIA-trained army of anti-Castro Cubans unsuccessfully invaded the island.
    d. both sides realized how close they had come to the brink, and tensions eased somewhat and a nuclear test ban treaty was signed.

16. Ngho Dinh Diem was probably an unfortunate choice as the basis of American hopes for creation of a viable noncommunist regime in the southern part of Vietnam because he:
    a. resisted serious political or economic reforms.
    b. failed to attract the support of the upper class in Saigon.
    c. was too willing to appease the Viet Cong.
    d. persecuted the nation's Roman Catholics.

17. The Gulf of Tonkin Resolution:
    a. aroused strong opposition and a lengthy debate in Congress before being narrowly passed.
    b. limited President Johnson to a one-time retaliatory bombing strike on the northern part of Vietnam.
    c. was claimed by President Johnson as legal authorization for the military escalation of the U.S. role in the conflict.
    d. marked the beginning of significant international support for the American response to communist aggression in Indochina.

18. By the end of 1967, the United States war efforts in Vietnam:
    a. had effectively reduced to a trickle the flow of communist soldiers and supplies in the southern part of Vietnam by intensive bombings of the north.
    b. involved roughly a half-million American military personnel in the war region.
    c. had succeeded in establishing an honest and efficient, if weak, government in South Vietnam.
    d. involved all of the above.

19. The American military forces in Vietnam seemed least capable of:

    a. winning a military victory in the major battles in which it became engaged.

    b. removing the Viet Cong and their Vietnamese allies from the north from such strongholds as Khesahn.

    c. sustaining a favorable "kill ratio."

    d. pacifying a captured region by winning "the hearts and minds" of the Vietnamese people.

20. In the 1968 presidential election, George Wallace enjoyed an unusually high degree of support for a third-party candidate because he argued that:

    a. the United States should immediately end its military involvement in Vietnam.

    b. the movement toward racial equality should be accelerated through "affirmative action" programs.

    c. programs to alleviate poverty should be fully funded by Congress and that defense spending should be cut sharply to get the money.

    d. busing of school children for racial integration, expanding government regulations and social programs, and soft treatment of rioters and demonstrators were destroying America.

<u>TRUE-FALSE QUESTIONS</u>

Read the statement carefully. Mark true statements "T" and false statements "F."

1. Richard Nixon, vice president to Dwight Eisenhower, was John F. Kennedy's Republican opponent in 1960.

2. President Kennedy supported the Army's Green Berets because the force could fight smaller, nontraditional wars.

3. The Peace Corps was composed of trained diplomats and negotiators that could be quickly dispatched to worldwide trouble spots to try to avoid war.

4. The Warren Commission on the assassination of President Kennedy concluded that Lee Harvey Oswald had acted alone.

5. Barry Goldwater was the last moderate to liberal candidate to be nominated for President by the Republican Party.

6. Medicare paid medical expenses for elderly Americans, regardless of income, and Medicaid provided medical benefits to welfare recipients, regardless of age.

7. The Immigration Act of 1965 eliminated the national origins system that had favored northern European immigrants.

8. Despite Johnson's "war on poverty," the rate of poverty actually increased in the 1960s.

9. The "freedom summer" efforts and the Selma march concentrated on voting-rights issues.

10. The term "*de jure* segregation" referred to racial segregation required by law, whereas "*de facto* segregation" referred to separation by practice not directly mandated by law.

11. Lyndon Johnson lost much of the support that he had previously enjoyed from blacks when he refused to endorse the concept of "affirmative action."

12. The U.S. government refused to give any support for the preparation of the band of Cuban exiles who planned to mount the Bay of Pigs invasion against Castro.

13. The Immigration Act of 1965 was designed to stem the flow of Asians and African immigrants who allegedly took jobs from Native Americans.

14. In the immediate post–World War II period, there was a major exodus of black population from the industrial cities of the Northeast back to the South because of urban riots and the loss of wartime jobs.

15. Malcolm X stressed that African Americans should band together and stress their racial pride through their Christian churches.

16. The Berlin Wall was erected in 1961 to prevent East Germans from fleeing to the West.

17. The "Ho Chi Minh Trail" was the nickname given to the supply routes that moved soldiers and material from the North part of Vietnam into the South during the Second Indochina War.

18. The Tet Offensive by the Viet Cong helped turn American opinion against the war in Vietnam even though the United States and allied Vietnamese forces repelled the invasion and inflicted serious losses on the Viet Cong.

19. Despite Martin Luther King, Jr.'s nonviolent philosophy, there were several riots and violent disturbances following his assassination.

20. Richard Nixon won the presidency in 1968 at least partly by appealing to the so-called "silent majority" of "middle Americans."

CHAPTER THIRTY-TWO
THE CRISIS OF AUTHORITY

Objectives

A thorough study of Chapter 32 should enable the student to understand

1. The reasons for the rise of the New Left and the counterculture.
2. The problems of Native Americans and Hispanics and the nature of their protest movements.
3. The meaning of the New Feminism.
4. The Nixon-Kissinger policy for terminating the Vietnam War, and the subsequent Paris peace settlement.
5. The changes in American foreign policy necessitated by the new perception of the world as multipolar.
6. The reasons for the decline of the American economy in the early 1970s, and President Nixon's reaction to the decline.
7. The ways in which the Supreme Court in the Nixon years began to change to a more conservative posture, and the reasons for this change.
8. The significance of Watergate as an indication of the abuse of executive power.
9. The significance of the environmental movement, how environmentalists sought political solutions to their demands, and how the American political system responded.

Main Themes

1. How Richard Nixon gradually reduced the American ground forces in Vietnam, but increased the air war as he and Henry Kissinger sought peace with honor, which turned out to be nothing more than a way for the United States to leave the war with a decent interval before North Vietnam's victory.
2. That Nixon and Kissinger believed that stability in a "multipolar" world could be achieved only by having the United States forge a bold new relationship with China and, at the same time, seek a detenté with the Soviet Union through grain sales and arms reductions.
3. That Nixon's efforts to build a policy of less federal dominance of the states and more respect for traditional values reaped more political gain than practical result.
4. How movements by youth, ethnic minorities, and women challenged social norms.
5. That Nixon's inconsistent economic policies failed to solve "stagflation," which was as much international as domestic in origin.
6. How Nixon's fear of opposition and assumption that his own fortunes were identical to those of the nation led to his downfall through the scandals collectively known as Watergate.
7. How the environment became an issue in American life.

Glossary

1. iconoclasm: The doctrine of those who attack cherished beliefs, traditions, or institutions. The term is derived from the Greek, referring to people who destroyed religious symbols (icons).

371

2. <u>hallucinogens</u>: Chemical substances (natural or synthetic drugs) that induce hallucinations. Hallucination is the repeated hearing, feeling, smelling, or seeing things that are not actually physically present.

Pertinent Questions

THE YOUTH CULTURE (852-857)

1. What forces led to the rise of the New Left and campus radicalism? How did the civil rights movement help give rise to this movement? How widespread was real radicalism?

2. Explain the ways that many young Americans went about resisting the draft. What eventually happened to the resisters?

3. In what ways did the counterculture exhibit its commitment to the idea of personal fulfillment through rejecting the inhibitions and conventions of middle-class culture?

4. How did rock music reflect the counterculture?

THE MOBILIZATION OF MINORITIES (857-863)

5. How did opposition to "termination" policy help inspire increasing Indian activism? What policy and attitude changes resulted from the Indian Civil Rights movement?

6. Describe the rapid increase in Hispanic population in the United States. What were the sources of growth and where did the immigrants tend to reside?

7. What were the political implications of the surge in Latino population?

8. What were the pros and cons of bilingualism in education?

9. How did Hispanics, blacks, Indians, and other ethnic groups challenge the "melting pot" ethic?

10. To what degree did the gay liberation movement change attitudes of the larger society toward homosexuality? How did it shape gays' views of themselves? In what ways did gay liberation produce a political backlash?

THE NEW FEMINISM (863-866)

11. What was it about Betty Friedan's *The Feminine Mystique* that sparked a revival of the women's movement?

12. What were the goals of the National Organization for Women (NOW)? How did NOW and the women's movement evolve?

13. What gains did women make in education, the professions, politics, and sports in the 1970s and 1980s?

14. What happened to the Equal Rights Amendment? Why?

ENVIRONMENTALISM IN A TURBULENT SOCIETY (866-869)

15. What factors combined to give birth to the environmentalism movement?

16. What is ecology? How does it differ from traditional conservationism?

17. Why did Rachel Carson's book, *Silent Spring*, not only lead to the banning of DDT but also help propel environmentalism into the public consciousness?

18. How did ecology lead to political and legal activism? How effective were ecological activists?

19. What specific examples of environmental degradation spurred public interest in ecological issues?

NIXON, KISSINGER, AND THE WAR (869-873)

20. How was Richard Nixon able to use Vietnamization and the draft lottery to defuse much of the opposition to the war?

21. Why did Nixon keep the bombing of Cambodia secret from Congress and the American people? What happened in the United States when the invasion of Cambodia was revealed?

22. What did the Pentagon Papers reveal about the true nature of the Vietnam War?

23. What did the bombings and negotiations from March 1972 to January 1973 accomplish? What was the main stumbling block to final agreement?

24. What were the main provisions of the Paris accords? Did they constitute "peace with honor"?

25. What were the costs of the war to Vietnam and the United States?

NIXON, KISSINGER, AND THE WORLD (873-874)

26. Why did Nixon and Henry Kissinger decide that the time had come for rapprochement with the People's Republic of China? What resulted from Nixon's visit and related initiatives?

27. What was the basic thrust of the Nixon Doctrine? What were its implications in Chile?

28. What dilemma of American Middle East policy did the Yom Kippur War make clear? What other lessons did the war teach?

POLITICS AND ECONOMICS UNDER NIXON (874-879)

29. To what constituency was Nixon trying to appeal with his attacks on liberal programs?

30. What major decisions of the Warren Court most outraged conservatives?

31. What successes and rebuffs did Nixon meet in his attempts to reshape the Supreme Court? Did the Court, with four Nixon appointees, perform as he had intended?

32. What advantages did Nixon have going into the 1972 election? What were George McGovern's liabilities?

33. What were the proximate and fundamental causes of the creeping inflation of the late 1960s and 1970s?

34. What were the causes and consequences of America's deindustrialization?

35. Describe the general outlines of Nixon's economic policy. Was it consistent? Was it effective?

THE WATERGATE CRISIS (879-882)

36. What aspects of Richard Nixon's personality and management style led to the Watergate scandal and the associated cover-up? How was Nixon's personal culpability discovered?

37. Why did Spiro Agnew resign? How did his removal and the appointment of Gerald Ford as vice president actually increase the pressure on Nixon?

38. On what charges would Nixon's probable impeachment and conviction have been based?

PATTERNS OF POPULAR CULTURE: ROCK MUSIC IN THE SIXTIES (854-855)

39. Why was 1960s rock music called "simultaneously subversive and liberating"? What differing views of the counterculture emerge from the Woodstock and Altamont festivals?

WHERE HISTORIANS DISAGREE: WATERGATE (878-879)

40. Is the Watergate scandal best understood as a product of an increasingly imperial presidency, a real radical threat, or the nature of Richard Nixon's own personality?

Identification

Identify each of the following, and explain why it is important within the context of the chapter.

1. Students for a Democratic Society (SDS)

2. Berkeley "People's Park"

3. Weathermen

4. hippies

5. sexual revolution

6. Rolling Stones

7. Beatles

8. Woodstock

9. American Indian Movement (AIM)

10. Wounded Knee

11. Chicano

12. United Farm Workers/César Chávez

13. "Stonewall Riot"

14. Ms.

15. Sandra Day O'Connor

16. Geraldine Ferraro

17. *Roe* v. *Wade*

18. Lady Bird Johnson

19. smog

20. acid rain

21. Environmental Protection Agency

22. Henry Kissinger

23. draft lottery

24. My Lai massacre

25. Ho Chi Minh City

26. Pol Pot and the Khmer Rouge

27. SALT I

28. Palestine Liberation Organization (PLO)

29. Warren Burger

30. *Bakke v. Board of Regents of California*

31. George Wallace

32. Organization of Petroleum Exporting Countries (OPEC)

33. "stagflation"

Document

Read the section of the text under the heading "The Watergate Crisis." All along, President Nixon had claimed that neither he nor any of his inner staff knew any of the details of the Watergate break-in. He also denied that he had been involved in any cover-up. Through July 1974, the evidence against Nixon was circumstantial or based on contradictory testimony. Although the pressure for his removal at that time was strong, the President still had many defenders. Then in August, Nixon was forced to release the tapes that are excerpted below. They cover conversations of June 23, 1972, only six days after the break-in. Read the excerpts, and consider these questions: Were these tapes necessary for Nixon's impeachment, or was there adequate evidence without them? What do the conversations reveal about the casual manner in which Nixon and Haldeman used federal agencies for political purposes?

HALDEMAN: Now, on the investigation, you know the Democratic break-in thing, we're back in the problem area because the FBI is not under control because Gray [Patrick Gray, acting director of the FBI] doesn't exactly know how to control it and they have—their investigation is now leading into some productive areas—because they've been able to trace the money—not through the money itself—but through the bank sources—the banker. And it goes in some directions we don't want it to go. . . . That the way to handle this now is for us to have Walters [General Vernon Walters, deputy director of the CIA] call Pat Gray and just say, "Stay to hell out of this—this is ah, business here we don't want you to go any further on it." That's not an unusual development, and ah, that would take care of it. . . .

374

NIXON: Well, what the hell, did Mitchell [John Mitchell, former attorney general and head of the president's campaign] know about this?

HALDEMAN: I think so. I don't think he knew the details, but I think he knew.

HALDEMAN (about three hours later): Well, it was kind of interesting. Walters made the point and I didn't mention Hunt [E. Howard Hunt, ex-CIA agent and White House consultant who was convicted in the Watergate conspiracy]. I just said that the thing was leading into directions that were going to create potential problems because they were exploring leads that led back into areas that would be harmful to the CIA and harmful to the government. . . .

Recorded presidential conversation submitted by Richard Nixon to the Committee on the Judiciary of the House of Representatives, April 30, 1974.

Map Exercise

Fill in or identify the following on the blank map provided. Use the map in the text as your source.

1. Israel, Lebanon, Syria, Jordan, Iraq, Iran, Turkey, Greece, Cyprus, Libya, Sudan, Saudi Arabia, and Kuwait.
2. Beirut, Jerusalem, Cairo, Teheran, and Mecca.
3. Territory occupied by Israel after the 1967 war and the part of that territory returned to Egypt.
4. Persian Gulf, Straits of Hormuz, and Suez Canal.
5. Major oil-producing area.

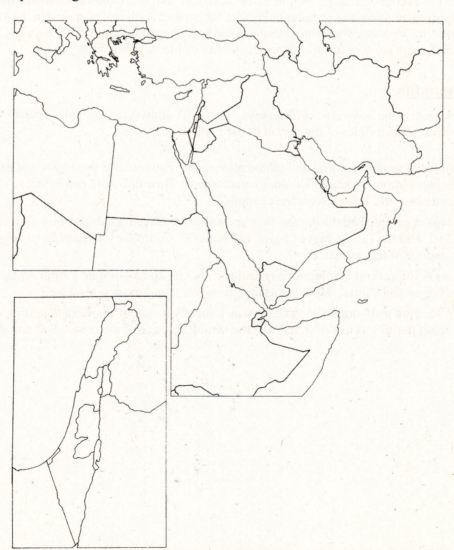

Interpretive Questions

Based on what you have filled in, answer the following. On some of the questions you will need to consult the narrative in your text for information or explanation.

1. What commitments did the United States have in the Middle East, and why was the area of such importance to the nation?

2. What were the geographic, military, and diplomatic results of the Six-Day War of 1967?

3. Describe the Yom Kippur War of 1973. What lessons did it hold for American foreign policy in the Middle East in particular and for other parts of the world in general?

Summary

Opposition to the war in Vietnam became the centerpiece of a wide-ranging political and cultural challenge to traditional American society. During this turbulent era, African Americans, women, Hispanics, and Native Americans organized to assert their rights. Richard Nixon inherited the war in Vietnam, and he brought it to an end. The cost of Nixon's four years of war was thousands of American lives and many more thousands of Asian lives, plus continued social unrest at home and an enduring strain on the economy. The end of American involvement did not mean that the goal of an independent, noncommunist South Vietnam had been secured. Nixon was more successful in his other foreign policy initiatives, opening meaningful contacts with China and somewhat easing tensions with the Soviet Union. He managed to stake out a solid constituency of conservative voters with his attacks on liberal programs and ideas. He never quite decided how to deal with a troubled economy that faced the unusual dual problem of slowed growth and rapidly rising prices. Less than two years after his overwhelming reelection in 1972, Nixon resigned from office under fire from a nation horrified by his arrogant misuse of presidential power for personal political purposes in the Watergate affair. Meanwhile, with the Vietnam War behind them, Americans began to look to other issues, particularly the environment, and raise more questions about the quality of life on our planet.

Review Questions

These questions are to be answered with essays. This will allow you to explore relationships between individuals, events, and attitudes of the period under review.

1. Chronicle the several cultural and ethnic movements that arose in the 1960s and early 1970s to challenge traditional white, male-dominated society. How did more conservative forces respond? How extensive and lasting were the changes?

2. What was accomplished during the four years that the Nixon administration carried on the war in Vietnam? Did the U.S. achieve "peace and honor"? Could the war have been concluded in a better manner at less human cost?

3. What were the several assumptions reflected in Nixon and Kissinger's rapprochement with the Soviet Union and China? Were the assumptions valid and the actions wise?

4. Was Watergate truly unprecedented, or was it merely a case of a president getting caught performing politics as usual? What was the lasting damage of the crisis? Did any good come from it?

Chapter Self Test

After you have read the chapter in the text and done the exercises in the Study Guide, take the following self test to see if you understand the material you have covered. Answers appear at the end of the Study Guide.

MULTIPLE-CHOICE QUESTIONS

Circle the letter of the response that best answers the question or completes the statement.

1. The "free speech movement" and the "peoples park" issue of the so-called New Left were centered in:
   a. New York City around Greenwich Village.
   b. Chicago under the "loop."
   c. Boston near Harvard and MIT.
   d. Berkeley around the University of California.

2. In 1967–1968 the issue that most unified the various people loosely known as the New Left was:
   a. support for environmental legislation
   b. opposition to the war in Vietnam.
   c. concern about nuclear power.
   d. rejection of capitalism.

3. Which of the following was *not* generally associated with the so-called counterculture?
   a. marijuana smoking
   b. long hair and nontraditional clothing
   c. rejection of the existence of a supreme being
   d. relaxed and open attitude about sexuality

4. Although the philosophy of the counterculture seemed to favor all of the following, the characteristic that most defined the movement was:
   a. rejecting the inhibitions and conventions of middle-class culture and concentrating on pleasure and fulfillment.
   b. striving for racial and social justice for all peoples.
   c. breaking the power of corrupt elites who controlled American corporations and governments.
   d. demanding an end to international wars and conflicts and substituting peaceful resolution.

5. The "termination" approach to federal Indian policy called for the end of:
   a. all economic aid to individual Indians.
   b. official recognition of tribes as legal entities.
   c. efforts to assimilate Indians into urban society.
   d. the movement to organize all tribes into a national Indian organization.

377

6. César Chávez is significant to American labor history as an organizer of what group of predominately Hispanic workers?

   a. janitors

   b. cigar makers

   c. agricultural laborers

   d. longshoremen

7. By the 1980s, Hispanic Americans had:

   a. become the fastest-growing large minority group in the nation.

   b. yet to make any efforts to organize themselves politically.

   c. consistently opposed the concept of bilingualism in education.

   d. uniformly championed the ideal of the "melting pot."

8. The "Stonewall Riot" is associated with:

   a. Puerto Rican anger at poor services in their neighborhoods.

   b. homosexual outrage at harassment by police and others.

   c. college students demanding legalization of drug use.

   d. African American clashes with new immigrants from Southeast Asia.

9. In *The Feminine Mystique* (1963), Betty Friedan:

   a. praised the ideal of women living happy, fulfilled lives in purely domestic roles.

   b. urged women to search for greater personal fulfillment.

   c. called for women to band together to assault the male power structure.

   d. rejected the whole notion of marriage, family, and even heterosexual intercourse.

10. The leading reason that the Equal Rights Amendment (ERA) failed to gain ratification was because of:

    a. public apathy and indifference.

    b. lack of time for proper organization of support groups.

    c. fears by many it would create a major disruption of traditional social patterns.

    d. inadequate evidence of sexual discrimination.

11. The largest and most influential feminist organization from the 1960s through the 1980s was the:

    a. Female Liberation League.

    b. American Women's Caucus.

    c. National Organization for Women.

    d. Gender Equity Society.

12. The first woman on the national ticket of one of the two major political parties was the 1984 Democratic vice presidential nominee:

    a. Sandra Day O'Connor.

    b. Bella Abzug.

    c. Kate Millet.

    d. Geraldine Ferraro.

13. The science of ecology stresses:

   a. the interplay among ethnic groups.

   b. the biological basis for human traits such as homosexuality and motherhood.

   c. the economic structure of social problems.

   d. the inter-relatedness of the natural world.

14. The term "Vietnamization" referred to the policy of:

   a. using propaganda to develop public support for the war.

   b. training United States troops to understand Vietnamese social customs.

   c. shifting the emphasis of the United States military from traditional to guerrilla warfare.

   d. shifting the burden of actual combat to the South Vietnamese army.

15. The invasion of Cambodia by U.S. and South Vietnamese forces in the spring of 1970:

   a. resulted in a crushing defeat of the U.S. forces.

   b. revived the domestic antiwar movement in the United States and led to large demonstrations.

   c. was the last major encounter of the war involving U.S. troops.

   d. led to Chinese intervention on the side of the North Vietnamese.

16. The Paris accords of January 1973 on Vietnam provided for three of the following. Which is the *exception?*

   a. an immediate cease-fire

   b. the return of American prisoners of war

   c. the Thieu regime to remain in power in South Vietnam

   d. North Vietnamese troops to be withdrawn from the southern part of Vietnam

17. Nixon and Kissinger's approach to foreign policy was based on the assumption that the world configuration of power had become:

   a. unipolar.

   b. bipolar.

   c. multipolar.

   d. nonpolar.

18. Richard Nixon's approach to China was to:

   a. isolate the mainland government because of its support for the north in the Vietnam War.

   b. open up contact for the first time since 1949 by visiting China and beginning diplomatic relations short of full recognition.

   c. pressure the nationalist government of Taiwan to seek reunification with the mainland.

   d. try to stir up Soviet-Chinese border conflict so that both nations would be preoccupied with each other and reduce tensions with the United States.

19. An important effect of America's support for Israel in the Yom Kippur War (1973) was:

   a. a reduction in unemployment.

   b. the strengthening of the dollar in international trade.

   c. the cancellation of the wheat deal with the Soviet Union.

   d. an Arab embargo on oil exports to the United States.

20. George McGovern, the Democratic candidate for president in 1972, could be most accurately described as:

    a. the most hawkish of the leading Democrats.

    b. an advanced liberal and outspoken critic of the Vietnam War.

    c. a conservative who appealed to the southern wing of the party.

    d. a suave politician who took no clear-cut stand on any major controversial issues.

TRUE-FALSE QUESTIONS

Read each statement carefully. Mark true statements "T" and false statements "F."

1. The New Left movement drew strength from the civil rights and anti-Vietnam War mood of many Americans.

2. Marijuana use, freer attitudes toward sex, and other attributes of the counterculture were confined to the movement and had no influence on the broader society.

3. In their later period, the Beatles moved away from the soft romantic songs that had led to their initial popularity, then recording music that reflected an interest in drugs and mysticism.

4. Woodstock, California was the most successful and long-lasting of the several free-love communes established by the counterculture.

5. The avowed goal of the American Indian Movement was to break down tribal allegiance and encourage Native Americans to assimilate into the mainstream of middle-class values.

6. Wounded Knee was, symbolically, an important place for a 1970s Indian protest because it had been the site of a massacre of Sioux Indians by federal troops some eighty years earlier.

7. The term "Chicano" came to be used with pride by many Hispanics in referring to themselves in the 1970s, even though it had previously been a term of derision.

8. The concept of "multiculturalism" or "cultural pluralism" challenged the "melting pot" vision often advanced by those who favored ethnic assimilation into America's dominant Anglo-European culture.

9. A major objective of the gay liberation movement was to get homosexuals to be more willing to make their sexual preference known publicly and unapologetically.

10. Betty Friedan's 1963 book *The Feminine Mystique* helped energize the women's liberation movement by showing that many college-educated women were frustrated by their limited opportunities.

11. The Equal Rights Amendment (ERA) became part of the U.S. Constitution in 1972 when Georgia became the thirty-eighth state to ratify it.

12. According to "Where Historians Disagree," historians have reached a consensus that Richard Nixon's paranoid and mean personality was the root cause of the Watergate scandal.

13. The *Roe v. Wade* decision of the U.S. Supreme Court used the "right to privacy" as the basis for ruling that states could not ban all abortions.

14. Conservative ecologists effectively demonstrated that the acid rain scare was a hoax perpetrated by companies wanting to sell protective coatings to consumers.

15. Although Henry Kissinger was officially President Nixon's principal foreign policy adviser, Secretary of State William Rogers and Secretary of Defense Melvin Laird actually had more influence in setting the direction of American policy.

16. The Department of Defense documents released as the so-called Pentagon Papers revealed that the U.S. government had been considerably less than fully honest in reporting to the American people about the military progress of the war in Vietnam.

17. The SALT I agreement called for freezing nuclear missile forces at present levels.

18. The United States agreed to protect Israel from further territorial losses following Israel's defeat in the Six-Day War of 1967.

19. The U.S. Supreme Court rulings in cases concerning abortion, prayer in school, and rights of the criminally accused aroused opposition from political conservatives.

20. President Nixon used the justification of protecting "national security" to stifle political dissent and undermine opposition.

CHAPTER THIRTY-THREE
FROM THE "AGE OF LIMITS" TO THE AGE OF REAGAN

Objectives

A thorough study of Chapter 33 should enable the student to understand:

1. The efforts of President Gerald Ford to overcome the effects of Richard Nixon's resignation.
2. The rapid emergence of Jimmy Carter as a national figure and the reasons for his victory in 1976.
3. Carter's emphasis on human rights and its effects on international relations.
4. Carter's role in bringing about the Camp David agreement and the impact of this agreement on the Middle East.
5. Why the United States had so much difficulty in freeing the hostages held by Iran and the effect of this episode on the Carter presidency.
6. The nature of the "Reagan revolution" and the meaning of supply-side economics.
7. The staunchly anticommunist Reagan foreign policy and the impact it had on the fall of the Soviet Union.
8. The changing demography of America from 1970 to 1990.
9. The increasingly conservative mood of the American electorate.
10. The emergence of a new era in foreign policy following the collapse of the Soviet Union.

Main Themes

1. That Gerald Ford managed to restore confidence in the presidency but remained unable to make significant breakthroughs in solving the nation's international and economic problems.
2. That the difficult problems faced by Jimmy Carter, including a sluggish economy, an energy crunch, and a Middle Eastern crisis, combined with his leadership style to ensure that he would be a one-term president.
3. That Ronald Reagan's personality soothed Americans and his brand of conservatism struck a responsive chord as he moved toward a reduced role for government in the economy and an increased emphasis on the military.
4. How the New Right challenged the liberal-moderate consensus that had dominated American politics since the New Deal.
5. How the fall of the Soviet Union and the end of the Cold War altered America's foreign policy and domestic goals, and turned American foreign policy focus to other matters, especially in the Middle East.

Glossary

1. demography: The study of population, including birth and death rates, residence patterns, and regional shifts.
2. Pentecostal Christianity: A type of fundamentalism that stresses faith healing and baptism by the Holy Spirit. The spirit manifests itself when followers speak in unknown tongues. Pentecost was an ancient Hebrew festival, and, according to the Book of Acts, on the first Pentecost after the

crucifixion of Jesus of Nazareth, the apostles spoke in tongues when they heard a sound like the rush of a mighty wind.

Pertinent Questions

POLITICS AND DIPLOMACY AFTER WATERGATE (886-889)

1. How did his pardon of Richard Nixon affect Gerald Ford's political standing?

2. What policies did the Ford administration employ to fight the recession of 1974–1975? How effective were they? How did the energy crisis complicate Ford's problems?

3. What themes and style did Jimmy Carter play on to win the nomination and presidency in 1976? How did that approach hamper him as president?

4. What role did "human rights" play in Carter's foreign policy?

5. How did Carter manage to help bring about a peace treaty between Egypt and Israel?

6. What led to the Iranian hostage crisis? What political effects did it have on the Carter administration? How was the crisis resolved?

7. How did the Carter administration react to the Soviet invasion of Afghanistan?

THE RISE OF THE NEW AMERICAN RIGHT (889-895)

8. Where is the "Sunbelt"? What were the political implications of its rise?

9. Describe the basis of Christian evangelicalism. How could it lead to both social liberalism, as in Jimmy Carter, and, more typically, cultural conservatism, as in Jerry Falwell?

10. What issues did the "Christian right" stress?

11. How did activists build the New Right? What was Ronald Reagan's role in the emergence of the movement? How did Gerald Ford's actions actually enhance the New Right even though he was not part of it?

12. To what extent was the tax revolt of the 1970s and 1980s as much an attack on government programs in principle as it was a frustration with high taxes?

13. Why did Ronald Reagan win such a decisive victory in 1980? What happened in the congressional races?

THE "REAGAN REVOLUTION" (895-901)

14. What were the key elements of the Reagan coalition? How did it differ from the traditional Republican constituency?

15. Explain the assumptions of supply-side economics ("Reaganomics") and how the Reagan administration implemented it. How did the economy respond?

16. Explain the concept of "deregulation." What steps were taken under Reagan?

17. What lifted the economy out of the 1982–83 recession? What contribution did Reagan's economic policy make to the recovery?

18. What long-term developments and short-term actions of the Reagan years led to the record federal budget deficits?

19. What stance toward the Soviets and communism in general constituted the so-called Reagan Doctrine? How was this approach applied in Latin America and the Caribbean?

20. How did the rise in terrorism as a political tactic shape American foreign policy in North Africa and the Middle East?

21. What did the election of 1984 reveal about the changing nature of American politics?

AMERICA AND THE WANING OF THE COLD WAR (901-907)

22. Describe the process by which the Soviet Union and its Eastern European bloc ceased to exist. What emerged in its place?

23. How did Ronald Reagan react to Mikhail Gorbachev? What concrete agreement resulted?

24. Describe the Iran-contra scandal and its political impact. What other scandals plagued the Reagan administration?

25. What main campaign strategy did George Bush use to come from behind and defeat Michael Dukakis? What happened in the congressional elections?

26. Even though President Bush lacked a clear domestic agenda, what significant measures did pass during his term of office? What was the most serious domestic challenge that faced Bush?

27. What precipitated the 1990–1991 Persian Gulf crisis and war? What role did the United Nations play? What was the outcome?

28. What broad issue was the key to Bill Clinton's victory in 1992? What role did Ross Perot play?

PATTERNS OF POPULAR CULTURE: THE MALL (890-891)

29. Why did shopping mall developers endeavor to control so many aspects of the environment? What did some observers perceive as the downside to the mall?

Identification

Identify each of the following, and explain why it is important within the context of the chapter.

1. Helsinki Conference
2. Mao Zedong
3. SALT II
4. Panama Canal Treaty
5. Camp David Accords
6. diplomatic relations with China
7. Ayatollah Ruhollah Khomeini
8. Billy Graham
9. Christian Coalition
10. Nelson Rockefeller
11. Proposition 13
12. "Teflon president"
13. "neo-conservatives"
14. "Star Wars"—SDI
15. "nuclear freeze"
16. Grenada
17. Sandinistas
18. Beirut barracks incident
19. Walter Mondale
20. Jesse Jackson
21. Geraldine Ferraro

22. Tiananmen Square

23. Savings and Loan crisis

24. Saddam Hussein

Document 1

Read the sections of the text dealing with the differing styles, personalities, and policies of Ronald Reagan and Jimmy Carter. The excerpts below, the first from Carter's so-called malaise speech of July 15, 1979, and the second from Reagan's State of the Union Address on February 4, 1986, illustrate the contrasting styles. Carter's address was given at a time when he was under considerable attack for his leadership, whereas Reagan's was delivered while his popularity was at a high point. Both speeches contain specific legislative agendas, but the speeches are more memorable for their general messages than for their specific proposals. Consider the following questions: How do the two documents illustrate the differences between the leadership styles of Reagan and Carter? Each speech cites experiences or opinions of supposedly typical Americans; compare and contrast the use of these examples. The America described by Reagan in 1986 was very different from that described by Carter in 1979; had America truly changed that much? Had Reagan restored national confidence through rhetoric or through long-term solutions to difficult problems? In light of the state of the nation and the world in the early 1990s, which speech was more realistic? Which was more prophetic?

[President Carter speaking.] . . . . I want to speak to you tonight about a subject even more serious than energy or inflation. I want to talk to you right now about a fundamental threat to American democracy.

I do not mean our political and civil liberties. They will endure. And I do not refer to the outward strength of America—the nation that is at peace tonight everywhere in the world with unmatched economic power and military might. The threat is nearly invisible in ordinary ways. It is a crisis of confidence. It is a crisis that strikes at the very heart and soul and spirit of our national will.

We can see this crisis in the growing doubt about the meaning of our own lives and in the loss of a unity of purpose for our nation.

The erosion of our confidence in the future is threatening to destroy the social and the political fabric of America. The confidence that we have always had as a people is not simply some romantic dream or a proverb in a dusty book that we read just on the Fourth of July. It is the idea which founded our nation and which has guided our development as a people. Confidence in the future has supported everything else—public institutions and private enterprise, our own families and the very Constitution of the United States. Confidence has defined our course and has served as a link between generations.

We've always believed in something called progress. We've always had a faith that the days of our children would be better than our own.

Our people are losing that faith. . . . But just as we are losing our confidence in the future, we are also beginning to close the door on our past.

In a nation that was proud of hard work, strong families, close-knit communities and our faith in God, too many of us now tend to worship self-indulgence and consumption. Human identity is no longer defined by what one does but by what one owns. . . .

Often you see paralysis and stagnation and drift. You don't like it. And neither do I.

What can we do? First of all, we must face the truth and then we can change our course. We simply must have faith in each other. Faith in our ability to govern ourselves and faith in the future of this nation. Restoring that faith and that confidence to America is now the most important task we face. . . .

And we are the generation that will win the war on the energy problem, and in that process rebuild the unity and confidence of America. . . .

Energy will be the immediate test of our ability to unite this nation. And it can also be the standard around which we rally. On the battlefield of energy we can win for our nation a new confidence, and we can seize control again of our common destiny. . . .

[At this point, the speech lists six specific points emphasizing conservation and reduced energy consumption.]

I do not promise you that this struggle for freedom will be easy. I do not promise a quick way out of our nation's problems when the truth is that the only way out is an all-out effort. . . . There is simply no way to avoid sacrifice. . . . In closing, let me say this: I will do my best, but I will not do it alone. Let your voice be heard. Whenever you have a chance, say something good about our country. With God's help and for the sake of our nation, it is time for us to join hands in America.

Let us commit ourselves together to a rebirth of the American spirit. Working together with our common faith, we cannot fail.

President Jimmy Carter, television address to the nation, July 15, 1979.

* * *

[President Reagan speaking.] I have come to review with you the progress of our nation, to speak of unfinished work and to set our sights on the future. I am pleased to report the state of the union is stronger than a year ago, and growing stronger each day. Tonight, we look out on a rising America—firm of heart, united in spirit, powerful in pride and patriotism. America is on the move.

But it wasn't long ago that we looked out on a different land—locked factory gates, long gasoline lines, intolerable prices and interest rates turning the greatest country on Earth into a land of broken dreams. Government growing beyond our consent had become a lumbering giant, slamming shut the gates of opportunity, threatening to crush the very roots of our freedom.

What brought America back? The American people brought us back—with quiet courage and common sense; the undying faith that in this nation under God the future will be ours, for the future belongs to the free. . . .

Family and community are the co-stars of this great American comeback. They are why we say tonight: private values must be at the heart of public policies.

What is true for families in America is true for America in the family of free nations. History is no captive of some inevitable force. History is made by men and women of vision and courage. Tonight, freedom is on the march. The United States is the economic miracle, the model to which the world once again turns. We stand for an idea whose time is now. . . .

We speak tonight of an agenda for the future, an agenda for a safer, more secure world. And we speak about the necessity for actions to steel us for the challenges of growth, trade, and security in the next decade and the year 2000. And we will do it—not by breaking faith with bedrock principles, but by breaking free from failed policies. . . . [At this point the speech goes into specific proposals for a balanced budget amendment, defense spending, tax reform, and other matters.]

America is ready, America can win the race to the future—and we shall.

The American dream is a song of hope that rings through the night winter air. Vivid, tender music that warms our hearts when the least among us aspire to the greatest things. . . . [At this point he introduces four young people and tells of their accomplishments in science, music, public service, and personal bravery.]

386

Would you four stand up for a moment. Thank you. You are heroes of our hearts. We look at you and know it's true—in this land of dreams fulfilled where greater dreams may be imagined, nothing is impossible, no victory is beyond our reach; no glory will ever be too great. So now it's up to us, all of us, to prepare America for that day when our work will pale before the greatness of America's champions in the 21st century.

The world's hopes rest with America's future. America's hopes rest with us. So let us go forward to create our world of tomorrow—in faith, in unity, and in love. God bless you, and God bless America.

President Ronald Reagan, State of the Union Address, February 4, 1986.

Document 2

Consider carefully the sections in the chapter concerning the end of the Cold War. The challenge facing American policymakers as we enter the twenty-first century is how to restructure foreign policy for the post–Cold War world. Secretary of State Warren Christopher confronted this challenge in his October 1993 address on the occasion of the opening of the new National Foreign Affairs Training Center, which will help prepare diplomats for the future. As you read excerpts from Secretary Christopher's speech, consider the following questions. What events during the Reagan, Bush, and Clinton administrations led to the "historic moment [that] requires a new diplomacy"? What are the "new priorities" that Christopher outlines?

Remaking American Diplomacy in the Post–Cold War World

The Clinton Administration is the first to take office since the end of the Cold War. We have an opportunity—indeed, a responsibility—to remake American diplomacy in a new world that is unburdened by superpower confrontation.

This historic moment requires a new diplomacy that advances the priorities reflecting the possibilities and the perils of the post–Cold War era. That is why President Clinton has placed economic policy at the center of our foreign policy; why he has made nonproliferation [of nuclear weapons] the arms control agenda of the 1990s; why he has committed America to enlarge the sway of democratic values around the world; and why he has moved global issues into the mainstream of American foreign policy—issues such as protecting the environment and reducing population growth.

These new priorities reflect a broader definition of our national security—and they will require an expanded role for American diplomacy—a role that can be cultivated in these wonderful new quarters.

For more than two centuries, diplomacy has been a vital instrument of our national security. But security during the Cold War was largely based upon our military's ability to contain Soviet power and to deter war. Now is the time when diplomacy—supported by a credible military force—can assume a new potency on behalf of a strong and secure America.

From *U.S. Department of State Dispatch,* October 18, 1993.

Map Exercise

Fill in or identify the following on the blank map provided. Use the maps in the text as your source.

1. States with a 1970–1990 growth rate of 15 percent or more.
2. Cities that were among the top ten in growth in 1950 but *not* in 1990.
3. Cities that were among the top ten in 1990 but *not* in 1950.

4. Cities that were among the top ten in both censuses but that lost relative rank.
5. States that *gained* representation in the House of Representatives, and thereby electoral votes, after the 1980 census and those that *lost*. (Compare the figures on the maps for the 1980 and 1984 presidential elections; the 1980 count was still based on the 1970 census. Remember, the electoral vote is equal to the number of representatives plus two. For further information you may also compare the electoral totals for 1948, based on the 1940 census, with those in 1984.)

Interpretive Questions

Based on what you have filled in, answer the following. On some of the questions you will need to consult the narrative in your text for information or explanation.

1. What were the congressional and presidential political implications of the growth of the Sunbelt?
2. What problems did the demographic shift to the Sunbelt leave for the Northeast, in general, and many of its central cities, in particular?

Summary

As president, Gerald Ford worked to heal the wounds of Watergate and restore respect for the presidency. His pardon of Richard Nixon was probably the most controversial act of his caretaker period in office. Jimmy Carter turned out to be a more effective campaigner than president. His administration was marked by an inability to set a tone of leadership. He made no significant strides toward solving the energy crisis and took only halting steps toward his goal of making the federal government more efficient. His last year in office was dominated by the Iranian hostage crisis, which at first boosted his popularity but later may have cost him another term. An upsurge in conservatism came from demographic shifts to the Sunbelt, the activism of the Christian right, the ideology of the neoconservatives, and effective organizational tactics. Ronald Reagan won the 1980 election by riding this conservative crest and by exploiting deep-seated feelings of resentment over America's seeming weakness abroad. Congress quickly passed his supply-side economics plan of tax reductions and spending cuts; however, a year later, the nation was mired in recession. Prosperity returned and Reagan won easy reelection. By now the Cold War, which had shaped national priorities since World War II, was waning. With the fall of the Soviet Union domestic issues again took center stage, and President George Bush, who followed Reagan, faced serious economic problems. At the same time foreign policy concerns shifted again to the Middle East, and though operation Desert Storm successfully stopped Iraqi aggression, victory did not solve the problems of the region.

Review Questions

These questions are to be answered with essays. This will allow you to explore relationships between individuals, events, and attitudes of the period under review.

1. Did Gerald Ford's pardon of Richard Nixon accomplish its purpose to "shut and seal the book" on Watergate? What else did Ford do to try to restore credibility to the presidency?

2. How effective was Jimmy Carter in applying the human-rights principle to American foreign policy? How did his approach differ from the actions taken by Ronald Reagan and George Bush?

3. How did the nation's energy needs complicate both the foreign and domestic policies of presidents Ford, Carter, Reagan, and Bush?

4. What were the political, economic, and social implications of the marked demographic changes in the American population during the 1970s and 1980s?

5. Describe the various elements of the rise of conservative politics in the 1970s and 1980s. How did they come together around the figure of Ronald Reagan?

Chapter Self Test

After you have read the chapter in the text and done the exercises in the Study Guide, take the following self test to see if you understand the material you have covered. Answers appear at the end of the Study Guide.

MULTIPLE-CHOICE QUESTIONS

Circle the letter of the response that best answers the question or completes the statement.

1. President Gerald Ford's popularity with the American public fell dramatically as a result of his:
   a. pardon of Richard Nixon.
   b. handling of the "Mayaguez" incident.
   c. vetoes of large numbers of congressional enactments.
   d. appointment of Nelson Rockefeller as vice president.

2. The death of Mao Zedong in China:
   a. led to a period of disruption, chaos, and violence.
   b. brought to power a more moderate government that wanted closer ties with the United States.
   c. intensified Chinese pressure on Taiwan inspiring the United States to increase military aid to the island regime.
   d. set off a wave of provincial revolutions that split China.

3. Ford's foreign policy included support for three of the following. Which is the *exception?*
   a. the SALT II agreement
   b. the Helsinki agreement on European boundaries
   c. the continued rapprochement with China after the death of Mao Zedong
   d. the abandonment of U. S. mediation efforts in the Middle East

4. Jimmy Carter's success in the election of 1976 resulted in large part because:
   a. Ford refused to choose a running mate who appealed to the Republican right.
   b. Carter's considerable service in Washington assured voters of an experienced administrator.
   c. Ford's acerbic personality had generated an atmosphere of bitterness and acrimony in Washington.
   d. Carter seemed to possess honesty, piety, and an outsider's skepticism of the federal government.

5. Which of the following best describes the nation's economy during Carter's final two years in office?
   a. modest inflation and stable interest rates
   b. modest inflation and declining interest rates
   c. rapid inflation and record high interest rates
   d. rapid inflation and stable interest rates

6. Carter had hoped to base American foreign policy on increased attention to:
   a. flexible military response whenever democratic governments were challenged.
   b. expansion of American economic interests overseas.
   c. reduction of American responsibility for involvement in world conflicts.
   d. the issue of how nations respect human rights.

7. The Camp David summit, hosted by President Carter, was a meeting between the leaders of Israel and:
   a. Egypt.
   b. Libya.
   c. Lebanon.
   d. the Palestine Liberation Organization.

8. Three of the following were significant features of Carter's foreign policy in the early years of his administration. Which is the *exception?*

   a. abandoning SALT II as futile

   b. completing negotiations to transfer the Canal Zone to Panama

   c. using diplomatic pressure to promote human rights in other countries

   d. continuing progress toward improving relations with China

9. In November 1979, Iranian militants took over the U.S. embassy in Teheran and held fifty-three embassy personnel hostage for more than a year. The immediate provocation for their act was the fact that the Carter administration:

   a. began to support Iraq in its war with Iran.

   b. refused to recognize Iran's new regime.

   c. attempted to restore the pro-American Shah to power in Iran.

   d. allowed the exiled former Shah of Iran to enter the United States.

10. In response to the Soviet invasion of Afghanistan in 1979, President Carter did three of the following. Which is the *exception?*

   a. He imposed economic sanctions on the Soviet Union.

   b. He called for a boycott of the 1980 Olympics in Moscow.

   c. He withdrew SALT II from consideration by the Senate.

   d. He invoked the SEATO treaty, by which member nations were to confer with one another in case of attack.

11. The rapid population growth in the "Sunbelt" shifted political power to the region and tended to strengthen which political viewpoint?

   a. conservative, antigovernment

   b. liberal, government activist

   c. moderate, middle-of-the-road

   d. none of the above; effect basically neutral

12. Which of the following is a common thread of evangelical Christianity?

   a. belief in personal conversion through direct communication with God

   b. conservative, right-wing politics, especially on social welfare issues

   c. belief in the literal, inerrant interpretation of the Bible, especially on evolution

   d. all of the above

13. Ronald Reagan and his administration received strong support from three of the following groups. Which is the *exception?*

   a. "neo-conservatives"

   b. New Right

   c. feminists and civil rights activists

   d. conservative business leaders

14. The "supply-side" economic theory that President Reagan sought to implement early in his administration called for:

    a. increasing government spending to stimulate consumption.

    b. maintaining high interest rates to control inflation.

    c. cutting taxes to encourage new investment.

    d. all of the above.

15. During the Reagan administration, the federal budget:

    a. experienced severe deficits.

    b. noticeably declined.

    c. shifted from reliance on the income tax to a national sales tax.

    d. rose markedly in domestic spending but remained flat on defense.

16. With respect to the civil war in El Salvador, the Reagan administration:

    a. maintained a strictly neutral position.

    b. sent in a peacekeeping force of American combat troops.

    c. supported the existing military regime with money and material.

    d. supported the revolutionaries, who were seeking to overthrow the military regime.

17. In Nicaragua, the Sandinistas were:

    a. pro-American forces.

    b. anti-American forces.

    c. essentially the same as the contras in Honduras.

    d. supporters of the former Somoza regime.

18. Reagan's policy toward Lebanon involved:

    a. supporting Lebanon with military aid for its border conflict with Saudi Arabia.

    b. sending in American marines as a peacekeeping force following Israeli-PLO clashes but removing them after over 200 were killed in a terrorist attack.

    c. backing Israel in the United Nations in its effort to make Lebanon part of the Left Bank area controlled by Israel.

    d. none of the above.

19. In the national elections of 1984, the Democrats made electoral history by, for the first time, nominating a vice presidential candidate who was:

    a. Jewish.

    b. female.

    c. African-American.

    d. Hispanic.

20. The leader of the Soviet Union who presided over its dissolution was

    a. Nikita Khrushchev

    b. Mikhail Gorbachev

    c. Helsinki Accord

    d. Michael Dukakis

TRUE-FALSE QUESTIONS

Read each statement carefully. Mark true statements "T" and false statements "F."

1. Gerald Ford's compassionate pardon of Richard Nixon for his role in the Watergate scandal improved Ford's standing in public opinion polls.

2. President Ford faced the relatively unusual problem of simultaneous inflation and recession.

3. Ronald Reagan mounted a strong effort to take the Republican nomination away from President Ford in 1976.

4. In his campaign for president, Jimmy Carter emphasized that he was a Washington "insider" who could be more effective with Congress than President Ford had been.

5. Jimmy Carter pledged that a major focus of his foreign policy would be the defense of "human rights."

6. President Carter canceled U.S. participation in the 1980 summer Olympic Games in Moscow in protest of the Soviet invasion of Afghanistan.

7. The treaty providing for transfer of control of the Panama Canal to the government of Panama won ratification in the U.S. Senate by a very close vote, despite President Carter's opposition.

8. The term "Sagebrush Rebellion" was used to describe the growing environmental consciousness in the West, where water was scarce and timber and mining interests were destroying natural areas.

9. The passage of "Proposition 13" in California was a manifestation of the growing popular mood often called the "tax revolt."

10. Evangelical Christianity could lead individuals to either liberal or conservative political activism, depending on which issues and concerns motivated them.

11. Gerald Ford's appointment of Nelson Rockefeller as vice president was designed to appease the New Right wing of the Republican party.

12. Although Ronald Reagan won a convincing victory over Jimmy Carter in 1980, the Republican Party made no significant gains in Congress.

13. Although Ronald Reagan was not able to fulfill his promise to balance the federal budget, he was able to reverse the trend of the Carter years and the amount of the annual deficit decreased significantly.

14. Ronald Reagan was sometimes called the "Teflon president" because it seemed to many observers that bad publicity never seemed to stick to him personally.

15. In the negotiations with Iran that eventually led to the freeing of the American hostages, the United States promised to release Iranian financial assets frozen in the United States.

16. The "supply-side" approach to economic policy was sometimes called "Reaganomics."

17. Although Reagan's opponents argued that his economic policies would lead to recession, the economy stayed on an expansion pace throughout his presidency.

18. Ronald Reagan took a hard-line stance toward the Soviet Union, even calling it, on one occasion, the "evil empire."

19. The Strategic Defense Initiative ("Star Wars") was designed as a defense against nuclear attack, using lasers and satellites to intercept incoming missiles.

20. The major accomplishment of the first Persian Gulf War was to depose Saddam Hussein from control of Iraq thereby removing a major destabilizing influence in the region.

CHAPTER THIRTY-FOUR
THE AGE OF GLOBALIZATION

Objectives

A thorough study of Chapter 34 should enable the student to understand:

1. The reasons Bill Clinton won the presidency in 1992, the successes and failures of his first administration, the factors behind the Republican resurgence in 1994, the reasons Clinton won re-election in 1996, and the issues that led to his impeachment and subsequent acquittal.

2. The issues in the election of 2000, the reasons behind the Republican victory, and how George W. Bush emerged victorious from one of the most controversial presidential elections in American history.

3. The reasons for the economic boom of the 1990s, the recession of 2001-2002, and how the George W. Bush administration responded to the economic downturn.

4. The emergence of a global economy, the technological revolution that made it happen, and the role the United States played in these developments.

5. The fundamental changes in the American and world economy after the 1970s.

6. The profound demographic changes the nation experienced in the last decades of the twentieth century.

7. The widening gulf between economically successful African Americans and the urban black underclass.

8. The troublesome issues of drugs, AIDS, homelessness, abortion, and environmental threats.

9. The tense and fragmented culture issues that affected American politics and social relations.

10. The issues that gave rise to the Islamic terrorism of this era, how and why terrorism was used against the United States, and the American response to terrorism.

Main Themes

1. How Bill Clinton won the presidency by focusing on the economy, and though the Republican Party rebounded in 1994, Clinton was re-elected in 1996.

2. How the 1990s was both a decade of intense party partisanship and rapid economic expansion.

3. That George W. Bush used his victories in 2000 and 2004 as a means to promote tax cuts and a conservative social agenda.

4. That fundamental changes in the United States and world economy led to significant changes in lifestyle and expectations for middle-class Americans.

5. That during this period a technology-driven, global economy emerged to shape relations between nations.

6. That America was becoming more diverse due to the changes in immigration after 1965 and the higher birth rates among many immigrant groups, especially Hispanics.

7. That the civil rights movement, affirmative action, and other liberal reforms had left a legacy of improved opportunities for educated middle-class blacks, but the urban African-American "underclass" seemed even worse off than before.

8.   That the nation, despite its prosperity, continued to face a rising number of seemingly intractable social problems including violent crime, drug addiction, homelessness, AIDS, environmental hazards, and a deprived underclass.

9.   That some Americans came to believe that defining American culture and its values was the most important problem facing the nation.

10.   That while globalization had its advantages, it also had its perils as ancient conflicts began to involve more people and more nations.

11.   That the events of September 11, 2001 awakened America to a new wariness and a new unity, and led to a war on terrorism that many contend to pose a threat to civil liberties.

Glossary

1.   "crack" cocaine: Cocaine in a concentrated form that is smoked rather than "snorted," as is typical for cocaine powder. "Crack" was more typical among central-city black addicts, while the powder form was more likely to be used by suburban abusers.

Pertinent Questions

A RESURGENCE OF PARTISANSHIP (910-916)

1.   What obstacles to effective leadership did Clinton face upon taking office? How did the administration's own actions compound its problems?

2.   What major domestic and trade legislation did the Clinton administration manage to push through in its first two years? Why did the health care initiative fail?

3.   What role did the United States play in the Bosnian civil war that emerged from the break up of Yugoslavia?

4.   Why were the Republicans able to win control of Congress in 1994? What were the Congressional Republicans able to accomplish? How did President Clinton react?

5.   What strategy did Clinton adopt for the 1996 election? What happened in the Congressional elections?

6.   What political and economic factors combined to make substantial reductions in the federal budget deficit during President Clinton's second term?

7   Explain the series of financial, political, and sexual scandals that plagued Bill Clinton. Why did Republicans push for impeachment? Why was Clinton acquitted?

8.   What was the result of America's involvement in the NATO intervention in the Yugoslavian province of Kosovo?

9.   Describe how the razor thin electoral margin in Florida was resolved in favor of George W. Bush in the 2000 election. Discuss the political agenda of the George W. Bush administration.

THE ECONOMIC BOOM (916-919)

10.   What new approaches to conducting business helped lead the American economy out of the doldrums of the 1970s and early 1980s? Specifically, what did businesses do to control labor costs?

11.   What were the hallmarks of the economic boom of the 90s? What caused the sudden downturn in the first years of the 21st Century?

12.   What is meant by the "two-tiered economy?" What factors contributed to this characteristic of the 1990s? What happened to the poverty rate over the post–World War II era?

13.   Explain how "globalization" transformed the American economy? In what economic sector were U. S. workers most affected?

SCIENCE AND TECHNOLOGY IN THE NEW ECONOMY (919-922)

14. What technological advance made possible the personal computer? How did the PC change business processes and even household activities?

15. Describe the rapid rise of the computer and software industry. How did Microsoft come to be so large and dominant?

16. What technological developments made the Internet and the World Wide Web possible? In what ways was the Internet a creature of government as well as private development?

17. What impact did the new medium of communications have on American life? How might the "digital divide" affect the American economy in the future?

18. Describe the rise of genetic engineering and the biotechnology industry. What are the future possibilities and controversies in this new field?

A CHANGING SOCIETY (922-927)

19. What factors led to the increase in the average age of Americans? What are the social, political, and economic consequences of this demographic change?

20. Describe the significant change in the nature and extent of immigration to the United States after 1965. What two groups had the most impact?

21. As Asian immigration swelled, what tensions developed? What helps explain why some Asian groups prospered?

22. Compare and contrast post-1960s accomplishments of the African American middle class with those of the underclass. What explains the stark disparity?

23. What precipitated the 1992 Los Angeles riot that was the largest racial disturbance of the twentieth century? What underlying problems did the outburst represent?

24. How did illegal drug use in the 1990s vary between the middle class and poor urban neighborhoods?

25. What are possible reasons that the crime rate fell in the 1990s reversing an upward trend since the end of World War II?

A CONTESTED CULTURE (927-933)

26. What were the key arguments on which the "right-to-life" movement rested its opposition to abortion? What gains did the movement make? How did the "pro-choice" forces respond?

27. What was accomplished in the struggle against sexual harassment in the workplace?

28. Describe the shift of the political left to emphasis on environmental and ecological concerns. What incidents and issues attracted the most attention?

29. How did environmental concerns blend with globalism issues? Why did the U.S. refuse to ratify the Kyoto Treaty?

30. Compare and contrast the forces of mass culture with the emerging more targeted or fragmented tendencies. How did new media technologies facilitate segmentation?

THE PERILS OF GLOBALIZATION (933-939)

31. Describe the differing perspectives of those who tended to resist globalization. What common concerns did they have?

32. Why did Islamic fundamentalism manifest itself in hatred against the West, especially the United States?

33. What encounters with terrorism did the United States experience prior to September 11, 2001?

34. Describe how the World Trade Center and Pentagon attacks combined with the anthrax scare thrust concern about terrorism to the forefront of American consciousness. How did the Bush administration respond?

35. In what ways did the national reaction to the terrorism of September 11 bring out the best in the American people?

36. How did the United States-led invasion of Iraq in 2003 signal a change in American foreign policy?

PATTERNS OF POPULAR CULTURE: RAP (928-929)

37. How does rap differ from earlier forms of African American music? Why can it be called "almost as much a form of language as a form of music"?

WHERE HISTORIANS DISAGREE: WOMEN'S HISTORY (930)

38. What revived interest in women's history in the 1960s and 1970s?

39. What is meant by the "contributionist" and "victimization" focus that characterized most women's history up to the 1990s?

40. How and why did gender studies shift from emphasis on the artificiality of gender distinction to a focus on the notion of gender as a source of social and culture difference?

Identification

Identify each of the following and explain why it is important within the context of the chapter.

1. North American Free Trade Agreement (NAFTA)

2. Hillary Rodham Clinton

3. Newt Gingrich

4. Robert Dole

5. welfare reform

6. Kosovo

7. Slobodan Milosevic

8. Saddam Hussein

9. Monica Lewinsky

10. Kenneth Starr

11. Katherine Harris

12. Richard Cheney

13. John Kerry

14. NASDAQ

15. "dot-coms" and the "tech bubble"

16. Enron Corporation

17. Apple

18. IBM

19. Microsoft

20. Silicon Valley

21. "digital divide"

22. Human Genome Project

23.	stem cell research
24.	the "underclass"
25.	O. J. Simpson trial
26.	HIV and AIDS
27.	"unsafe sex"
28.	caregiver leave
29.	global warming
30.	World Trade Organization
31.	Timothy McVeigh
32.	Osama Bin Laden
33.	Al Qaeda
34.	Taliban
35.	Saddam Hussein

Document

Read the sections of the chapter under the headings "The Two-Tiered Economy," "Globalization," and "Science and Technology in the New Economy." Trade and technology are among the forces that contribute toward making the American economy increasingly two-tiered in nature. Some social commentators have expressed fears that the technological revolution may accentuate the division of the nation into structurally separate haves and have-nots. Many politicians and some economists have expressed fears that U.S. prosperity is threatened by increasing globalization that leads corporations to shift jobs and capital abroad. President Clinton addressed both of these issues—not trying to restrict trade and hold back technology but by actively promoting both as indicated in the excerpts from two speeches below. He took up the theme of computer technology in his commencement speech at Massachusetts Institute of Technology in June 1998, and he addressed globalization at the Summit of the Americas in December 1994 in Miami. How accurate are the President's appeals to history that he uses to shape his vision of the future?

[M.I.T., June 1998] I come today not to talk about the new marvels of science and engineering. . . . Instead, I come to MIT, an epicenter of the seismic shifts in our economy and society, to talk about how we can and must apply enduring American values to this revolutionary time—about the responsibilities we all have as citizens to include every American in the promise of this new age. . . . Today, I ask you to focus on the challenges of the Information Age. . . . We can extend opportunity to all Americans or leave many behind. We can erase lines of inequity or etch them indelibly. . . . The tools we develop today are bringing down barriers of race and gender, of income and age. . . . For the very first time in our history, it is now possible for a child in the most isolated inner-city neighborhood or rural community to have access to the same world of knowledge at the same instant as the child in the most affluent suburb. Imagine the revolutionary democratizing potential this can bring. Imagine the enormous benefits to our economy, our society, if not just a fraction, but all young people can master this set of twenty-first century skills. . . .

Yet today, affluent schools are almost three times as likely to have Internet access in the classroom; white students more than twice as likely as black students to have computers in their homes. We know from hard experience that unequal education hardens into unequal prospects. We know the Information Age will accelerate this trend. . . .

History teaches us that even as new technologies create growth and new opportunity, they can heighten economic inequalities and sharpen social divisions. That is, after all, exactly what happened with the mechanization of agriculture and in the Industrial Revolution. As we move into the

Information Age, we have it within our power to avoid these developments. . . . But until every child has a computer in the classroom and a teacher well-trained to help, until every student has the skills to tap the enormous resources of the Internet, until every high-tech company can find skilled workers to fill its high-wage jobs, America will miss the full promise of the Information Age. . . . [At this point President Clinton lays out his plans for funding computers in every school and related educational initiatives.]

All students should feel as comfortable with a keyboard as a chalkboard, as comfortable with a laptop as a textbook. It is critical to ensuring that they all have opportunity in the world of the twenty-first century.

* * *

[Miami, Dec. 1994] . . . the truth is that the United States have never been in a stronger economic position to compete and win in the world. We are also taking bold steps to open new markets and to make the global economy work for our people. For 40 years, our markets have been more open than those of many other nations. . . . Just a year ago yesterday, I signed into law NAFTA—the North American Free Trade Agreement. When Congress voted for NAFTA, that even committed the United States to continuing leadership and engagement in the post–Cold War world. . . .

Just yesterday, I signed into law the bill implementing the General Agreement on Tariffs and Trade, the largest agreement ever for free and fair trade. GATT, like NAFTA before it, passed because we had strong bipartisan support in Congress. That is a pattern that must prevail as we continue to pursue open markets and prosperity in this hemisphere and around the world. . . . Once, the United States and its neighbors were clearly divided by seemingly unbridgeable cultural and economic gulfs. But today, superhighways, satellite dishes, and enlightened self-interest draw us together as never before.

MIT Tech Talk, June 10, 1998, and U. S. Dept. of State Dispatch Supplement, May 1995, vol. 6, No. 2, pp. 7–8.

Document 2.

Scarcely six weeks after the attack on the World Trade Centers and the Pentagon, Congress passed at the behest of President George W. Bush a new anti-terrorism bill. The President's remarks at the bill signing ceremony give a flavor of how quickly the American consciousness was transformed by terrorism. Read the speech and consider the following questions. (1) Is the anger, resolve, and unity reflected in the fall of 2001 likely to persist? (2) Is responding to terrorism principally a process of law enforcement and military response or does it require an effort to change the hearts and minds of the potential terrorists? (3) How does the war on terrorism differ from other challenges that Americans faced in the past?

President Signs Anti-Terrorism Bill

George W. Bush, President
Remarks at Signing of the Patriot Act, Anti-Terrorism Legislation
The East Room, Washington, DC
October 26, 2001

THE PRESIDENT: Good morning and welcome to the White House. Today, we take an essential step in defeating terrorism, while protecting the constitutional rights of all Americans. With my signature, this law will give intelligence and law enforcement officials important new tools to fight a present danger. . . . [The President thanks the Vice President and others.]

The changes, effective today, will help counter a threat like no other our nation has ever faced. We've seen the enemy, and the murder of thousands of innocent, unsuspecting people. They recognize no barrier of morality. They have no conscience. The terrorists cannot be reasoned with. Witness the recent anthrax attacks through our Postal Service. . . .

But one thing is for certain: These terrorists must be pursued, they must be defeated, and they must be brought to justice. And that is the purpose of this legislation. Since the 11th of September, the men and women of our intelligence and law enforcement agencies have been relentless in their response to new and sudden challenges.

We have seen the horrors terrorists can inflict. We may never know what horrors our country was spared by the diligent and determined work of our police forces, the FBI, ATF agents, federal marshals, Custom officers, Secret Service, intelligence professionals and local law enforcement officials, under the most trying conditions. They are serving this country with excellence, and often with bravery.

They deserve our full support and every means of help that we can provide. We're dealing with terrorists who operate by highly sophisticated methods and technologies, some of which were not even available when our existing laws were written. The bill before me takes account of the new realities and dangers posed by modern terrorists. It will help law enforcement to identify, to dismantle, to disrupt, and to punish terrorists before they strike.

For example, this legislation gives law enforcement officials better tools to put an end to financial counterfeiting, smuggling and money-laundering. Secondly, it gives intelligence operations and criminal operations the chance to operate not on separate tracks, but to share vital information so necessary to disrupt a terrorist attack before it occurs.

As of today, we're changing the laws governing information-sharing. And as importantly, we're changing the culture of our various agencies that fight terrorism. Countering and investigating terrorist activity is the number one priority for both law enforcement and intelligence agencies.

Surveillance of communications is another essential tool to pursue and stop terrorists. The existing law was written in the era of rotary telephones. This new law that I sign today will allow surveillance of all communications used by terrorists, including e-mails, the Internet, and cell phones.

As of today, we'll be able to better meet the technological challenges posed by this proliferation of communications technology. Investigations are often slowed by limit on the reach of federal search warrants.

Law enforcement agencies have to get a new warrant for each new district they investigate, even when they're after the same suspect. Under this new law, warrants are valid across all districts and across all states. And, finally, the new legislation greatly enhances the penalties that will fall on terrorists or anyone who helps them.

Current statutes deal more severely with drug-traffickers than with terrorists. That changes today. We are enacting new and harsh penalties for possession of biological weapons. We're making it easier to seize the assets of groups and individuals involved in terrorism. The government will have wider latitude in deporting known terrorists and their supporters. The statute of limitations on terrorist acts will be lengthened, as will prison sentences for terrorists.

This bill was carefully drafted and considered. Led by the members of Congress on this stage, and those seated in the audience, it was crafted with skill and care, determination and a spirit of bipartisanship for which the entire nation is grateful. This bill met with an overwhelming -- overwhelming agreement in Congress, because it upholds and respects the civil liberties guaranteed by our Constitution.

This legislation is essential not only to pursuing and punishing terrorists, but also preventing more atrocities in the hands of the evil ones. This government will enforce this law with all the urgency of a nation at war. The elected branches of our government, and both political parties, are united in our resolve to fight and stop and punish those who would do harm to the American people.

<u>Map Exercise</u>

Fill in or identify the following on the blank map provided.

1.   Identify and label the following Eastern European nations: Russia, Poland, Hungary, Czechoslovakia, Bulgaria, Romania, Ukraine, and Belarus.

2. Identify and label Germany and Berlin.
3. Mark the old western border of the Soviet Union and shade the nations that were under Soviet dominance during the Cold War.
4. Circle the area of the former Yugoslavia which broke up into smaller republics, including Bosnia.
5. Identify and label Afghanistan, Iran, Iraq, Kuwait, Saudi Arabia, and the Persian Gulf.

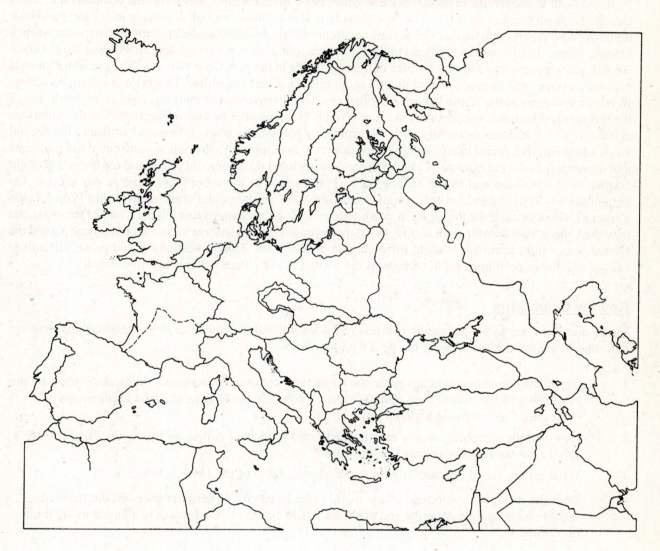

Interpretive Questions

Based on what you have filled in, answer the following. On some of the questions you will need to consult the narrative in your text for information or explanation.

1. How did the borders and sphere of influence of the old Soviet Union compare with the situation following removal of Soviet dominance from Eastern European nations and the independence of former Soviet republics?
2. Why was having a friendly government in Kuwait so important to the United States and the Western European nations?

3. Why were other European nations so concerned about the civil war in Bosnia and the conflict in Kosovo?

Summary

With the Cold War over, the economy became Americans' main concern, and it was the economy that led to George H. Bush's defeat in 1992. The new president, Bill Clinton, set out to reverse many Reagan-Bush policies. As a result, with neither Democrats nor Republicans dominating the government, partisan politics became bitter. Issues such as the "graying" of America, population diversity, and differing cultural values were to many people more important than defining our role in the post Cold War era. The president himself became an issue, was impeached, and though acquitted, remained embattled. Despite a booming economy, Republicans regained the White House in 2000, when, by the narrowest of margins, George W. Bush, son of the former president, became president in his own right. Not long after he took office, however, the American economy, which had grown rapidly with the expanding technology market, began to slow and the second Bush administration found itself facing serious domestic problems. As the nation confronted the problems that accompanied the emergence of a technology-driven global economy, old issues and old hatreds brought conflict to the Balkans and to the Middle East. Finally, one of these conflicts came to our shores. On September 11, 2001, Islamic militants took control of three airplanes and crashed them into World Trade Center in New York and the Pentagon in Washington, D. C. Other nations had felt the wrath of terrorists, but now the United States was in their sights. What means could Americans use to combat terrorism? Could the United States fight terrorism without infringing on civil rights? These questions would prove difficult to answer and foster prolonged public debate as the United States entered the twenty-first century.

Review Questions

These questions are to be answered with essays. This will allow you to explore relationships between individuals, events, and attitudes of the period under review.

1. Explain the fundamental changes in the nature of the American economy that were evident by the mid 1990s. What caused such transformation? What are the long term social implications of a "two-tiered" economy in a global setting?

2. How had the computer already transformed many aspects of American life by the early 1990s? What does the Internet promise for the future?

3. What groups failed to share fully in the economic boom of the 1990s? Why?

4. Does the new century portend a new world order of terror? What grievances do the terrorists seem to have against America and the West? How has the United States responded to the threat of terrorism?

Chapter Self Test

After you have read the chapter in the text and done the exercises in the Study Guide, take the following self test to see if you understand the material you have covered. Answers appear at the end of the Study Guide.

MULTIPLE-CHOICE QUESTIONS

Circle the letter of the response that best answers the question or completes the statement.

1. Which of the following was *not* an episode that tarnished President Clinton's early popularity?
   a. His effort to end the ban on homosexuals serving in the military.

b. His controversial appointments to major government positions in the Justice Department and elsewhere.

c. His wholesale replacement of the Federal Reserve Board with liberals.

d. His clumsy handling of the investigation into his banking and real estate ventures.

2. What major domestic initiative of the first two years of the Clinton administration was a political failure?

a. mental health

b. child welfare

c. educational improvements

d. health care reform

3. The Clinton administration involved the U.S. militarily in the Civil War in:

a. Afghanistan.

b. Belarus.

c. Turkey.

d. Bosnia.

4. During Clinton's second term, the federal budget deficit:

a. declined significantly due mainly to economic growth.

b. increased significantly due to increased social spending.

c. fluctuated widely due to the series of short military interventions.

d. remained at the approximate levels of the first Bush administration despite tax cuts.

5. The combative Republican congressman who became Speaker of the House in the early 1990s and helped lead his party to control of Congress was:

a. Bob Dole.

b. Newt Gingrich.

c. Arthur Anderson.

d. Dick Cheney.

6. The White House intern whose sexual involvement with President Clinton led to his impeachment was:

a. Jennifer Flowers.

b. Paula Jones.

c. Janet Reno.

d. Monica Lewinski.

7. Hillary Rodham Clinton went from first lady to politics in her own right by becoming:

a. Governor of Arkansas.

b. Attorney General of Florida.

c. U.S. Senator from New York.

d. Secretary of Energy.

8. George W. Bush:

a. continued to support the Clinton assault-weapons ban.

b. opposed efforts to establish federally funded "faith-based" organizations.

c. presented an ambitious plan to restructure Social Security.

d. refused to state a position on gay marriage.

9. The "two tiered" economy referred to a situation characterized by:

   a. a prosperous industrial north and a lagging Sunbelt dependent on a service economy.

   b. the U.S. leading the world and other nations being noticeably behind in GNP and other measures of prosperity.

   c. the increasingly wide and seemingly intractable gap between the educated American middle class and above compared with the so-called underclass.

   d. the contrast between the consumer economy and the investment economy as manifested in a volatile stock market.

10. The American economy in the period of the late 1980s and early 1990s was characterized by all of the following *except*:

    a. the lowest rate of poverty in the post–World War II era.

    b. a decline in the relative importance of heavy manufacturing.

    c. an increase in the number of families needing more than one income to maintain their desired standard of living.

    d. an unequal distribution of wealth and income, with the middle 40 percent experiencing a decline in wealth.

11. From 1965 to the early 1990s there was significant relative and actual increase in immigration by all of the following groups *except:*

    a. Asians.

    b. Mexicans.

    c. Puerto Ricans.

    d. Europeans.

12. Which of the following best represents the economic status of African Americans by the 1980s?

    a. Despite the efforts of the 1960s, all classes of blacks were falling further behind whites.

    b. The black middle class made significant gains, but the gap between the black middle class and underclass was accentuated.

    c. Working-class blacks made significant strides but white-collar options remained closed, so middle-class blacks made little gain.

    d. Except in the South, average family income for blacks matched that of whites by the 1990 census.

13. What technological advance ushered in the personal computer (PC) revolution?

    a. microprocessor

    b. transistors

    c. vacuum tubes

    d. circuit breakers

14. The nickname given to a region of northern California known as a center for computer development is:

    a. Silicon Valley.

    b. Research Triangle.

    c. Dot-com Row.

    d. PC Village.

15. What entity undertook the original research and development that led to the creation of the Internet?

    a. the New York Stock Exchange to keep track of stocks

    b. the railroad industry to monitor rolling stock and loads

    c. the telephone industry to facilitate long distance calling

    d. the Department of Defense to provide rapid military communication and command

16. In the early stages of the AIDS epidemic, which of the following groups showed the greatest incidence?

    a. homosexual men

    b. homosexual women

    c. heterosexual men

    d. heterosexual women

17. The forces opposed to legalized abortion were generally known as the _____ movement.

    a. "abstinence"

    b. "birthright"

    c. "baby alive"

    d. "right-to-life"

18. Activists who protested against globalism focused their attention on the meetings of:

    a. the World Trade Organization.

    b. the United Nations.

    c. the U.S. Congress.

    d. the Pan American Union.

19. Which TWO of the following structures were attacked by terrorists on September 11, 2001?

    a. White House

    b. Capitol

    c. Pentagon

    d. World Trade Center

20. George W. Bush decided to invade Iraq in March 2003 for all of the following reasons *except*:

    a. he believed Iraq was developing "weapons of mass destruction."

    b. Iraq was supporting terrorist groups.

    c. Iraq planned to invade Israel in the late spring.

    d. the Hussein regime was responsible for major human-rights violations.

True-False Questions

Read each statement carefully. Mark true statements "T" and false statements "F."

1. Although the investigation widened considerably, the "Whitewater affair" originally involved allegations that President Clinton had been sexually involved with a woman that he met on a rafting trip through the Grand Canyon.

2. Despite persistent effort by Republicans in the House of Representatives, President Clinton was never impeached.

3. Kenneth Starr was the special prosecutor charged with investigating Bill Clinton.

4. After the first two years of the Clinton administration, the Republicans won control of both houses of Congress for the first time since the early Eisenhower years.

5. Most political analysts argue that Bill Clinton's return to his activist liberal roots was responsible for his reelection victory in 1996.

6. Although he lost in the Electoral College, John Kerry outpolled George W. Bush in the 2004 presidential election.

7. By 2005 stock prices had recovered and exceeded those of early 2001.

8. NASDAQ was established to investigate corporate accounting scandals.

9. Microsoft Corporation became one of the largest companies in the world by establishing a near monopoly on the operating system used on most PCs.

10. The Human Genome Project was designed to fight environmental degradation from smog, water pollution, industrial output, etc.

11. The economic boom of the 1990s was based to a great extent on the wide use of computers, and the improved technology resulted in a lessening of economic disparities between lower and upper class Americans.

12. By the mid 1990s American global market competitiveness had been restored in the manufacturing sector so exports once again exceeded imports.

13. The U.S. birth rate began to slow in the 1970s and at the same time life expectancy increased, so the average age of Americans was noticeably higher by 1990 than it had been in 1970.

14. Asians constituted the largest group of illegal immigrants to the United States in the 1970s and 1980s.

15. The "O.J. trial" pitted the citrus growers of Florida against those of California because the latter undercut juice prices by using illegal aliens to pick the fruit.

16. The major riot in South Central Los Angeles in 1992 was sparked by turf conflict between black and Hispanic gangs.

17. Safe sex advocates promoted the use of abstinence or condoms to reduce the spread of AIDS.

18. The advocates of making abortion legal chose to call themselves "pro-choice" rather than "pro-abortion" in order to stress that they were defending the woman's right to make her own decision.

19. Timothy McVeigh worked with Osama Bin Laden to plan the Oklahoma City bombing in 1995.

20. Soon after the United States-led invasion of Iraq in 2003, United Nations inspectors found several nuclear weapons built by Saddam Hussein.

Answers to Chapter Self Tests

Chapter Fifteen

MULTIPLE-CHOICE QUESTIONS

1. b
2. c
3. a
4. e
5. c
6. d
7. d
8. c
9. a
10. d
11. a
12. b
13. e
14. a
15. d
16. a
17. b
18. d
19. c
20. b
21. c

TRUE-FALSE QUESTIONS

1. F
2. F
3. F
4. T
5. F
6. F
7. F
8. F
9. F
10. T
11. T
12. F
13. T
14. F
15. F

16.	T
17.	F
18.	F
19.	T
20.	F
21.	T

Chapter Sixteen
MULTIPLE-CHOICE QUESTIONS

1.	d
2.	c
3.	c
4.	b
5.	b
6.	d
7.	d
8.	c
9.	a
10.	c
11.	d
12.	a,c
13.	d
14.	d
15.	b,c
16.	a
17.	d
18.	d
19.	b
20.	a,c,d

TRUE-FALSE QUESTIONS

1.	F
2.	F
3.	F
4.	T
5.	F
6.	T
7.	F
8.	T
9.	F
10.	T
11.	T
12.	T
13.	F
14.	F

15.	F
16.	F
17.	F
18.	T
19.	F
20.	F

Chapter Seventeen
MULTIPLE-CHOICE QUESTIONS

1.	d
2.	b
3.	a
4.	d
5.	a
6.	d
7.	a
8.	c
9.	d
10.	d
11.	a
12.	d
13.	b
14.	d
15.	b
16.	c
17.	c
18.	c
19.	d
20.	c

TRUE-FALSE QUESTIONS

1.	T
2.	T
3.	F
4.	F
5.	T
6.	T
7.	F
8.	F
9.	T
10.	T
11.	T
12.	T
13.	F
14.	F

15. F
16. F
17. T
18. T
19. F
20. F

Chapter Eighteen
MULTIPLE-CHOICE QUESTIONS
1. d
2. b
3. d
4. a
5. d
6. a
7. b
8. b
9. a,b
10. c
11. a
12. a,d
13. d
14. d
15. b
16. b
17. b
18. b.
19. d
20. b
21. d

TRUE-FALSE QUESTIONS
1. T
2. T
3. T
4. F
5. F
6. T
7. T
8. T
9. T
10. F
11. F
12. F
13. F

14.	T
15.	F
16.	F
17.	T
18.	F
19.	T
20.	F
21.	F

Chapter Nineteen

MULTIPLE-CHOICE QUESTIONS

1.	d
2.	d
3.	a
4.	b
5.	c
6.	d
7.	c
8.	b
9.	c
10.	b
11.	d
12.	b
13.	c
14.	b
15.	a
16.	c
17.	a
18.	d
19.	c
20.	a

TRUE-FALSE QUESTIONS

1.	T
2.	T
3.	F
4.	F
5.	T
6.	T
7.	F
8.	F
9.	T
10.	F
11.	F
12.	T

13. T
14. F
15. F
16. T
17. F
18. T
19. T
20. T

Chapter Twenty
MULTIPLE-CHOICE QUESTIONS

1. d
2. c
3. a
4. b
5. c
6. d
7. d
8. c
9. d
10. c
11. a,d
12. b
13. b
14. a
15. c
16. c
17. b
18. a
19. d
20. b

TRUE-FALSE QUESTIONS

1. T
2. T
3. F
4. F
5. F
6. F
7. F
8. F
9. F
10. F
11. F
12. T

13. T
14. F
15. F
16. T
17. T
18. T
19. T
20. F

Chapter Twenty-one
MULTIPLE-CHOICE QUESTIONS
1. d
2. a
3. b
4. a
5. d
6. c
7. d
8. d
9. d
10. d
11. c
12. c
13. d
14. b
15. d
16. c
17. c
18. c
19. a
20. d
TRUE-FALSE QUESTIONS
1. F
2. F
3. T
4. F
5. T
6. F
7. T
8. T
9. F
10. T
11. T
12. F

13.	T
14.	F
15.	F
16.	F
17.	T
18.	T
19.	F
20.	T
21.	T
22.	T

Chapter Twenty-two
MULTIPLE-CHOICE QUESTIONS

1.	b
2.	d
3.	c
4.	b
5.	a
6.	d
7.	a
8.	b
9.	c
10.	b
11.	d
12.	b
13.	c
14.	b
15.	a
16.	c
17.	c
18.	a
19.	a
20.	c

TRUE-FALSE QUESTIONS

1.	T
2.	F
3.	T
4.	F
5.	F
6.	T
7.	T
8.	F
9.	F
10.	F

11. T
12. F
13. F
14. T
15. F
16. F
17. F
18. T
19. T
20. F

Chapter Twenty-three
MULTIPLE-CHOICE QUESTIONS
1. a
2. a
3. d
4. d
5. c
6. a
7. b
8. d
9. a
10. b,c
11. b
12. c
13. a
14. d
15. b
16. c
17. d
18. b
19. a
20. b
TRUE-FALSE QUESTIONS
1. T
2. T
3. F
4. F
5. F
6. T
7. F
8. F
9. T
10. T

11.	F
12.	F
13.	F
14.	T
15.	F
16.	F
17.	T
18	T
19.	F
20.	T

Chapter Twenty-four
MULTIPLE-CHOICE QUESTIONS

1.	c
2.	d
3.	c
4.	b
5.	a
6.	a
7.	a
8.	c
9.	d
10.	d
11.	d
12.	b
13.	c
14.	a
15.	c
16.	b
17.	b
18.	a
19.	d
20.	a

TRUE-FALSE QUESTIONS

1.	T
2.	T
3.	F
4.	F
5.	T
6.	T
7.	F
8.	T
9.	F
10.	T

11.	F
12.	f
13.	T
14.	T
15.	t
16.	F
17.	f
18.	T
19.	t
20.	f

Chapter Twenty-five
MULTIPLE-CHOICE QUESTIONS

1.	d
2.	d
3.	b
4.	d
5.	c
6.	d
7.	a
8.	b
9.	b
10.	c
11.	a
12.	b
13.	c
14.	a
15.	c
16.	a
17.	b
18.	a
19.	d
20.	b

TRUE-FALSE QUESTIONS

1.	T
2.	T
3.	T
4.	F
5.	F
6.	F
7.	T
8.	T
9.	F
10.	F

11. F
12. T
13. F
14. F
15. F
16. F
17. F
18. T
19. F
20. f

Chapter Twenty-six
MULTIPLE-CHOICE QUESTIONS

1. b
2. a
3. c
4. a
5. d
6. b
7. a
8. c
9. c
10. b
11. b
12. a
13. c
14. a
15. d
16. b
17. a
18. c
19. d
20. c

TRUE-FALSE QUESTIONS

1. F
2. F
3. F
4. F
5. F
6. T
7. F
8. T
9. F
10. F

11.	T
12.	F
13.	T
14.	F
15.	T
16.	T
17.	T
18.	F
19.	T
20.	T

Chapter Twenty-seven
MULTIPLE-CHOICE QUESTIONS

1.	a
2.	c
3.	c
4.	a
5.	d
6.	b
7.	d
8.	c
9.	c
10.	d
11.	b
12.	a
13.	b
14.	d
15.	d
16.	a
17.	c
18.	b
19.	d
20.	a

TRUE-FALSE QUESTIONS

1.	T
2.	T
3.	F
4.	F
5.	F
6.	F
7.	F
8.	F
9.	T
10.	T

11. T
12. F
13. F
14. F
15. T
16. T
17. T
18. T
19. T
20. F

Chapter Twenty-eight
MULTIPLE-CHOICE QUESTIONS
1. b
2. c
3. d
4. b
5. b
6. d
7. b
8. c
9. a
10. d
11. a
12. a
13. b
14. b
15. d
16. c
17. c
18. b
19. a,d
20. d

TRUE-FALSE QUESTIONS
1. T
2. F
3. T
4. F
5. T
6. F
7. T
8. F
9. T
10. F

11.	T
12.	F
13.	F
14.	F
15.	F
16.	T
17.	T
18.	F
19.	F
20.	F

Chapter Twenty-nine
MULTIPLE-CHOICE QUESTIONS

1.	b
2.	a
3.	d
4.	b
5.	c
6.	c
7.	b
8.	d
9.	a
10.	b
11.	b
12.	a
13.	d
14.	a
15.	a
16.	c
17.	c
18.	a
19.	d
20.	d

TRUE-FALSE QUESTIONS

1.	F
2.	T
3.	F
4.	T
5.	F
6.	T
7.	F
8.	F
9.	T
10.	F

11. F
12. T
13. T
14. T
15. F
16. T
17. T
18. F
19. F
20. F

Chapter Thirty
MULTIPLE-CHOICE QUESTIONS
1. d
2. d
3. a
4. d
5. b
6. c
7. a,d
8. c
9. d
10. b
11. c
12. c
13. c
14. a
15. c
16. d
17. d
18. d
19. d
20. d

TRUE-FALSE QUESTIONS
1. F
2. T
3. F
4. F
5. T
6. T
7. F
8. F
9. T
10. T

11. T
12. F
13. T
14. T
15. F
16. F
17. T
18. F
19. F

Chapter Thirty-one
MULTIPLE-CHOICE QUESTIONS

1. d
2. c
3. a
4. a
5. c
6. d
7. b
8. d
9. b
10. c
11. a
12. b
13. c
14. d
15. d
16. a
17. c
18. b
19. d
20. d

TRUE-FALSE QUESTIONS

1. T
2. T
3. F
4. T
5. F
6. T
7. T
8. F
9. T
10. T
11. F

12. F
13. F
14. F
15. F
16. T
17. T
18. T
19. T
20. T

Chapter Thirty-two
MULTIPLE-CHOICE QUESTIONS
1. d
2. b
3. c
4. a
5. b
6. C
7. a
8. b
9. b
10. c
11. c
12. d
13. d
14. d
15. b
16. d
17. c
18. b
19. d
20. b

TRUE-FALSE QUESTIONS
1. T
2. F
3. T
4. F
5. F
6. T
7. T
8. T
9. T
10. T
11. F

12.	T
13.	T
14.	F
15.	F
16.	T
17.	T
18.	F
19.	T
20.	T

Chapter Thirty-three
MULTIPLE-CHOICE QUESTIONS

1.	a
2.	b
3.	d
4.	d
5.	c
6.	d
7.	a
8.	a
9.	d
10.	d
11.	a
12.	d
13.	c
14.	c
15.	a
16.	c
17.	b
18.	b
19.	b
20.	b

TRUE-FALSE QUESTIONS

1.	F
2.	T
3.	T
4.	F
5.	T
6.	T
7.	F
8.	F
9.	T
10.	T
11.	F

12.	F
13.	F
14.	T
15.	T
16.	T
17.	F
18.	T
19.	T
20.	F

Chapter Thirty-four

MULTIPLE-CHOICE QUESTIONS

1.	c
2.	d
3.	d
4.	a
5.	b
6.	d
7.	c
8.	c
9.	c
10.	d
11.	d
12.	b
13.	a
14.	a
15.	d
16.	a
17.	d
18.	a
19.	c, d
20.	c

TRUE-FALSE QUESTIONS

1.	F
2.	F
3.	T
4.	T
5.	F
aa.	F
bb.	F
6.	F
7.	T
8.	F
9.	F

10. F
11. T
12. F
15. F
16. F
17. T
19. T
20. F
cc. F